VISIONS OF GOD IN EZEKIEL
PENTECOSTAL EXPLORATIONS OF THE GLORY AND
HOLINESS OF YAHWEH

וַיְהִ֣י ׀ בִּשְׁלֹשִׁ֣ים שָׁנָ֗ה בָּֽרְבִיעִי֙
בַּחֲמִשָּׁ֣ה לַחֹ֔דֶשׁ וַאֲנִ֥י בְתֽוֹךְ־
הַגּוֹלָ֖ה עַל־נְהַר־כְּבָ֑ר נִפְתְּחוּ֙
הַשָּׁמַ֔יִם וָאֶרְאֶ֖ה מַרְא֥וֹת
אֱלֹהִֽים׃ בַּחֲמִשָּׁ֖ה לַחֹ֑דֶשׁ
הִ֚יא הַשָּׁנָ֣ה הַחֲמִישִׁ֔ית
לְגָל֖וּת הַמֶּ֥לֶךְ יוֹיָכִֽין׃ הָיֹ֣ה
הָיָ֣ה דְבַר־יְהוָ֗ה אֶל־יְחֶזְקֵ֨אל
בֶּן־בּוּזִ֧י הַכֹּהֵ֛ן בְּאֶ֥רֶץ כַּשְׂדִּ֖ים
עַל־נְהַר־כְּבָ֑ר וַתְּהִ֥י עָלָ֛יו
שָׁ֖ם יַד־יְהוָֽה׃ וָאֵ֡רֶא וְהִנֵּה֩

Ezekiel 1:1-3
The Aleppo Codex – c. 930 CE

VISIONS OF GOD IN EZEKIEL

PENTECOSTAL EXPLORATIONS OF THE GLORY AND HOLINESS OF YAHWEH

A. REBECCA BASDEO HILL

CPT

CPT Press
Cleveland, Tennessee

Visions of God in Ezekiel
Pentecostal Explorations of the Glory and Holiness of Yahweh

Published by CPT Press
900 Walker ST NE
Cleveland, TN 37311
USA
email: cptpress@pentecostaltheology.org
website: www.cptpress.com

Library of Congress Control Number: 2018960682

ISBN-13: 978-1-935931-799

CONTENTS

ACKNOWLEDGEMENTS

The completion of this monograph could not have been accomplished without the prayers, support, and encouragement of several individuals. I owe my greatest gratitude to my beloved husband, Jason Hill, who not only bore the brunt of my long hours spent on research and writing, but also provided the love and support that made this work meaningful. Your faithful love and limitless patience were with me to the end. To my daughter, Maddi Hill, I pray that God will bless you for your understanding and stir within you a desperate longing for God's holy presence.

Words cannot express the tremendous gratitude I have for Lee Roy Martin, my mentor and friend. His gentle spirit, intellectual expertise, and spiritual wisdom have guided and assisted me all the way through my research. Special thanks go to my doctoral supervisor, Willie J Wessels, who provided helpful opportunities that enabled me to complete this study.

I owe great thanks to John Christopher Thomas who demonstrated his friendship and encouragement by giving me a seat at the table of fellowship and Pentecostal scholarship. To the Bangor PhD candidates, thank you for your helpful insights and feedback. My colleagues at the Pentecostal Theological Seminary have been a source of constant support. To Ayodeji Adewuya, thank you for readily sharing your resources with me.

Finally, I express gratitude to my parents, siblings, nieces, and nephews. My parents have always urged me to pursue the holy presence of God. My siblings and their children have always been my cheerleaders. Their devotion to God has continually encouraged me.

My prayer is that this monograph will ignite a zeal and passion to see, hear, and encounter the glorious and holy God of Ezekiel.

ABBREVIATIONS

AB	Anchor Bible
ANE	Ancient Near East
AOAT	Alter Orient Und Altes Testament
AOTC	Abingdon Old Testament Commentary
BDB	Francis Brown, *et al.*, *The New Brown, Driver, Briggs, Gesenius Hebrew and English Lexicon: With an Appendix Containing the Biblical Aramaic* (trans. Edward Robinson; Peabody, MA: Hendrickson, 1979).
BETL	*Bibliotheca Ephemeridum Theologicarum Lovaniensium*
BLE	Bulletin de Littérature Ecclésiastique
BWANT	Beiträge zur Wissenschaft vom Alten und Neuen Testament
BZAW	*Beihefte zur Zeitschrift für die alttestamentliche Wissenschaft*
CBQ	*Catholic Biblical Quarterly*
CBR	*Currents in Biblical Research*
CCur	*Cross Currents*
CR:BS	*Currents in Research: Biblical Studies*
DCB	David J.A. Clines (ed.), *The Dictionary of Classical Hebrew* (Sheffield: Sheffield Academic Press; Sheffield Phoenix Press, 1993–2011).
DTIB	*Dictionary for Theological Interpretation of the Bible*
EHB	*Ezekiel and His Book*
EHS	Europäishe Hochschulschriften
FOTL	Forms of the Old Testament Literature
FzB	Forschung zur Bibel
HAR	*Hebrew Annual Review*
HKAT	Handkommentar zum Alten Testament
HSM	Harvard Semitic Monographs
HTR	*Harvard Theological Review*
HUCA	*Hebrew Union College Annual*
IB	The Interpreter's Bible
IBC	Interpretation: A Bible Commentary for Teaching and Preaching

ICC   International Critical Commentary
IDBSup   *The Interpreter's Dictionary of the Bible*: Supplementary
           Volume
Int   *Interpretation*
ISBE   *International Standard Bible Encyclopedia*
ITC   International Theological Commentary
JAAR   *Journal of the American Academy of Religion*
JAOS   *Journal of the American Oriental Society*
JBL   *Journal of Biblical Literature*
JETS   *Journal of the Evangelical Theological Society*
JBPR   *Journal of Biblical and Pneumatological Research*
JEPTA   *Journal of the European Pentecostal Theological*
           Association
JNSL   *Journal of North West Semitic Languages*
JPT   *Journal of Pentecostal Theology*
JPTSup   Journal of Pentecostal Theology Supplement
JSNTSup   Journal for the Study of the New Testament Supplement
           Series
JSOT   *Journal for the Study of the Old Testament*
JSOTSup   Journal for the Study of the Old Testament Supplement
JSS   *Journal of Semitic Studies*
JTS   *Journal of Theological Studies*
LHB/OTS   Library of Hebrew Bible/Old Testament Studies (for-
           merly JSOTSup)
LS   H.G. Liddell *et al.*, *A Greek-English Lexicon* (Oxford:
           Clarendon Press, 1996).
LXX   Septuagint
NEchtB   Neue Echter Bibel
NICOT   New International Commentary on the Old Testament
NIDOTTE *New International Dictionary of Old Testament Theology and*
           Exegesis
NIV   New International Version of the Bible
NSKAT   Neuer Stuttgarter Kommentar Altes Testament
OBO   Orbis Biblicus et Orientalis
OEBI   Steven L. McKenzie (ed.), *The Oxford Encyclopedia of Bib-*
           lical Interpretation (New York, NY: Oxford University
           Press, 2013).
OTE   *Old Testament Essays*
OTL   Old Testament Library

SAT   Die Schriften des Alten Testaments
SBL   Society of Biblical Literature
SBLDS   Society of Biblical Literature Dissertation Series
SBLSS   Society of Biblical Literature Semeia Studies
SBLSymS   Society of Biblical Literature Symposium Series
SJLA   Studies in Judaism in Late Antiquity
SR   *Studies in Religion*
StC   *Studia Catholica*
TBT   *The Bible Today*
TDOT   J.G. Botterweck, H. Ringgren, and H.-J. Fabry (eds.),
             Theological Dictionary of the Old Testament (15 vols.; Grand
             Rapids, MI: Eerdmans, 1974-2004).
ThT   *Theology Today*
THAT   Jenni and Westermann, *Theologisches Handwörterbuch Zum
             Alten Testament*
TOTC   Tyndale Old Testament Commentaries
TWOT   Harris, Waltke, and Archer (eds.), *Theological Wordbook of
             the Old Testament*
VT   *Vetus Testamentum*
VTSup   Supplements to Vetus Testamentum
WBC   Word Biblical Commentary
ZAW   *Zeitschrift für die Alttestamentliche Wissenschaft*

1

INTRODUCTION

The glory of YHWH and the holiness of YHWH are prominent threads that run throughout the book of Ezekiel. This work articulates the literary and theological relationship between these two themes, focusing primarily on the narratives that depict the prophet's sequential visions of the glory of YHWH (Ezekiel 1-3; 8-11; and 40-48). These visionary experiences of YHWH's glory provide the structural framework that supports the theological theme of YHWH's holiness. This study of Ezekiel emerges out of my own Pentecostal socio-religious milieu. My context and experience certainly influence my interpretation of Scripture. I am an East Indian woman from the Caribbean islands of Trinidad and Tobago, living in North America for almost twenty years, and teaching at a North American educational institution, Pentecostal Theological Seminary, for the past four years. Having been raised in a Pentecostal community of faith, I identify with, and am a member of, a Pentecostal church. However, I also identify with, and am a member of, the academic community. Therefore, as a result of this context, I concede that my experiences as a Pentecostal woman will have a compelling effect on my interpretation of Scripture.[1] This does not suggest, however, that I will allow my

---

[1] It is becoming increasingly clear that the interpretive context of the reader of Scripture provides a paradigm for interacting with the dynamic meaning of the biblical texts. The most widespread readings that acknowledge their contextual location have been feminist readings, African American readings, and non-Western readings. Cf. Madipoane Masenya, 'An African Methodology for South African Biblical Sciences: Revisiting the Bosadi (Womanhood) Approach', *OTE* 18.3 (2005), pp. 741-51; Stephen Breck Reid, 'Endangered Reading: The African-American Scholar between Text and People', *CCur* 44.4 (1994), pp. 476-88; and F.F.

experiences as a Pentecostal woman to command my reading and understanding of Scripture, but will rather allow my context as a Pentecostal woman to produce a *pro nobis* study that will reflect the distinctive character of the Pentecostal community, as well as contribute to the academic conversation of Ezekiel.[2]

Ezekiel's prophecy is a creative visual and aural message that is closely linked to the glory of YHWH and the holiness of YHWH. The prophecy opens almost immediately with a striking and vivid description of the glory of YHWH. The hearers[3] of this vision are told that the prophet Ezekiel is in exile when he receives the vision, but before they are able to consider the prophet's captivity, their attention is immediately arrested by the colorful and dramatic vision of YHWH's glory. The prominence of Ezekiel's initial vision of YHWH's glory (Ezek. 1.28), along with the appearance of similar references of YHWH's glory throughout the book (3.12, 23; 8.4; 9.3; 10.4, 18-19; 11.22-23; 39.11, 21; 43.2-5; and 44.4), suggest that the

---

Segovia and M.A. Tolbert, *Reading from This Place: Social Location and Biblical Interpretation in the United States* (Minneapolis: Fortress, 1994). Pentecostal biblical scholars also contend for an integration of their Pentecostal context with their academic study of Scripture. See J.C. Thomas, *The Spirit of the New Testament* (Leiden/Blandford Forum: Deo, 2005), pp. 3-6, who discloses the critical issues confronting previous Pentecostal scholars as they engaged Scripture and the traditional lines of academic disciplines; J.C. Thomas, *1 John, 2 John, 3 John* (Pentecostal Commentary Series; London: T&T Clark International, 2004); Robby Waddell, *The Spirit of the Book of Revelation* (JPTSup 30; Blandford Forum: Deo Publishing, 2006); Lee Roy Martin, *The Unheard Voice of God: A Pentecostal Hearing of the Book of Judges* (JPTSup 32; Blandford Forum: Deo Publishers, 2008); Rickie D. Moore, *The Spirit of the Old Testament* (JPTSup 35; Blandford Forum: Deo Publishing, 2011); and Rickie D. Moore, 'A Pentecostal Approach to Scripture', *Seminary Viewpoint* 8.1 (1987).

[2] Kenneth Archer, *A Pentecostal Hermeneutic for the Twenty-First Century: Spirit, Scripture and Community* (JPTSup 28; New York: T&T Clark International, 2004), p. 156.

[3] I choose to use the term 'hearers' rather than 'readers' because Ezekiel is a prophetic message that needs to be heard. In the *Unheard Voice of God*, Martin shows that 'hearing is the most frequent method of encounter with the word of God'. Per Martin, the command 'to hear' occurs 201 times in the Old Testament and all forms of the verb occur 1,159 times in the Old Testament. He cites Deut. 5.1, Josh. 3.9, 1 Kgs 22.19, Jer. 2.4, 2 Kgs 20.16, and Isa. 55.3 as evidence of a person(s) who is/are commanded 'to hear' God or his word in the Old Testament. Martin also argues that the biblical term, *hearing*, involves more than merely *listening* because to hear the word of God is to obey the word of God (cf. Exod. 7.16, Deut. 30.17-18, 2 Kgs 14,11, 2 Kgs 17.13-14, Ezek. 12.2, and Neh. 9.17), p. 68. In Chapter 3 of this monograph, I build upon Martin's concept of 'hearing' and argue that Ezekiel is a message that must be seen and heard by the hearers of Ezekiel.

glory of YHWH is a preeminent theme in the book of Ezekiel. The presence and absence of YHWH's glory narrated in chs. 1-3, 8-11, and 40-43 provide a coherent structure and give unity and movement to the themes and dramatic events of Ezekiel. Even the city's name, 'יהוה שׁמה', drives the theme of YHWH's glory to the very end of the book (48.35). Thus, the visions of YHWH's glory advance the narrative of Ezekiel.[4] Although the glory of YHWH is a dominant motif in Ezekiel, it is not independent of the significant motif of YHWH's holiness. Ezekiel's visions of the glory of YHWH paint a masterful portrait of YHWH's character, namely YHWH's holiness, and so an interdependent relationship between the glory of YHWH and the holiness of YHWH emerges. In this study, therefore, I will argue that the glory of YHWH and the holiness of YHWH interrelate with each other in order to produce a unique theological vision of YHWH.

My study focuses primarily on chs. 1-3, 8-11, and 40-48 because these vision narratives bear witness to YHWH's glorious splendor as well as provide a backdrop for the mutually dependent relationship between the glory of YHWH and the holiness of YHWH that emerges in the book of Ezekiel. Additionally, these vision accounts clearly relate to one another as they tell the story of the appearance, departure, and return of YHWH's glory. Although this monograph will give primary attention to the vision narratives, it will not be limited to the aforementioned texts, but will refer to other texts in Ezekiel that overtly contribute to the themes of YHWH's glory and holiness.

The Task

Previous studies acknowledge the innate complexities of the visions of Ezekiel and the interpretive challenges that result from those complexities.[5] The church father Jerome claimed that the book of Ezekiel was so obscure that it was impossible to understand it or explain it.[6]

---

[4] Cf. James M. Hamilton, *God's Glory in Salvation through Judgment: A Biblical Theology* (Wheaton, IL: Crossway, 2010), pp. 222-23.

[5] Cf. Brian Neil Peterson, *Ezekiel in Context: Ezekiel's Message Understood in Its Historical Setting of Covenant Curses and Ancient Near Eastern Mythological Motifs* (Princeton Theological Monograph Series; Eugene: Pickwick Publications, 2012), p. 3.

[6] Cf. Iain M. Duguid, *Ezekiel* (Grand Rapids: Zondervan, 1999), p. 17.

Prior to Jerome, rabbis also wrestled with the chariot vision and the final temple vision of Ezekiel, and so they prohibited anyone under the age of thirty from studying the book of Ezekiel.[7] Like Jerome and the rabbis, many Pentecostals fail to understand adequately the odd components that comprise the book of Ezekiel. Hence, Ezekiel remains an illogical, perplexing, bizarre, and relatively unknown book to the Pentecostal community. Undoubtedly Ezekiel is a difficult book,[8] and not simply because of its length. The irrational, encumbered, and often sensational language of Ezekiel is usually shrouded in inexplicable symbols, and so the book of Ezekiel can become a frustrating encounter for the Pentecostal hearer. The prophet's sign acts are often eccentric, secluded from everyday familiarity, and occasionally deliberately repugnant.[9] The prophecy's lexis is chronically ambiguous, and the stark fierceness of adverse emotion – anger, derision, resentment[10] – found in the book may also be troubling to the Pentecostal community.

Ezekiel's cryptic language and equivocal symbols have created an impenetrable mystery, which have generated more questions than answers for most readers of the book. For example, the dispensational eschatology of many Pentecostals leads them to ask the following questions about the book of Ezekiel: Is Ezekiel a prophecy for the end time? What does Ezekiel's vision of the wheel within a wheel mean? Does Ezekiel 38-39 foretell of an imminent end time invasion of Israel by a coalition of nations under the leadership of present-day Russia (Gog of Magog)?[11] Does the vision of the valley of dry

---

[7] S.G. Dempster, 'Canon, Canonization', in Mark J. Boda and J. Gordon McConville (eds.), *Dictionary of the Old Testament Prophets: A Compendius of Contemporary Biblical Scholarship* (Downers Grove, IL: InterVarsity Press, 2012), p. 74.

[8] Duguid, *Ezekiel*, p. 18.

[9] Voltaire, for example, declared repulsion when God commanded Ezekiel to eat cakes baked with dung: F.M.A de Voltaire, *The Complete Works of Voltaire,* xxxv. *Dictionnaire philosophique, ii* (Oxford: University Press, 1994), cited in Andrew Mein, *Ezekiel and the Ethics of Exile* (Oxford Theological Monographs; Oxford, NY: University Press, 2001), p. 1.

[10] Joseph Blenkinsopp, *Ezekiel* (IBC; Louisville: John Knox Press, 1990), p. 3; Mein, *Ezekiel and the Ethics of Exile*, p. 1.

[11] Ezekiel 38-39 records a fierce battle between Israel and the nations of the world headed by Gog of the land of Magog. Gog of Magog has often been associated with the leader of present-day Russia. C.I. Scofield, *The Scofield Reference Bible* (New York: Oxford Univeristy Press, 1917), appears to be primarily responsible for the proliferated view that the invading army of Gog is Russia; cf. A.C. Gaebelein,

bones in Ezekiel 37 signify God's plan for Israel's future national restoration? Will there be a reinstitution of the Old Testament animal sacrificial system in the millennial kingdom?[12] Is the King of Tyre prophecy in Ezekiel 28 referring to Satan? Such questions reflect the views of those who tend to focus on Ezekiel's eschatological vision, the participation of Gog and Magog in the final battles, and the role of the temple and its cult in the millennium.[13]

Despite Ezekiel's eminent theology and the applied character of his message, dispensationalists view the prophet's message through their very narrow eschatological lens. The primary cause for this mistreatment of the book of Ezekiel cannot be ascribed only to the bizarre vision that introduces the book. Not many readers can competently cope with the prophet's vehement and unremitting denunciations, his eccentric and grotesque acts, his monotonous style, and his incomprehensible assortment of issues. However, for those who are willing to engage the prophecy beyond the first chapter, the rewards are inestimable.[14] This study will redirect the Pentecostal community toward a more literary and theological interpretation that emerges from Ezekiel's original context rather than from the lens of a dispensational eschatology.

The interrelationship between YHWH's glory and YHWH's holiness in the book of Ezekiel has been substantially overlooked by previous academic approaches to the book. An extensive review of pre-

The Prophet Ezekiel: An Analytical Exposition (New York: Our Hope, 1918), p. 259. H. Lindsey added momentum to this view in *The Late Great Planet Earth* (Grand Rapids, MI: Zondervan, 1970), p. 59-60. The fulfillment of the prophesied invasion is most often regarded as taking place after the rapture and during the tribulation period preceding the second advent of Christ. This has been the prevailing opinion of dispensational premillennialism. While the teachings of dispensationalism can be heard in Pentecostal churches today, Pentecostalism and dispensationalism are actually quite at interpretive odds with one another.

12 Ezekiel's vision in chs. 40-48 provide the interpretive lens for the futurists' interpretation of prophecy concerning Israel. These chapters detail God's instructions for the building of a new temple to be constructed as part of Israel's future restoration. Although a Jewish remnant from the exile built the second temple, they did not follow the specific blueprint for the construction of the temple found in chs. 40-48, and so futurists believe that there will be an eschatological fulfillment of this prophecy – a construction of the temple in the earthly Millennial Kingdom.

13 C.L. Feinberg, *The Prophecy of Ezekiel: The Glory of the Lord* (Chicago: Moody, 1969), and Lindsey's *The Late Great Planet Earth*, which has sold millions of copies.

14 Daniel Block, *The Book of Ezekiel Chapters 1-24* (NICOT; Grand Rapids, MI: Eerdmans, 1997), p. 91.

vious studies indicates that the majority of commentators allot mea-
ger space for a discussion of the interrelationship between YHWH's
glory and YHWH's holiness. A few commentaries devote space in
the introduction for a brief and insubstantial discussion of the interdependent relationship between the glory of YHWH and the holiness of YHWH. John B. Taylor, for example, dedicated three para-
graphs in his introduction to the relationship between Ezekiel's vision
of God's glory and the holiness of God.[15] In 13 lines Daniel Block
describes how YHWH's holiness can be seen in Ezekiel's 'inaugural
vision'.[16] After his exegetical review of ch. 1, Preston A. Taylor sums
up Ezekiel's initial vision of YHWH's glory in one line: 'Ezekiel's vision shows that God is "here," and He is holy, powerful and majestic'.[17] Other commentaries[18] are devoid of any mention of the
relationship between the glory of YHWH and the holiness of
YHWH. The most significant academic studies on these two subjects
have either viewed the relationship as a derivative of YHWH's concern for his holy name,[19] or they have divorced the apparent interrelationship between the glory of YHWH and the holiness of YHWH
and have treated these themes independently of each other.[20] Despite

---

[15] John B. Taylor, *Ezekiel: An Introduction and Commentary* (TOTC; Downers
Grove, IL: Inter-Varsity Press, 1969), pp. 40-42.

[16] Block, *The Book of Ezekiel Chapters 1-24*, pp. 47-48, 107; Daniel Block, *The
Book of Ezekiel: Chapters 25-48* (NICOT; Grand Rapids: Eerdmans, 1998).

[17] Preston A. Taylor, *Ezekiel: God's Prophet and His Puzzling Book* (Xulon Press,
2006), p. 31.

[18] William H. Brownlee, *Ezekiel 1-19* (WBC; Waco, TX: Word Books, 1986);
Blenkinsopp, *Ezekiel*; Bruce Vawter and Leslie J. Hopp, *Ezekiel: A New Heart* (ITC;
Grand Rapids: Eerdmans Publishing Company, 1991); John W. Wevers, *Ezekiel*
(London: Butler & Tanner LTD, 1969).

[19] I disagree with Luc who claims that 'Yahweh's name was more important
than his glory', p. 137.

[20] For an investigation on the glory of Yahweh in Ezekiel see George Ricker
Berry, 'The Glory of Yahweh and the Temple', *JBL* 56 (1937), pp. 115-17; Daniel
Block, 'Divine Abandonment: Ezekiel's Adaptation of an Ancient near Eastern
Motif', in Margaret S. Odell and John T. Strong (eds.), *The Book of Ezekiel:
Theological and Anthropological Perspectives* (SBLSymS 9; Atlanta: SBL, 2000), pp. 15-
42; John T. Strong, 'God's Kabod: The Presence of Yahweh in the Book of
Ezekiel', in Margaret S. Odell and John T. Strong (eds.), *The Book of Ezekiel:
Theological and Anthropological Perspectives* (SBLSymS 9; Atlanta: SBL, 2000), pp. 69-
96; Steven Tuell, 'Divine Presence and Absence in the Book of Ezekiel', in
Margaret S. Odell and John T. Strong (eds.), *The Book of Ezekiel: Theological and
Anthropological Perspectives* (SBLSymS 9; Atlanta: SBL, 2000), pp. 96-117; John F.
Kutsko, *Between Heaven and Earth: Divine Presence and Absence in the Book of Ezekiel*
(Biblical and Judaic Studies; Winona Lake, IN: Eisenbrauns, 2000); Elizabeth Keck,

of various observations which recognize that a reciprocal relationship exists between the glory of YHWH and the holiness of YHWH, no monographs have fully explored this area of study. I contend that a presentation of Ezekiel's theology of YHWH is not complete without a full elucidation of the interdependent relationship between the glory of YHWH and the holiness of YHWH.

Review of Previous Research on the Book of Ezekiel

The ample scholarly research on the book of Ezekiel in the preceding 80 years has been well documented. Yet, I find myself agreeing with G.A. Cooke's sage observation that 'no one who has worked at Ezekiel can feel satisfied that all the problems have been solved'.[21] As I have already observed, the relationship between the glory of YHWH and the holiness of YHWH have not been fully investigated, and inasmuch as these two topics are central to Pentecostal theology, my location as a Pentecostal hearer may provide an opportunity for a fresh reading of Ezekiel's visions.

Visions and dreams, glossolalia, interpretations, and prophecy were the pulse of early Pentecostal spirituality. According to W.J. Hollenweger, 'dreams and visions in personal and public forms of worship'[22] were added as a basic component of early Pentecostal worship. In fact, dreams and visions 'function as a kind of icon for the individual and the community'.[23] The most reasonable place for seeing, hearing, testing, and discerning visions and dreams was the context of worship within the Pentecostal community. While individuals experienced visions and dreams outside of the communal

---

'Beside the Chebar River: The Glory of Yahweh, Name Theology, and Ezekiel's Understanding of Divine Presence' (PhD thesis; Boston College, 2011). For a survey of the interpretations of holiness in Ezekiel see Tova Ganzel, 'Transformation of Pentateuchal Descriptions of Idolatry', in William A Tooman and Michael A. Lyons (eds.), *Transforming Visions: Transformations of Text, Tradition, and Theology in Ezekiel* (Eugene, OR: Pickwick Publications, 2010), pp. 33-49; Alex Luc, 'A Theology of Ezekiel: God's Name and Israel's History', *JETS* 26.2 (1983), pp. 137-43; and Rimon Kasher, 'Anthropomorphism, Holiness and Cult: A New Look at Ezekiel 40-48', *ZAW* 110 (1998), pp. 192-208.

   [21] G.A. Cooke, 'Review of G. Hölscher, Hesekiel: Der Dichter und das Buch', *JTS* 27 (1925), p. 202.

   [22] W.J. Hollenweger, *Pentecostalism: Origins and Developments Worldwide* (Peabody, MA: Hendrickson Publishers, 1997), p. 18.

   [23] Hollenweger, *Pentecostalism*, p. 19.

worship, they brought those prophetic revelations to the community of faith for judgment. The community would then discern the legitimacy of those prophetic experiences.

Pentecostals also view visions and dreams as a result of the outpouring of the Holy Spirit experienced by the disciples on the day of Pentecost in Acts 2, as well as a fulfillment of the last days' prophecy of Joel 2.28-32. Pentecostals understand that the dreams and visions referenced in Joel 2.28-32 are the manifestations of the eschatological gift of the Spirit,[24] and 'this eschatological pouring out of the Spirit is the pouring out of the Spirit of prophecy'.[25] According to Roger Stronstad, in both the Old and New Testaments, visions and dreams were recognized as means of communicating a prophetic revelation (cf. Num. 12.6).[26] Ezekiel's initial vision of YHWH's glory inaugurates him into his role as a prophet. As the book unfolds, the prophet will continue to see visions of YHWH's glory that reveal the holiness of YHWH. Recognizing the prophetic nature of Ezekiel's visionary experiences of YHWH's glory would go a long way toward defining how the hearers encounter the book of Ezekiel.

Scholars have approached the book of Ezekiel from various perspectives, prior theories, and methodologies, and have argued for a particular position based on literary content and historical setting. Historical-critical scholars debate the unity of the book, the prophet's setting, his sanity, and his authorship of the book.[27] The historical/sociological works illuminate Ezekiel's moral and ethical actions by placing the text in a historical and social context. The form-critical approach places the biblical text of Ezekiel in a framework that reflects its interrelationship with Ancient Near Eastern texts.[28] Rhetorical criticism employs a synchronic approach to study the book of

[24] Steven Jack Land, *Pentecostal Spirituality: A Passion for the Kingdom* (Cleveland, TN: CPT Press, 2010), p. 9.

[25] Roger Stronstad, *The Prophethood of All Believers: A Study in Luke's Charismatic Theology* (JPTSup 16; New York: Sheffield Academic Press, 2003), p. 69.

[26] Stronstad, *The Prophethood of All Believers*, pp. 69, 98, 108.

[27] R. Kraetzschmar, *Das Buch Ezechiel* (HKAT 3: Göttingen: Vandenhoeck & Ruprecht, 1900), and G. Hölscher, *Hesekiel, Der Dichter und das Buch* (BZAW 39; Giessen: Töpelmann, 1924) focused on the compositional process (redaction criticism) of the book of Ezekiel.

[28] Walther Eichrodt, *Ezekiel* (trans. Cosslett Quin; OTL; Philadelphia: Westminster, 1970), and Walther Zimmerli, *Ezekiel 1: A Commentary on the Book of*

Ezekiel in an effort to analyze the persuasive effect of the prophet's message. Although this method views the text in its final form, it typically favors a selective reading of certain sections of the text of Ezekiel, rather than the entire book.[29] While each of the above critical approaches contributes significantly to the discussion on the book of Ezekiel, none of them views the text through the traditional and cultural lens of the Pentecostal community. Due to the fact that current interpretations of Ezekiel have overlooked the specific beliefs and practices of the Pentecostal community, there remains a need for this study.

Furthermore, as noted above, previous academic studies have either divorced the apparent interrelationship between the glory of YHWH and the holiness of YHWH and have treated these themes independently of each other, or they have viewed this relationship as a derivative of YHWH's concern for his holy name. Since no monograph has attempted to explore the interdependent relationship between the glory of YHWH and the holiness of YHWH in the book of Ezekiel, my review of literature will focus on a survey of scholarship that has either investigated the theme of YHWH's glory or the theme of YHWH's holiness in Ezekiel. This survey will begin with an examination of the major interpretations of the role of YHWH's glory followed by the major contributions to the motif of YHWH's holiness in the book of Ezekiel. This review of scholarship will clarify the attention given to these themes and will unveil an area in which a fresh and constructive view of the interrelationship between the glory of YHWH and the holiness of YHWH might critically advance the Old Testament discussion of the book of Ezekiel, as well as stimulate the interests of the Pentecostal community.

The Glory of YHWH
In his revision of his doctoral thesis (Harvard 1997), John F. Kutsko argues that the enigma of divine presence and absence motivates

---

the Prophet Ezekiel, Chapters 1-24 (trans. Ronald E. Clements; Hermeneia; Philadelphia: Fortress, 1979), p. 2, offer the best paradigms for a form and redaction critical approach to Ezekiel.
[29] See Thomas Renz, *The Rhetorical Function of the Book of Ezekiel* (Leiden: Brill, 1999); and Michael V. Fox, 'The Rhetoric of Ezekiel's Vision of the Valley of the Bones', in R.P. Gordon (ed.), *'The Place Is Too Small for Us': The Israelite Prophets in Recent Scholarship* (Winona Lake: Eisenbrauns, 1995), first published as Michael V. Fox, 'The Rhetoric of Ezekiel's Vision of the Valley of the Bones', *HUCA* 51 (1980).

Ezekiel's approach to three critical issues of the exile: theodicy (the reason for exile), theophany (where is God?), and theonomy (the scope of God's rule). He understands the structure of the book of Ezekiel to revolve around YHWH's glory, and he interprets the theme of YHWH's absence and presence against the backdrop of the Mesopotamian idol texts and his exploration of the language of idolatry. While Kutsko contends that Israel's sin of idolatry is the basis for their exile and the departure of YHWH's glory from the temple, he does not view Israel's sin and the departure of YHWH in relation to the glory and holiness of YHWH in the book of Ezekiel. Rather, the goal of Kutsko's study is to reveal that Ezekiel used the theme of divine presence and absence to react to the scornful mocking of Israel's enemies that their God was absent.[30]

Daniel Block's analysis provides a review of Mesopotamian sources such as Sumerian laments, the Tikulti-Ninurta epic, and Assyrian and Neo-Babylonian texts, which offer ample extra-biblical evidence of the Ancient Near East's understanding of the curse of divine abandonment. Block's research illustrates a Mesopotamian mindset of divine abandonment of cities and lands, usually caused by cultic and moral offenses. He views Ezekiel 8-11 as a 'divine departure narrative' and indicates subtle variations between Ezekiel and the extra-biblical materials.[31]

John T. Strong's work surveys previous academic research on the inherited beliefs encircling Zion and the glory of YHWH. Strong argues that Ezekiel is a theological conservative who aspires to uphold YHWH's presence for the exilic community. He infers, therefore, that the glory of YHWH was never 'de-throned' when it exited the temple in Ezekiel 8-11; but, rather, YHWH's glory departed in order to engage in battle for YHWH against chaos and to return triumphantly to the temple at the end of the book. Strong's interpretation of Ezekiel 8-11 is based upon the parallels he sees between Ezekiel's text and the Baal cycle from Ugarit. The text of Ezekiel never indicates that YHWH's glory abandons the temple to do battle against any opposing power.[32]

---

[30] Kutsko, *Between Heaven and Earth*.
[31] Block, 'Divine Abandonment', pp. 15-42.
[32] Strong, 'God's Kabod', pp. 69-96.

The goal of Steven Tuell's study is to determine the dwelling place of YHWH's presence once his glory departs from the temple in Jerusalem. By comparing the concepts of divine presence in the text of Ezekiel and priestly texts, he concludes that YHWH's abandonment from the temple is a response to the sins of the people. He expands on his proposal that Ezekiel 40-42 depicts the heavenly sanctuary and is a 'verbal icon' that arbitrates the presence of YHWH to the exiles in Babylon. Tuell presents a provocative argument, reinforced by comparing the exilic community's use of Ezekiel's text with Christian iconographic beliefs and practices, the significance of textuality in Ezekiel's sign act of eating the scroll (Ezek. 3.1-3), and associations between the text of Ezekiel, Qumran texts, and rabbinic literature. However, there is still no compelling proof that the book of Ezekiel was used in worship settings to mediate YHWH's presence for the exilic community.[33]

Elizabeth Keck asserts that there are two ways to view the divine presence of YHWH in the Old Testament. Ezekiel's depiction of the glory of YHWH contrasts with the Deuteronomistic view of YHWH's earthly divine presence. Ezekiel portrays YHWH's glory as having no affiliation with the temple or the land in Jerusalem. The glory of YHWH moves out of Jerusalem and appears to Ezekiel in Babylon where YHWH reveals the sins of the people. This delineation of YHWH's glory sharply opposes the Deuteronomistic theology of the one 'chosen place'. Ezekiel's schema of YHWH's glory is influenced by the Priestly account of the Exodus wanderings in the wilderness before the construction of the Tabernacle. According to Priestly tradition, the pre-Tabernacle accounts in Exodus record the only times YHWH's glory ever appeared outside a sanctified structure. The glory of YHWH appeared outside of Israel while the people were displaced in the wilderness with no physical sanctuary – a situation that was homologous to Ezekiel's current circumstances.[34]

The Kābôd of YHWH in the Old Testament: With Particular Reference to the Book of Ezekiel is a published revision of Pieter de Vries' 2010 PhD dissertation. Employing both a synchronic and a canonical approach, De Vries provides a comprehensive study of the semantic usage of the word כבד in the Old Testament. De Vries concludes that Ezekiel uses the word כבד distinctively and solely as a hypostasis

---

[33] Tuell, 'Divine Presence and Absence', pp. 96-117.
[34] Keck, 'Beside the River Chebar'.

of YHWH and asserts that the word כבד underscores the dual and anomalous character of the glory of YHWH. De Vries' research places accent on the visible aspect of YHWH's כבד.[35]

The Holiness of YHWH

Michael A. Lyons explains that Ezekiel's frequent use of the vocabulary and ideologies of the priestly legislatures attests to the pervasive literary similarities found in the book of Ezekiel and the Holiness Code. Lyons offers impressive criteria for ascertaining the path of literary reliance and effectively shows that it was Ezekiel who borrowed from the Holiness Code and not vice-versa. The main part of his study analyzes the ways in which Ezekiel documents and alters his original text into categories of accusation, judgment, instruction, and hope. Lyons pioneers this subject on the prophet's use of the Holiness Code found in the priestly traditions of Leviticus 17-26 and establishes the foundation for future discussions.[36]

Tova Ganzel contends that Ezekiel's language for Israel's idolatry seems to be more inspired by Deuteronomy than by the Holiness Code since Ezekiel mainly uses language characteristic of Deuteronomic Torah when referring to Israel's idols. Ganzel observes that Ezekiel infrequently refers to the priestly legislation (Leviticus 26) when he depicts Israel's idolatry. The copious literary correlation between Ezekiel and Deuteronomy leads Ganzel to conclude that Ezekiel intentionally borrowed Deuteronomy's language to portray Israel's idolatry. She discovers numerous links between the prophet's visions of idolatry in Ezekiel 8 and Moses' firm reproof against idolatry in Deuteronomy 4. Ganzel's study appropriately questions the widespread view that the Deuteronomic Torah has little or no influence on Ezekiel's distinctive priestly theology.[37]

According to Paul Joyce's innovative essay, 'Ezekiel and Moral Transformation', Israel's moral failure is not simply an individual responsibility but is considered to be the responsibility of the entire

---

[35] Pieter de Vries, *The Kābôd of YHWH in the Old Testament: With Particular Reference to the Book of Ezekiel* (trans. Alexander Thomson; Leiden: Koninklijke Brill, 2016).

[36] Michael A. Lyons, 'Transformation of Law: Ezekiel's Use of the Holiness Code (Leviticus 17–26)', in William A. Tooman and Michael A. Lyons (eds.), *Transforming Visions: Transformations of Text, Tradition, and Theology in Ezekiel* (Eugene, OR: Pickwick Publications, 2010), pp. 1-31.

[37] Ganzel, 'Transformation', pp. 33-49.

nation of Israel. The collective emphasis is palpable in Ezekiel 18, where Joyce indicates that the three hypothetical figures do not represent three individuals but instead corporate entities, namely, generations. Joyce finds Ezekiel's distinctive contribution elsewhere: the prophet's theocentric view of moral transformation. In Ezekiel's mind, Israel's moral transformation will not give rise to their restoration; rather, a divinely initiated restoration will effect Israel's moral transformation.[38]

As observed from this review, previous academic research on Ezekiel has inadequately explored the relationship between the glory of YHWH and the holiness of YHWH in the book of Ezekiel. The lack of attention given to the interrelationship between YHWH's glory and YHWH's holiness further justifies the need for this work. Since previous studies have shown little interest in exploring the relationship between the glory of YHWH and the holiness of YHWH in Ezekiel, I offer that a Pentecostal approach which desires to see and hear the voice of YHWH in the text may provide opportunity for the hearer to encounter the glorious majesty and holiness of YHWH.

Pentecostals and the Book of Ezekiel

For the past thirty years, the theological message(s) of Ezekiel has been virtually ignored by Pentecostals, a fact that is paradoxical considering Pentecostalism's interest in the Holy Spirit and Ezekiel's frequent mention of the Holy Spirit. Certain Pentecostal and Charismatic scholars such as George T. Montague, Stanley Horton, John Rea, Wilf Hildebrandt, and French Arrington have written on the Spirit's role in relation to Ezekiel's prophecy.[39] In addition to these older works on the Spirit in Ezekiel, Pieter de Vries' article analyzes the relationship between the glory of YHWH and the Spirit of

---

[38] Paul M. Joyce, 'Ezekiel and Moral Transformation', in William A. Tooman and Michael A. Lyons (eds.), *Transforming Visions: Transformations of Text, Tradition, and Theology in Ezekiel* (Eugene, OR: Pickwick Publications, 2010), pp. 139-58.
[39] George T. Montague, *The Holy Spirit: Growth of a Biblical Tradition* (New York: Paulist Press, 1976); Stanley M. Horton, *What the Bible Says About the Holy Spirit* (Springfield, MO: Gospel Publishing House, 1986); John Rea, *The Holy Spirit in the Bible* (Lake Mary, Florida: Creation House, 1990); Wilf Hildebrandt, *An Old Testament Theology of the Spirit of God* (Peabody, MA: Hendrickson Publishers, 1995); and French Arrington, *Encountering the Holy Spirit: Paths of Christian Growth and Service* (Cleveland, TN: Pathway Press, 2003).

YHWH in Ezekiel.[40] However, apart from these studies on the Spirit, Ezekiel has essentially been overlooked by the Pentecostal community.

Although Ezekiel may be one of the least known Old Testament prophets within the Pentecostal community today, early Pentecostals paid some attention to certain passages in Ezekiel, particularly to Ezek. 36.16–48.1-35. Most of their interpretations of these passages utilized either an allegorical hermeneutic or a literal dispensational eschatological hermeneutic. Only a few have appreciated the theological implications that may be discerned from a historical, contextual, or literary approach to the prophet. To analyze how early Pentecostals' approached the book of Ezekiel, I examined almost 90 references to Ezekiel in the early Pentecostal periodicals, beginning from 1906 to the end of 1916. I focused on this material because many scholars are agreed that the first ten years of the Pentecostal movement is the theological 'heart' of the movement.[41]

Allegorical Interpretations of Ezekiel

The early Pentecostals who followed an allegorical approach to Scripture fixed upon certain details in the text and applied them directly to their present-day context of Spirit baptism. The four living creatures in Ezekiel's inaugural vision, therefore, were identified as the 'Bride of Christ' and 'fire-baptized sons of God'[42] because these four creatures came out of the wind and fire of Ezekiel's vision. To be

---

[40] Pieter de Vries, 'The Relationship between the Glory of Yahweh and the Spirit of Yahweh in Ezekiel 33-48', *OTE* 28.2 (2015), pp. 326-50.

[41] See W.J. Hollenweger, *The Pentecostals* (Peabody, MA: Hendrickson, 1988), p. 551; Land, *Pentecostal Spirituality*, p. 27; Kimberly E. Alexander, *Pentecostal Healing Models in Theology and Practice* (JPTSup 29; Blandford Forum, UK: Deo Publishing, 2006), p. 66; Larry McQueen, *Toward a Pentecostal Eschatology: Discerning the Way Forward* (JPTSup 39; Blandford Forum, UK: Deo Publishing, 2012); C.E.W. Green, *Toward a Pentecostal Theology of the Lord's Supper: Foretasting the Kingdom* (Cleveland: CPT Press, 2012); Melissa L. Archer, *'I Was in the Spirit on the Lord's Day': A Pentecostal Engagement with Worship in the Apocalypse* (Cleveland, TN: CPT Press, 2014); Lee Roy Martin, *Fasting: A Centre for Pentecostal Theology Short Introduction* (Cleveland, TN: CPT Press, 2014), p. 116.

[42] *The Latter Rain Evangel* 3.2 (Nov 1910), p. 2. *The Latter Rain Evangel* was published monthly between 1908 and 1911 by the Stone Church in Chicago, IL. See also *The Bridegroom's Messenger* 6.121 (Nov 1912), p. 4. *The Bridegroom's Messenger* was published by G.B. Cashwell in Atlanta, Georgia in 1907. Some of the magazine's early contributors became leaders of the Church of God (Cleveland, Tennessee), the International Pentecostal Holiness Church, and the Pentecostal Free Will Baptist Church.

baptized with the Spirit meant to be baptized with the fire of God. To retain the fire of God, Christian believers should take their cue from the four living creatures who dwelled continuously in the presence of God.[43] The baptism of the Spirit was also 'typified by the deep river' in Ezek. 47.5.[44] Ezekiel's vision of a restored temple was the body of the Christian believer in which the Holy Spirit dwelled (1 Cor. 3.16; Eph. 3.17-18). Therefore, 'Just as the body is immersed in water in the rite of baptism, so the soul of the believer is immersed in the Holy Ghost when he is baptized in the Spirit'.[45] The river was also seen by some as a symbol of the 'latter rain' that will bring life to the saints of God,[46] and by others as a sign of the Holy Spirit working in an individual from new birth to baptism of the Holy Spirit.[47]

The interpretation of Ezekiel's vision of the valley of dry bones (37.1-25) varied depending upon the local context of the early Pentecostal. For a Pentecostal missionary, the dry bones in ch. 37 exemplified unbelievers who needed God's Spirit to breathe into them so that they may live and become an army.[48] For those Pentecostals living in North America, the dry bones characterized the state of some North American churches who needed the breath of the Holy Spirit to revive them and raise them up into a mighty army.[49] These two interpretations of Ezekiel 37 coalesced in Mrs. J.F. Greer's testimony of the Missouri revival in 1916:

> For two months it looked like Ezekiel's vision and the resurrection of the dry bones. Surely God did send his servants with the word of the Lord, and there was a noise and shaking and the dry bones came together. There was blessed victory among the saints. Surely it was a time of refreshing in the Lord, and precious souls were born into the Kingdom of God.[50]

---

[43] *The Pentecostal Evangel* 146 (Jul 1, 1916), p. 5. *The Pentecostal Evangel* was first published as *The Christian Evangel* in 1913. The weekly magazine for the Assemblies of God, USA was founded by J. Roswell and Alice Flower to report on revivals and mission activities.

[44] *Pentecostal Evangel* 146, p. 5.

[45] *Pentecostal Evangel* 146, p. 5.

[46] *Bridegroom's Messenger* 2.42 (Jul 1909), p. 1.

[47] *Bridegroom's Messenger* 3.48 (Oct 1909), p. 1.

[48] *Pentecostal Evangel* (Dec 16, 1916), p. 6.

[49] *Pentecostal Evangel* (Nov 25, 1916), p. 5.

[50] *Pentecostal Evangel* (Apr 1, 1916), p. 15.

A Literal Dispensational Interpretation of Ezekiel

At variance with the allegorical method of interpretation is the literal dispensational hermeneutic of Ezekiel. The literal dispensational view pivots on the literal fulfillment of the eschatological visions of Ezekiel in the future, and therefore pays special attention to chs. 38-39, which describe a climactic battle between Gog and Magog and the God of Israel, and to chs. 40-48, which according to dispensationalists, form a description of the restoration of the temple and its cultic worship during the millennium. Therefore, many early Pentecostals' view of Ezekiel chs. 36-48 was contingent on the current activities of the people of Israel and the Jews. Dispensationalists believed that the church must first understand God's plan for the Jews in order to understand God's plan for the church, the world, and the last days: 'The Jew is the proof of the inspiration of the scriptures. The scriptures uphold the Jew, and the Jew reacts upon the scriptures and proves its truth ... the Jew depends on the Bible, and the Bible is dependent upon the Jew'.[51] The Zionist movement occurring in the early 1900s was recognized as a fulfillment of Ezek. 39.27-29.[52] The Jews' return to their homeland would set in motion the rapture, the reign of the Antichrist, the judgments of God during the Great Tribulation, and the return of Christ to defeat the Antichrist in the final battle of Armageddon.[53]

A Historical and Doctrinal Interpretation of Ezekiel

In addition to the allegorical and literal dispensational approaches to Ezekiel, some early Pentecostals used Ezek. 36.25-27 to help form a historical and doctrinal theology of sanctification and holiness. Emerging from the Wesleyan-Holiness tradition, early Pentecostals adopted John Wesley's teaching on sanctification as part of their own theological system of beliefs. In essence, they believed a sanctified

---

[51] *Latter Rain* 2.6 (Mar 1910), p. 5.

[52] *The Pentecostal Herald* 1.4 (Jul 1915), p. 1. *The Pentecostal Herald*, an independent monthly paper, was first published in 1915 by George Brinkman, a Pentecostal leader in Chicago. In 1919, Brinkman became one of the founding officers of the Pentecostal Assemblies, USA in 1919, later renamed as Pentecostal Church of God in 1922. Brinkman donated his paper to the new organization.

[53] See also *Latter Rain* 2.1 (Oct 1909), pp. 17-23; *Latter Rain* 2.7 (Apr 1910), pp. 2-6; *Latter Rain* 2.8 (May 1910), pp. 3-8; *Latter Rain* 2.11 (Aug 1910), pp. 2-5; *Latter Rain* 4.5 (Feb 1912), pp. 6-11; *Latter Rain* (Jan 3, 1915), pp. 6-7; *Bridegroom's Messenger* 5.119 (Oct 1912), p. 4; *Bridegroom's Messenger* 8.175 (Oct 1915), p. 4.

'clean heart' was subsequent to justification and a necessary require-
ment for the baptism in the Holy Spirit. Thus, Ezek. 36.25-27 exemplified the 'threefold aspect of cleansing' that was necessary for every
Christian believer – 'justification by faith, or the cleansing by blood;
sanctification or the cleansing by the water of the Word; and the full-
ness of the Holy Ghost, or purging by fire'.[54]

Toward a Literary and Theological Interpretation of Ezekiel
This review of early Pentecostal literature reveals that the early Pentecostals utilized an allegorical, a dispensational, or a historical and
doctrinal method of interpreting the book of Ezekiel. Although the
allegorical and dispensational methods seem to dominate the early
Pentecostals' interpretation of Scripture, I propose that they are inadequate, and even incompatible with a Pentecostal approach to
Scripture. The allegorical hermeneutical paradigms of the early Pentecostals sought to uncover the hidden meaning of the text through
a spiritualization of Scripture.[55] One of the primary reasons for using
an allegorical approach to Scripture was to teach spiritual truths from
the Old Testament texts such as Ezekiel. The early Pentecostals who
employed an allegorical approach to Scripture viewed the book of
Ezekiel as a demonstration of the Holy Spirit's power to baptize believers, revive barren and lifeless churches, and to save unbelievers.
However, they did not focus on the theology found in the narratives
of the biblical texts. Although a Pentecostal approach can appreciate
the spiritual interpretation of Ezekiel, I would recommend that it is
not advantageous, judicious, or even practical to return to such a
passé method of biblical interpretation as the allegorical hermeneutical paradigm.[56] A restoration of antiquated biblical hermeneutics
rejects the scholarly consensus of postcritical methodologies.

Like the early Pentecostals, the dispensational eschatological view
of Ezekiel continues to inform many modern Pentecostals' theology
concerning Israel and the end times. However, as stated earlier, Pentecostalism and dispensationalism are actually quite at interpretive

---

[54] *Latter Rain* 4.3 (Dec 1911), pp. 6-8. See also *The Church of God Evangel* 6.49
(Dec 1915), p. 3. *The Church of God Evangel* began as *The Evening Light and the Church
of God Evangel* in 1910 under the leadership of A.J. Tomlinson. The title was short-
ened to *The Church of God Evangel* in 1911. This publication is the official periodical
for the Church of God (Cleveland, TN).
[55] Elliott E. Johnson, *Expository Hermeneutics: An Introduction* (Grand Rapids, MI:
Academie Books Zondervan Publishing House, 1990), p. 216.
[56] Martin, *The Unheard Voice of God,* pp. 49-51.

odds with one another. Dispensationalism rejects any ongoing activity and spiritual gifts of the Holy Spirit, including glossolalia, prophecy, and divine healing. The doctrine of dispensationalism, therefore, is antithetical to the ethos, tradition, and theology of Pentecostalism.

Since allegory and dispensationalism are not appropriate methods of a Pentecostal approach to Scripture, a literary and theological approach to Ezekiel will steer the interpretation of Ezekiel away from the aforementioned bygone views, and towards a message that is relevant to the contemporary Pentecostal community of faith. Ezekiel is not merely a manuscript that simply interprets the current events concerning the Jews and Palestine, and it is not a countdown timer to the battle of Armageddon. A fresh interpretation of the book of Ezekiel that is free from allegory and dispensationalism will reveal a God who is sovereign, glorious, and holy, and will lead the Pentecostal community to encounter and engage the God of Ezekiel. In addition to reshaping Ezekiel's message for the Pentecostal community, this study will serve the field of Old Testament studies by advancing the discussion of the interrelationship between the glory of YHWH and the holiness of YHWH in the book of Ezekiel.

Problem Formulation and Research Question

In this monograph I examine the role of the relationship between the glory of YHWH and the holiness of YHWH in the book of Ezekiel through a close literary-theological reading of key texts in Ezekiel. As stated above, I argue that the glory of YHWH and the holiness of YHWH interrelate in order to produce a unique theological vision of YHWH. Therefore, this research addresses three questions: (1) How does YHWH's glory and YHWH's holiness interrelate in the book of Ezekiel? (2) How does this interrelationship contribute to the characterization of YHWH in the book of Ezekiel? (3) How is the relationship between the glory of YHWH and the holiness of YHWH theologically significant for the Pentecostal community and the academy?

Goal and Objectives of this Study

The initial vision of Ezekiel is set at the opening of the prophecy so as to validate Ezekiel as YHWH's prophet to the exiles (Ezek. 33.33).

However, that endorsement should not be viewed only as a sanctioned mandate for Ezekiel's prophecy. The details of the inaugural vision are preserved so that we may see it with our imagination and be overwhelmed with complete astonishment and may meditate upon it so that we may respond affectively and with keen understanding. 'The seeing is here for the sake of hearing the word of [YHWH] through the prophecy – the very word of [YHWH] who translates himself into visions that he may approach us. Ezekiel saw, fell on his face, and [heard the Word of YHWH].'[57] The goal and objective of this study, therefore, is to see and hear the word of YHWH in the prophecy of Ezekiel by forging an adequate and properly applied method that is consistent with the ethos of the Pentecostal community as well as contribute to the current academic conversation on the book of Ezekiel.

Introductory Remarks on Methodology

My endeavor in this study is to pay explicit attention to how the depiction of YHWH's glory is emblematic of YHWH's holiness and how that portrait paints a theology of YHWH in the book of Ezekiel. Therefore, this study primarily utilizes a literary and theological approach to Ezekiel, rather than one that focuses on the redactional work or compositional history of Ezekiel. While I acknowledge the significant contributions of historical-critical scholarship to the book of Ezekiel, the interpretive aim of this examination is not to supply knowledge about the historical setting of the book of Ezekiel, nor will it seek the historical development of Ezekiel. The texts investigated in this monograph are interpreted as part of a larger literary whole – the book of Ezekiel. It is indubitably not this study's goal to reconstruct the historical figure and events of Ezekiel, but instead to construct a theological reading based on the literary contents of the book of Ezekiel.

General literary criticism studies, evaluates, and interprets any genre of literature,[58] and when the tools and principles of literary criticism are applied to biblical narrative texts, it may be known as

---

[57] James Luther Mays, *Ezekiel, Second Isaiah* (Proclamation Commentaries; Philadelphia: Fortress Press, 1978), p. 28.
[58] Martin, *The Unheard Voice of God*, p. 245.

'narratology'[59] or 'narrative criticism'.[60] The primary focus of literary criticism is to study the text in its finished form. The form, shape and structure of a text are studied as a 'complete tapestry, an organic whole'.[61] Although literary criticism is not a theological method,[62] it considers the text as a coherent whole, and it is an encouraging ally to canonical and theological methodologies. Although the entire book of Ezekiel is not a strict narrative, the book as a whole has a narrative structure.[63] Brevard Childs, for example, observes that 'the backbone of the [book of Ezekiel's] structure is provided by a chronological framework which extends throughout the book and joins the sections together'.[64] Daniel Block also notes that the

---

[59] Mieke Bal, *Narratology: Introduction to the Theory of Narrative* (Toronto: University of Toronto Press, 1985), pp. 1-6.

[60] Mark Allan Powell, *What Is Narrative Criticism?* (Minneapolis: Fortress, 1990), pp. 1-6. The term 'narrative criticism' was introduced by David Rhoads in an article 'Narrative Criticism and the Gospel of Mark', *JAAR* 50 (1982), pp. 411-34; repr. in David Rhoads, *Reading Mark, Engaging the Gospel* (Minneapolis: Fortress, 2004), Chapter 1. For a general overview of the application of literary theory to the analysis of biblical narrative text see Robert Alter, *The Art of Biblical Narrative* (New York: Basic Books, 1981), pp. 3-22; Meir Sternberg, *The Poetics of Biblical Narrative; Ideological Literature and the Drama of Reading* (Bloomington, IN: Indiana University Press, 1985); Shimon Bar-Efrat, *Narrative Art in the Bible* (Bible and Literature Series 17; Sheffield: Almond, 1989); David Aune, 'Narrative Criticism', *The Westminster Dictionary of New Testament and Early Christian Literature and Rhetoric* (Louisville: Westminster John Knox, 2003), pp. 315-17; Stanley E. Porter, 'Literary Approaches to the New Testament: From Formalism to Deconstruction and Back', in Stanley E. Porter and David Tombs (eds.), *Approaches to New Testament Study* (JSNTSup 120; Sheffield: Sheffield Academic Press, 1995), pp. 77-128; Wesley A. Kort, *Story, Text and Scripture: Literary Interests in Biblical Narrative* (University Park: Pennsylvania State University Press, 1988); Petri Merenlahti, *Poetics for the Gospels? Rethinking Narrative Criticism* (London: T&T Clark, 2002); Kenneth R.R. Gros Louis, James Stokes Ackerman, and Thayer S. Warshaw, *Literary Interpretations of Biblical Narratives* (2 vols.; Nashville: Abingdon, 1974-1982); Elizabeth Struthers Malbon, 'Narrative Criticism: How Does the Story Mean?', in Janice Capel Anderson and Stephen D. Moore (eds.), *Mark & Method: New Approaches in Biblical Studies* (Minneapolis: Fortress, 1992), pp. 23-49; Michael Fishbane, *Text and Texture: Close Readings of Selected Biblical Texts* (New York: Schocken Books 1979); Daniel and Yvan Bourquin Marguerat, *How to Read Bible Stories: An Introduction to Narrative Criticism* (London: SCM, 1999).

[61] J.L. Resseguie, *Narrative Criticism of the New Testament: An Introduction* (Grand Rapids, MI: Baker Academic, 2005), p. 19.

[62] Adele Berlin, 'Characterization in Biblical Narrative: David's Wives', *JSOT* 23 (1982), p. 69.

[63] See Chapter 4 for a more detailed discussion on the narrative structure of Ezekiel.

[64] Brevard Childs, *Introduction to the Old Testament as Scripture* (Philadelphia: Fortress, 1979), p. 365.

sequential dates of the oracles construct a 'chronological framework' for the prophet's ministry.[65] The thirteen chronological dates (1.1; 8.1; 20.1; 24.1; 26.1; 29.1; 29.17; 30.20; 31.1; 32.1; 32.17; 33.21; and 40.1) that Ezekiel provides with careful precision[66] give a coherent reading to the entire book of Ezekiel. Finally, since narrative critics describe narrative as 'any work of literature that tells a story',[67] Ezekiel is a narrative that tells the story of a glorious and holy God who is committed to redeeming his people and restoring his relationship with them. YHWH's devotion to saving 'the house of Israel' arises out of his ardent love for them. Thus, my methodology will focus on the holistic literary reading of the prophetic book of Ezekiel as a narrative with special emphasis upon language and exegesis.

Narrative criticism[68] examines how the content and structure of a biblical text function as literature. Biblical narrative critics employ the same elements of contemporary literary theories such as narrator, plot, character, etc. to study biblical texts. Scripture, therefore, can be read in the same way one would read a short story, a play, or a novel.[69]

Literary criticism is a departure from the long established historical-critical methodology that endeavored to discover the historical composition – the life and rationalization behind the pericope – to the literary meaning and the arresting emotive effects of the texts themselves. Literary criticism views the final, finished form of a text as a coherent whole,[70] sees how the nuances and various narrative qualities of a text – its structure, characters, rhetorical designs, setting, time and space, symbolism, etc. – are interrelated through close reading of the text[71] and acknowledges the affective dimensions of the text upon its hearers/readers.[72] Literary

---

[65] Block, *The Book of Ezekiel Chapters 1-24*, p. 6.
[66] Ezekiel usually recorded each date by the year, the month, and the day of the month.
[67] Powell, *What Is Narrative Criticism?*, p. 23.
[68] The terms 'narrative criticism' and 'literary criticism' are used synonymously in this study.
[69] Resseguie, *Narrative Criticism*, p. 19.
[70] Powell, *What is Narrative Criticism?*, p. 7.
[71] M.H. Abrams, *A Glossary of Literary Terms* (Fort Worth: Harcourt Brace College Publishers, 7th edn, 1999), p. 181.
[72] For more on the affective aspect of Scripture, see Robert O. Baker, 'Pentecostal Bible Reading: Toward a Model of Reading for the Formation of the Affections', *JPT* 7 (1995), pp. 34-38; Land, *Pentecostal Spirituality*, pp. 32-48, 131-61; and Lee Roy Martin, '"Oh give thanks to the Lord for he is good": Affective

criticism understands that the genesis, source, and evolution of a text are irrelevant for the interpretation of a text. The hermeneutical process no longer relies on the historical, social, cultural, and psychological factors of the text but finds meaning within the current, present form of the text.[73] The adoption of a literary and theological approach to the book of Ezekiel for this study does not discredit the immense contribution of the various historical-critical methodologies; neither does it imply that this method is the only key to interpreting Scripture or contend that literary criticism is a theological method; but, rather, it acknowledges that it is a complimentary ally to the theological hermeneutical process.[74]

This study's approach will start with the 'being' of the Ezekiel texts in their final form rather than on their 'becoming', will include emphasis upon language and exegesis, and the interpreter's 'personal voice'[75] on the relationship between the glory of YHWH and the holiness of YHWH in Ezekiel. Any interpretation that views Scripture 'as an organic whole, a unity that needs to be examined on its own terms and pays close attention to the words [of the text]'[76] is bound to engage the methods and techniques of literary scholarship.

Narrative texts can be identified by their inclusion of five literary characteristics. The first crucial characteristic of a narrative is the narrator, the voice who tells the story. It is essential to observe that the narrator is not the same as the author, but is the character devised by the author to relate the events of the narrative to the audience.[77] Through the narrator we observe, gain knowledge of, and 'direct access to the characters of the narrative ... We see and hear only through the narrator's eyes and ears.'[78] We are unable to know anything the narrator does not know.

Hermeneutics, Psalm 107, and Pentecostal Spirituality', *Pneuma* 36.3 (Fall 2014), pp. 1-24.

[73] Powell, *What Is Narrative Criticism?*, p. 2; Resseguie, *Narrative Criticism*, p. 19.

[74] Robert Morgan and John Barton, *Biblical Interpretation* (Oxford Bible Series; New York: Oxford University Press, 1988), p. 203.

[75] Daniel Patte, 'The Guarded Personal Voice of a Male European-American Biblical Scholar', in Ingrid Rosa Kitzberger (ed.), *Personal Voice in Biblical Interpretation* (London: Routledge, 1999), pp. 12-24.

[76] Resseguie, *Narrative Criticism*, p. 22.

[77] David Gunn and Danna Nolan Fewell, *Narrative in the Hebrew Bible* (Oxford: Oxford University Press, 1993), p. 52.

[78] Bar-Efrat, *Narrative Art in the Bible*, p. 13.

Biblical narrators are also omniscient and authoritative.[79] The all-seeing and all-knowing narrator has complete access to covert conversations and unseen events and is able to reveal the most intimate thoughts and feelings of the characters to the readers. 'Nothing remains hidden from the omniscient narrator'.[80] The narrator's omniscience prepares the readers to accept her/his voice as reliable and authoritative. Since the readers are expected to believe everything the narrator says – and not challenge the reliability of the narrator – the narrator is able to influence the readers' views of the characters in the narrative.[81]

The second characteristic of a narrative is the plot. The plot is the causal sequence of related events that formulate the narrative's story.[82] These events are not haphazardly strung together, but are painstakingly chained together by cause and effect, parallelism, and contrast to construct a logical and unified whole. No event is a nugatory link in the chain. The withdrawal of one of the events may cause a break in the chain and blemish the aesthetic development of the plot.[83]

The plot's sequential events have a discernible beginning, middle, and end; and these events are structured in such a way that provoke readers' interest and engage their emotions. Between the beginning and the end, the plot progresses through conflicts among characters that create rising tension and suspense in the story. This tension continues to escalate until it reaches the climax, or the highest point of the story, which is then followed by a denouement. Here, the conflicts descend, and the story concludes with either a resolution or a tragedy. Often times, a story may contain subsidiary plots or auxiliary plots that coexist with the main plot. Usually, biblical narratives consist of multiple individual stories that are intricately woven together to form a macro plot.

Unlike other prophetic books of the Old Testament, the book of Ezekiel unfolds in a sequential arrangement of events that include visions, sign acts, and prophetic utterances. Its plot begins with the

[79] Martin, *The Unheard Voice of God*, p. 246.
[80] Bar-Efrat, *Narrative Art in the Bible*, p. 18.
[81] Alter, *The Art of Biblical Narrative*, p. 59.
[82] William Harmon and C. Hugh Holman, *A Handbook to Literature* (Upper Saddle River: Prentice Hall, 8th edn, 1999), p. 393-94.
[83] Bar-Efrat, *Narrative Art in the Bible*, p. 93.

account of the prophet's initial vision of YHWH's glory that summons Ezekiel to his prophetic calling. Ezekiel's sign acts that portray the foreboding siege of Jerusalem and the disclosure of the people's sins reach a climax when YHWH's glory departs from the temple. Not only do Israel's[84] sins conflict with the majesty and holiness of YHWH, but his departure from the temple collides with Israel's confident assumption that YHWH's presence would reside forever in the temple of Jerusalem. How then can YHWH's glory depart from the temple? By this point of the story, the readers are fully immersed in the conflict and are captivated by the desire to know the ending. Would the ending provide meaning, closure, and resolution? Or would the ending spell tragedy? The plot of Ezekiel concludes with the prophet's vision of salvation, the restored temple, and the return of YHWH's glory to the temple. The concluding line of the story, 'YHWH is there', reflects God's restoration of his people, and so provides resolution to the exile and YHWH's previous departure from the temple.

The third feature of narrative, characters, are distinctive actors involved in the events of the story, and their individual personalities are created by a process called characterization. Characters are extremely important because they are the *dramatis personae* who enact the various events that constitute the plot. Many of the significant themes of the narrative are uttered through the characters. We may engage biblical characters directly through information mediated through the narrator or by other characters, or we may experience characters indirectly through their speech, actions, thoughts, environment, clothing, social status, and the way in which they present themselves. We should not restrain our conception of characters to only individuals. Characters may also be animals or creatures (such as the four living creatures in the prophet's initial vision) or non-human entities (such as the four wheels in Ezekiel 1).

---

[84] Ezekiel applies the name Israel to the northern kingdom, to Jews living in Babylon, and to the remnant in Jerusalem. For a detailed discussion on Ezekiel's use of the terms 'house of Israel', 'sons of Israel', and 'Israel' see Daniel Block, '"Israel" – "Sons of Israel": A Study in Hebrew Eponymic Usage', *SR* 13 (1984), 301-26. This study will employ the various expressions of Israel as they appear in the text. Like Ezekiel, this work will use the expression 'Israel' and 'Israelite' as a theological and ethnic reference to the people of YHWH, whether they be the original twelve tribes, the kingdom of Judah, the exiles in Babylon, or the remnant in Jerusalem.

Characters are developed based on the amount of information that is conveyed about them. Characters may be described as either flat or round. Flat characters are two-dimensional and possess a limited number of personality traits; we may see only one side or aspect of them. Consequently, they have no mysterious complexities, do not undergo development, and are predictable. By contrast, round characters are three-dimensional, displaying an aggregation of complex traits, undergo several changes and development, and are capable of surprising the reader.[85]

Additionally, characters may be analyzed according to the way in which they engage other characters, the change and development a character experiences through the course of the story, and by the role she/he plays in the events of the narrative.[86]

Since the events of the story are told by a narrator, characters become known to us through the narrator. In order to preserve mystery in the character, the narrator conceals critical information from the reader.[87] The narrator may choose to reveal information about a character by either indirect or direct presentation.[88] In indirect presentation, the narrator authoritatively interjects in order to make direct descriptions, comments, and observations about the motive and personality traits of the characters. Indirect presentation may show 'the characters talking and acting and leaves the reader to infer the motives and dispositions that lie behind what they say and do'.[89] The inward speech of a character as well as the 'narrator's explicit statement of what the characters feel, intend, desire'[90] can be accepted as infallible information. Direct presentation may be voiced by other characters or by the characters themselves. Since characters

---

[85] See Powell, *What Is Narrative Criticism?*, pp. 51-54; Resseguie, *Narrative Criticism*, pp. 121-26; Gunn and Fewell, *Narrative in the Hebrew Bible*, pp. 46-89; Shlomith Rimnon-Kenan, *Narrative Fiction: Contemporary Poetics* (London: Methuen, 1983), pp. 59-71.

[86] Bal, *Narratology: Introduction to the Theory of Narrative*, pp. 25-37, 79-93.

[87] Alter, *The Art of Biblical Narrative*, p. 126.

[88] Rimnon-Kenan, *Narrative Fiction*, p. 59; Powell, *What Is Narrative Criticism?*, pp. 52-53 and; Resseguie, *Narrative Criticism*, pp. 126-30, prefer the terms 'showing' and 'telling' rather than 'direct and indirect presentation' to describe the two narrative techniques of characterization; Bal, *Narratology*, p. 89, uses the terms 'qualification' and 'qualification by function'.

[89] Abrams, *'A Glossary of Literary Terms'*, pp. 33-34.

[90] Alter, *The Art of Biblical Narrative*.

are not always trustworthy, direct presentation should be carefully analyzed because it may or may not be reliable.[91]

In view of the foregoing discussion, how does the narrative role of YHWH in Ezekiel's visions (chs. 1-3; 8-11 and 40-43) portray that he is glorious and holy? This question will be explored fully in Chapter 5, but a brief response is in order at this point. Lee Roy Martin suggests that the narrative role of God may be determined by the following six elements:

> (1) the presence or absence of God throughout the narrative; (2) the actions of God within the narrative; (3) the role of God as described by the narrator; (4) the role of God as described by other characters in the narrative; (5) the role of God when compared and contrasted to the role of other characters; (6) the role of God as characterized by his own speech (either direct or inward speech).[92]

From the prophet's visions in chs. 1-3, 8-11, and 40-43, it seems clear that the presence and absence of God uncover an interrelated link between the glory of YHWH and the holiness of YHWH in Ezekiel. Ezekiel's riveting vision of YHWH's glory in ch. 1 was an unveiling of God himself. YHWH was infinitely exalted above the earth and was arrayed with beauty, radiance, splendor, and majesty. YHWH's glorious presence at the outset of the book is used as a backdrop to feature the depravity of Israel's sins. Their vitiable worship of other gods is contrasted heavily with the glory of YHWH. As a consequence of the abominations being done in the temple and the promiscuous and idolatrous heart of Israel, YHWH withdrew his glorious presence from the temple. This departure from the temple reveals a holy God, a God who could not reside with sin. The revelation of YHWH's glory and holiness is God's own witness of himself. The return of YHWH's glory to the temple in 40-43 underlines the holy character of YHWH because Israel has been purified (36.25), transformed (36.26), and reconciled (36.26) unto their God. The return of YHWH's glory also shows a God who is loving, merciful, and faithful. He's not simply a God who judges, punishes, and abandons his people, but a God who desires to have intimate relationship with his people. God is the most compelling

---

[91] Alter, *The Art of Biblical Narrative*, p. 117.
[92] Martin, *The Unheard Voice of God*, p. 250.

character in the book of Ezekiel. He is, in fact, the one figure whose presence (and even absence) gives the book a coherent structure.

The portrayal of YHWH's character 'is one of the great challenges of the Hebrew Bible'[93] because the attributes of God are not overtly delineated in an orderly form. So, we sketch God's character by compiling the features extrapolated from 'dramatic manifestations'.[94] The narrator refrains from direct presentation of God. There is no precise physical description of God and no explanation of his 'social status, personal history [and] local habitation'.[95] Although Ezekiel sees a vision that he describes as the glory of God, there is no description of God himself, but only of the elements around God. This dearth of direct description of God provides a 'qualitative distance that separates God from humans and pagan gods, both existing in matter and time and space and society'.[96] Direct presentation of God will simply place him in the same class as the other characters 'rather than a unique and enigmatic power, knowable only through his incursions into history'.[97] Uncovering God's character through indirect presentation 'reveals enough to make the divine order intelligible and impressive while concealing it enough to leave it mysterious, transcendent, irreducible to terms other than itself'.[98]

While the word 'compassion' (רחם) is found only once in 39.25, during Ezekiel's description of the restoration of Israel (chs. 33-48), and the words 'forgiveness' (סלח), 'mercy' (חסד), and 'pity' (חום) are not found at all, God shows his love to his people by restoring them and returning his glory to the new temple. The return of the glory of YHWH indicates that the covenant is renewed, and the people are cleansed (Ezek. 36.25-27). God's love for Israel demonstrates the holy character of God. God loves Israel not because Israel loves God. God forgives Israel not because Israel repents and turns away from idolatry. God loves and forgives Israel because God is holy. For God to be holy means that every aspect of God's nature, character,

---

93 Gunn and Fewell, *Narrative in the Hebrew Bible*, p. 89.
94 Sternberg, *The Poetics of Biblical Narrative*, p. 323.
95 Sternberg, *The Poetics of Biblical Narrative*, p. 323.
96 Sternberg, *The Poetics of Biblical Narrative*, p. 323.
97 Sternberg, *The Poetics of Biblical Narrative*, p. 323.
98 Sternberg, *The Poetics of Biblical Narrative*, p. 323.

and being is holy. Thus, the holiness of God effects the holy love of God.

The fourth characteristic of narrative is 'point of view', which is the outlook from which a story is narrated. The point of view decides and influences the perspective and insight of the unfolding story. It is the vantage point from which reality is viewed or action and information are conveyed. A story can be communicated from the standpoint of the narrator, the characters, or the reader. Just as a movie director selects from a number of different camera angles to create the right image to depict the scene, the point of view thus chosen controls the content of the narration and how it will be narrated.[99] Understanding the point of view is crucial to grasping the meaning of the narrative; it is the means by which the events of a story, and, in some instances, emotions and motives of the characters are relayed.[100]

The fifth characteristic of narrative, setting, is the context in which the story takes place, and it includes the spatial, temporal, and social locations of the story.[101] Elements of spatial setting in Ezekiel include geographical locations (Tel Abib, Judah); topographical locations (the River Chebar); and architectural (or man-made structures such as the temple) locations. The temporal aspects of setting consist of three types of time discourse: (1) time (length of time) required for telling the narrative;[102] (2) 'narrated time', the time within the plot or the length of an event or action; and (3) chronological time, which refers to the sequential order of events constituting the plot. Chronological time, however, does not mean that the events in the narrative are always presented in the successive order in which they occur.[103] Temporal citation in Ezekiel includes the dates of the prophet's vision. The final component of setting is the social milieu of the narrative. The social backdrop includes the political, cultural, class, and economic conditions of the story.[104] The political climate of Ezekiel is an exilic community of Israel in

---

[99] Bar-Efrat, *Narrative Art in the Bible*, p. 15.
[100] J.P. Fokkelman, *Reading Biblical Narrative: An Introductory Guide* (Louisville, KY: Westminster John Knox Press, 1999), pp. 143-47.
[101] Powell, *What Is Narrative Criticism?*, pp. 69-74.
[102] Fokkelman, *Reading Biblical Narrative*, pp. 35-44.
[103] Bar-Efrat, *Narrative Art in the Bible*, pp. 141-67.
[104] Resseguie, *Narrative Criticism*, p. 110; Powell, *What Is Narrative Criticism?*, p. 74.

Babylon. Setting is an important element of narrative because it establishes the mood or atmosphere of the narrative,[105] influences plot development, and intensifies the central conflict in a narrative.[106]

Although narrative criticism focuses on the five formal characteristics of literature – narrator, plot, characters, point of view, and setting – attention is also given to the narrative's linguistic style and techniques such as semantics, rhetorical devices, figures of speech, synonyms, antonyms, and theological movement. My employment of literary criticism will also comprise a close reading of the text and a comprehensive analysis of the Hebrew language. Additionally, while my methodology will consider the five formal literary characteristics, these five elements will not control my analysis of the text. Instead, my examination of Ezekiel will be directed by the text itself, applying the five formal characteristics when appropriate.

It is crucial to grasp at the start that the book of Ezekiel is not composed of one genre but consists of many different genres. These include prophecy, visions, dramas, poetry, parables, and apocalyptic writing. The convergence of these heterogeneous literary styles in the book of Ezekiel adds to the complexity of its interpretation. Certain sections of the book are considered to be narrative, and the book as a whole displays a narrative structure.[107] The 'prophetic book is shaped from the beginning as a narrative … [and] in many respects, the book of Ezekiel can be viewed as one long narrative'.[108] The discernable narrative texts include chs. 1.1–3.15; 8.1–11.25; 20.1; 33.21-22; and 40.1–48.35. The narrative may include only a temporal setting such as the date, a complete vision, or a significant proclamation such as the fall of Jerusalem in 33.21-22.

This study focuses primarily on those narrative texts that depict the prophet's sequential visions of the glory of YHWH (chs. 1-3, 8-11, and 40-43); therefore, I have chosen a literary-theological reading of the book of Ezekiel from a Pentecostal perspective. The application of my methodology will probe and sculpt the

---

105 Seymour Chatman, *Story and Discourse: Narrative Structure in Fiction and Film* (New York: Cornell University Press, 1980), p. 140.

106 David Rhoads, Joanna Dewey and Donald Michie, *Mark as a Story: An Introduction to the Narrative of a Story* (Minneapolis, MN: Fortress Press 2012), p. 63.

107 Chapter 4 will further discuss the narrative structure of the book of Ezekiel.

108 Tyler D. Mayfield, *Literary Structure and Setting in Ezekiel* (Tübingen, Germany: Mohr Siebeck, 2010), p. 94.

interrelationship between the glory of YHWH and the holiness of YHWH in the narrative, and may facilitate the narratives' ability to 'order and reorder our experience … reflect a given culture … [or] create the real world … [be] performative … give meaning to life … be subversive … [criticize] dominant patters of thought and institution'.[109] Accordingly, this approach to the book of Ezekiel may endorse or examine, sustain or stimulate the Pentecostal community of faith and the academy. We should be completely prepared to experience all possible effects generated by Ezekiel's visions.[110]

Research Approach and Technique

As I investigate the interrelationship between the glory of YHWH and the holiness of YHWH in the book of Ezekiel, my research approach and technique will progress in two major stages. The first stage involves the development of an interpretive lens for the visions of the glory of YHWH. This stage includes a review of preceding scholarship on the book of Ezekiel and an explication on the purpose of a Pentecostal hermeneutic.

The second stage applies my methodology to the book of Ezekiel. In this stage, I will offer a brief overview of the book of Ezekiel, an analysis of the glory of YHWH and the holiness of YHWH, a theological reflection on the interrelationship between the glory of YHWH and the holiness of YHWH, and a conclusion that summarizes my discoveries and highlights this study's significant contributions to the Pentecostal community and the academy.

Chapter Outline

This study begins with an introductory chapter that will delineate my motivations, aspirations, and strategies for my examination of how the themes of YHWH's glory and YHWH's holiness interrelate in the book of Ezekiel. Chapter 1 introduces this study as a Pentecostal literary-theological reading of the book of Ezekiel that gives special attention to the narratives that depict the prophet's sequential visions

---

[109] Gunn and Fewell, *Narrative in the Hebrew Bible*, p. 1.
[110] Martin, *The Unheard Voice of God*, p. 253.

of the glory of YHWH (Ezekiel 1-3; 8-11, and 40-43). These visionary experiences of YHWH's glory provide the structural framework
that supports the theological theme of YHWH's holiness. My primary motivation for this research is to redirect the Pentecostal community away from the dispensational eschatology perspective of Ezekiel toward a more literary-theological interpretation that emerges
from the book's original context. The need for this work is also justified by the inadequate scholarly attention given to the interrelationship between the glory of YHWH and the holiness of YHWH in the
book of Ezekiel. This chapter describes the literary-theological
method as a helpful tool for interpreting Ezekiel and presents a Pentecostal approach to biblical study.

Chapter 2 surveys previous academic approaches to the book of
Ezekiel and reveals a paradigm shift from the historical-critical methods of interpreting Ezekiel to literary/rhetorical studies in the book
of Ezekiel. The development of synchronic methods has allowed
contemporary scholarship to be more inclusive, to acknowledge numerous methods of study, and to be more receptive to the various
voices of interpretation. This shift indicates that a Pentecostal literary
and theological approach to the book of Ezekiel is consistent with
current Ezekielian scholarship.

In Chapter 3 I will refine my Pentecostal hermeneutical strategy
by integrating it with the book of Ezekiel. In this chapter I propose
that the themes of *seeing* and *hearing* serve as a suitable biblical model
for a Pentecostal approach to Ezekiel.

Chapter 4 presents the book's literary structure, a brief overview
of Ezekiel's message, and the theological themes of the book of Ezekiel.

Chapters 5 through 7 form the heart of this study. These chapters
explore the theme of the glory of YHWH as depicted in the book
of Ezekiel. As part of the process, I will show how the visions of
YHWH's glory play a crucial structural role in the entire book. The
visions of YHWH's glory lay the groundwork for the message of
covenant curses and are a vital part of the structural framework that
holds the entire prophecy together. Additionally, it is the appearance
of the glory of YHWH in ch. 43 that gives the prophetic message its
cohesive final form. The book begins with the departure of YHWH's
glory, but ends with the return of YHWH glory, which is evident in
the final phrase of the book, 'YHWH is there' (Ezek. 48.35). These

chapters will also discuss the motif of YHWH's holiness in the book of Ezekiel. Through Ezekiel's oracles, it is evident that he has a high regard for YHWH's holiness. This radically God-centered point of view finds its sharpest expression in 36.22–23: 'It is not for your sake, O house of Israel, that I am about to act, but for the sake of my holy name ... And I will vindicate the holiness of my great name ... And the nations will know that I am YHWH'. These chapters will demonstrate how the glory of YHWH and the holiness of YHWH interrelate in the book of Ezekiel to provide a unique theological vision of YHWH. The crucial theme for the exilic community is that YHWH doesn't just possess holiness, but YHWH is holy, and as a result YHWH's glory, which is symbolic of YHWH's divine presence, will not dwell among unholy people.

Chapter 8 presents the conclusions and implications of a Pentecostal seeing and hearing of the word of YHWH in the book of Ezekiel.

2

APPROACHES TO EZEKIEL

Introduction

This chapter will provide an overview of the most significant scholarly approaches to the book of Ezekiel. A detailed review of the literature on Ezekiel is unnecessary because an exhaustive presentation
of that material has already been offered elsewhere.[1] Nevertheless,
this limited survey is necessary in order to show how various developments in Ezekielian scholarship have constructed a path that per-
mits a Pentecostal literary–theological method of interpretation.
Therefore, the bulk of this review examines the works of key scholars in the twentieth century and concludes with the current state of
Ezekielian scholarship. It will also include some of the pertinent
studies of the late nineteenth century as they relate to the historic
moves within the scholarship on Ezekiel. Some scholars have argued
for a particular hermeneutical paradigm based upon the historical setting; others have approached the book in terms of its compositional

---

[1] For a comprehensive review of literature until 1950, the reader should confer
with H.H. Rowley, 'The Book of Ezekiel in Modern Study', in *Men of God: Studies
in Old Testament History and Prophecy* (London: Nelson, 1963), pp. 169-210; Zimmerli,
Ezekiel 1-24, pp. 3-8; Henry McKeating, *Ezekiel* (Sheffield: Sheffield Academic
Press, 1993), pp. 30-42; Childs, *Introduction*. For a history of scholarship after 1950,
see McKeating, *Ezekiel*, pp. 43-61; Katheryn Pfisterer Darr, 'Ezekiel among the
Critics', *CR:BS* 2 (1994), pp. 9-24; Risa Levitt Kohn, 'Ezekiel at the Turn of the
Century', *CBR* 2 (2003), pp. 9-31. See also Paul M. Joyce, *Divine Initiative and Human
Response in Ezekiel* (JSOTSup 51; Sheffield: JSOT Press, 1989), pp. 21-31; Renz, *The
Rhetorical Function of the Book of Ezekiel*, pp. 27-38.

history; still others have taken a canonical approach and have examined Ezekiel based on the literary unity and integrity of the final form of the book. This chapter, therefore, will move from the most notable history-oriented studies to the advocates of the literary/rhetorical methods, and it will conclude that the current direction of scholarship on Ezekiel is moving toward a literary/rhetorical approach and, therefore, offers room for a Pentecostal literary–theological study of the book of Ezekiel.[2]

Historical and Critical Approaches

The impact of a diachronic analysis of the book of Ezekiel was slow to develop in the twentieth century. For the first quarter of the century, no one offered convincing arguments against the literary unity or authorship of the book of Ezekiel. This does not imply that all scholars were agreed on the unity of the book and its authorship for the first twenty-five years of the twentieth century. The works of R. Kraetzschmar[3] and J. Herrmann[4] had already alluded to the possibility of multiple authors or editors.[5] However, the publication of G. Hölscher's *Hesekiel Der Dichter und das Buch*[6] in 1924 is credited with polarizing the critical debate on the book of Ezekiel.[7] Hölscher contends that the original words of the prophet make up only about seven percent of the book of Ezekiel and that the rest of the book was written by a Zadokite redactor who lived in Jerusalem in the early fifth century.[8] Hölscher's controvertible work signified a clear turning

---

[2] A few examples of this contemporary move toward literary/rhetorical methods include Peterson, *Ezekiel in Context*; Jurrien Mol, *Collective and Individual Responsibility: A Description of Corporate Personality in Ezekiel 18 and 20* (Boston: Brill, 2009); Mayfield, *Literary Structure and Setting in Ezekiel*; and Keck, 'Beside the Chebar River'.

[3] Kraetzschmar, *Das Buch Ezechiel*.

[4] J. Herrmann, *Ezechielstudien* (BWANT 2; Leipzig: J.C. Hinrich, 1908).

[5] Cf. Ellen F. Davis, *Swallowing the Scroll: Textuality and the Dynamics of Discourse in Ezekiel's Prophecy* (Bible and Literature Series 21; Sheffield: Almond Press, 1989), p. 12; Joyce, *Divine Initiative*, p. 22.

[6] Hölscher, *Hesekiel, der Dichter und das Buch*.

[7] Cf. Childs, *Introduction*, p. 357; Davis, *Swallowing the Scroll*, pp. 12-13; Iain M. Duguid, *Ezekiel and the Leaders of Israel* (VTSup 56; Leiden: Brill, 1994), p. 3; Renz, *The Rhetorical Function of the Book of Ezekiel*, p. 30.

[8] Childs, *Introduction*, p. 358; Davis, *Swallowing the Scroll*, p. 13; Joyce, *Divine Initiative*, p. 22. It is worth mentioning that before critical approaches to biblical interpretation were fully in use, Georg Ludwig Oeder in 1756 questioned the unity

point in the history of Ezekielian scholarship. Since his publication, the compositional history of the book has been a matter of debate, and while there are certain points upon which scholars can agree, there is still no established consensus among them.[9]

The range of opinions among historical-critical scholars has been condensed by Thomas Renz into six main arguments. Renz notes that the core of the historical debate revolves around two questions. First, 'was the book meant for a specific audience, and if so was the audience an exilic one? Secondly, does the book portray the ministry of a prophet who was (exclusively) active in Babylonia, or, more precisely … is the picture drawn by the book accurate?'[10] Scholars have responded to these questions from diverse perspectives and presumptions and have aggressively defended a particular stance that was contingent on literary content, location, and perspective of the prophet. In order to avoid reiterating the historical debate that has already been chronicled elsewhere, I will present the main points of Renz's methodical work and will apprise his research from the date of his publication in 1999.[11] The six popular historical arguments and their advocates are as follows:

1. Currently, it seems the majority of scholars believe that most of the book of Ezekiel was written in Babylon with minor redactions occurring in the post-exilic era. This argument has been adopted by G.A. Cooke, Georg Fohrer, John W. Wevers, Walther Eichrodt, Solomon B. Freehof, Moshe Greenberg, Walther Zimmerli, B. Maarsingh, Ronald M. Hals, Leslie C. Allen, Daniel Block, John F. Kutsko, Andrew Mein, Christopher J.H. Wright, Margaret S. Odell, Paul M. Joyce, Thomas Renz, Dale F. Launderville, and Brian Neil Peterson.[12]

---

of the book of Ezekiel. He argued that Josephus was responsible for chs. 40-48. Oeder's work was published after his death by Georg Vogel, *Freye Untersuchung über einige Bücher des Alten Testaments* (1771).

[9] Duguid, *Ezekiel and the Leaders of Israel*, p. 3.

[10] Renz, *The Rhetorical Function of the Book of Ezekiel*, p. 28.

[11] The subsequent six perspectives and references have been adapted from Renz, *The Rhetorical Function of the Book of Ezekiel*, pp. 28-31.

[12] Renz, *The Rhetorical Function of the Book of Ezekiel*, pp. 28-31; G.A. Cooke, *A Critical and Exegetical Commentary on the Book of Ezekiel* (ICC; Edinburgh: T&T Clark, 1936); Georg Fohrer, *Die Hauptprobleme des Buches Ezechiel* (BZAW 72; Berlin: Töplemann, 1952); Zimmerli, *Ezekiel 1-24*; John W. Wevers, *Ezekiel*; Walther Eichrodt, *Ezekiel*; Solomon B. Freehof, *Book of Ezekiel: A Commentary* (Jewish Commentary for Bible Readers; New York: Union of American Hebrew

2. Ezekiel ministered in Jerusalem before the Babylonian exile in 597 BCE, and afterwards he was among the exiles in Babylon where the majority of the book was written.[13] Those who were willing to accept that the prophet ministered in Palestine, albeit disinclined to forsake the idea of a Babylonian ministry, provided impetus for this view in the 1930s to the 1950s. While this is no longer a popular view, a few scholars such as Hans F. Fuhs, Joseph Blenkinsopp, and Chaim von Rabinowitz still tend to imply that certain texts were written by Ezekiel in Judah.[14]

3. Ezekiel only ministered in Babylon; however, while the book has Babylonian origins, the majority of the book was revised by a redactor in Palestine. This view was recognized by Hölscher in 1924 and was built upon by Irwin in 1943.[15] Hölscher argued that only 170 verses were the original words of the prophet in Babylon.[16]

Congregations, 1978); Moshe Greenberg, *Ezekiel 1-20: A New Translation with Introduction and Commentary* (AB 22; Garden City, NY: Doubleday, 1983); B. Maarsingh, 'Das Schwertlied in Ez 21, 13-22 und das Erra-Gedicht', in Johan Lust (ed.), *Ezekiel and His Book: Textual and Literary Criticism and Their Interrelation* (BETL, 74; Leuven: Leuven University Press 1986); Ronald M. Hals, *Ezekiel* (FOTL 19; Grand Rapids: Eerdmans, 1989); Leslie C. Allen, *Ezekiel 1-19* (WBC 28; Dallas: Word, 1994); Block, *The Book of Ezekiel 1-24* ; Block, *The Book of Ezekiel: Chapters 25-48*; Kutsko, *Between Heaven and Earth*; Andrew Mein, *Ezekiel and the Ethics of Exile* (Oxford Theological Monographs; Oxford: Oxford University Press, 2001); Christopher J.H. Wright, *The Message of Ezekiel: A New Heart and a New Spirit* (The Bible Speaks Today; Leicester: Inter-Varsity, 2001); Margaret S. Odell, *Ezekiel* (The Smith & Helwys Bible Commentary; Macon: Smith & Helwys, 2005); Joyce, *Divine Initiative*; Renz, *The Rhetorical Function of the Book of Ezekiel*; and Dale F. Launderville, *Spirit and Reason: The Embodied Character of Ezekiel's Symbolic Thinking* (Waco: Baylor University Press, 2007); and Peterson, *Ezekiel in Context*.

[13] Scholars who favored this approach to the book of Ezekiel include S. Spiegel, 'Toward Certainty in Ezekiel', *JBL 54* (1935), pp. 145-71; Paul Auvray, *Ezéchiel. Sainte Bible/ Traduite En Français Sous La Direction De L'ecole Biblique De Jérusalem* (Paris: Cerf, 1949), pp. 503-19; Henry Wheeler Robinson, *Two Hebrew Prophets: Studies in Hosea and Ezekiel* (London: Lutterworth, 1948), pp. 75-79; Mays, *Ezekiel, Second Isaiah*, pp. 51-53; and Jean Steinmann, *Ézéchiel* (Connaître La Bible; Paris: Brouwer, 1953), p. 16.

[14] Renz, *The Rhetorical Function of the Book of Ezekiel*, pp. 28-31. Hans F. Fuhs, *Ezechiel 1-24* NEchtB (Würzburg: Echter, 1986); Blenkinsopp, *Ezekiel*; and Chaim Dov Rabinowitz, *Da'ath Sofrim: The Book of Yehezkel* (Jerusalem: Vagshal, 2001).

[15] D.M.G. Stalker, *Ezekiel* (Torch Bible Commentaries; London: SCM, 1974), p. 20.

[16] Hölscher, *Hesekiel, der Dichter und das Buch*, p. 5; Renz, *The Rhetorical Function of the Book of Ezekiel*, pp. 28-30.

4. Ezekiel ministered only in Jerusalem, and so the origins of the book is not associated with Babylon. The Palestinian book was later adapted by a Palestinian redactor in the post-exilic era who coalesced a Babylonian setting with Babylonian themes. This stance was taken by Berry[17] and Herntrich[18] in the 1930s, but their view was generally rejected when C.G. Howie,[19] Mullo Weir,[20] and Fohrer[21] published convincing arguments against a Palestinian setting.[22]

5. The Palestinian pseudepigraphic approach argues that the book is from a much later period and that the prophet Ezekiel never existed. This idea was perhaps first advanced by Leopold Nunz in 1832,[23] and was continued by Charles Cutler Torrey,[24] Nils Messel,[25] Laurence E. Browne,[26] Adrianus van den Born,[27] and Joachim Becker[28] (each of these scholars dated the book to different time periods). More recently, Karl-Friedrich Pohlmann[29] and Udo Feist[30] have presented the pseudepigraphical approach.[31]

6. The majority of Ezekiel's ministry was in Babylon, but he might have also ministered in Jerusalem before the exile. While the book may have its origins in Babylon, some argue that the long history

---

[17] George Ricker Berry, 'Was Ezekiel in the Exile?', *JBL 49* (1930), pp. 83-93.

[18] Volkmar Herntrich, *Ezechielprobleme* (BZAW 61; Giessen: Töpelmann, 1932), pp. 64-67.

[19] C.G. Howie, *The Date and Composition of Ezekiel* (JBL Monograph Series 4; Philadelphia: SBL, 1950).

[20] Cecil J. Mullo Weir, 'Aspects of the Book of Ezekiel', *VT 2* (1952), pp. 97-112.

[21] Fohrer, *Die Hauptprobleme des Buches Ezechiel*.

[22] Renz, *The Rhetorical Function of the Book of Ezekiel*, pp. 28-30.

[23] See Freehof, *Book of Ezekiel*, p. 3, and Udo Feist, *Ezechiel: Das literarische Problem des Buches forschungsgeschichtlich betrachtet* (BWANT 138; Stuttgart: Kohlhammer, 1995), pp. 104-15.

[24] Charles Cutler Torrey, *Pseudo-Ezekiel and the Original Prophecy* (New York: KTAV, 1970).

[25] Nils Messel, *Ezechielfragen* (Oslo: Dybward, 1945).

[26] Laurence E. Browne, *Ezekiel and Alexander* (London: S.P.C.K., 1952).

[27] Adrianus van den Born, 'Ezechiel-Pseudo-Epigraaf?', *StC 28* (1953), pp. 94-104.

[28] Joachim Becker, 'Erwägungen zur ezechielischen frage', in Lothar Ruppert *et al.* (eds.), *Künder des Wortes* (Würzburg: Echter, 1982), pp. 137-49.

[29] Karl-Friedrich Pohlmann, *Ezechiel: Der Stand der theologischen Diskussion* (Darmstadt: Wissenschaftliche Buchgesellschaft, 2008).

[30] Feist, *Ezechiel. Das literarische Problem des Buches forschungsgeschichtlich betrachtet*.

[31] Renz, *The Rhetorical Function of the Book of Ezekiel*, pp. 28-31.

of redaction affirms a 'Deutero-Ezekiel'.[32] Other scholars such
as Horacio Simian-Yofre,[33] Frank- Lothar Hossfeld,[34] Franz Sedlmeier,[35] and Stefan Ohnesorge[36] have adopted a mediating position between the first argument above and this final position.[37]

Although the majority of scholars at the present maintain that the
bulk of the book of Ezekiel was written in Babylon with few post-
exilic redactions, those who vigorously defend the Palestinian view
appear to have valid arguments for espousing this view.

First, scholars who advocate a Palestinian ministry of Ezekiel and
a Palestinian origin of the book state that chs. 1-24 target the 'house
of Israel', a phrase that is synonymous with the entire nation of Israel
(either the whole Northern Israelite kingdom, or the whole Judean
kingdom, as it was known as after the destruction of Israel). If Ezekiel's prophecies are aimed at the entire nation, then he could not
have ministered to all of Israel from exile because only a minority of
the population was exiled to Babylon in 597 BCE. Additionally, Ezekiel, at times, directly addresses the sins of Jerusalem (16.2; 22.2), and
so it is only logical to conclude that he was in Jerusalem during this
time.[38]

Second, Jeremiah 24 and 29 seem to indicate that the exilic community was faithful to Yahweh, but the oracles of chs. 1-24 of Ezekiel are addressed to the 'rebellious house'. Since Ezekiel's messages
accuse the hearers of idolatry and rebelliousness against Yahweh, the
term 'rebellious house' characterizes the community living in Jerusalem better than it describes the exilic Jews.[39]

---

[32] Schulz, H., *Das Todesrecht im Alten Testament* (BZAW 114; Berlin: de Gruyter, 1969), pp. 163-87; Jörg Garscha, *Studien zum Ezechielbuch: Eine redaktionskritische Untersuchung von Ez 1-39* (EHS XXIII, 23; Frankfurt: Lang, 1974).

[33] Horacio Simian-Yofre, *Die theologische Nachgeschichte der Prophetie Ezechiels: form- und traditionskritische Untersuchung zu Ez 6; 35; 36* (Würzburg: Echter, 1974).

[34] Frank-Lothar Hossfeld, *Untersuchungen zur Kompositon und Theologie des Ezechielbuches* (Würzburg: Echter, 1977).

[35] Franz Sedlmeier, *Das Buch Ezechiel* (NSKAT, 21; Stuttgart: Katholisches Biblewerk, 2002).

[36] Stefan Ohnesorge, *Jahwe gestaltet sein Volk neu: Zur Sicht der Zukunft Israels nach Ez 11, 14-21; 20,1-44; 36,16-38; 37,1-14.15-28* (FZB, 64; Würzburg: Echter, 1991).

[37] Peterson, *Ezekiel in Context*, p. 10.

[38] Renz, *The Rhetorical Function of the Book of Ezekiel*, pp. 32-33. Cf. Mullo Weir, 'Aspects of the Book of Ezekiel', p. 102, and Fohrer, *Die Hauptprobleme des Buches Ezechiel*, pp. 209-12.

[39] Renz, *The Rhetorical Function of the Book of Ezekiel*, pp. 32-33.

Third, the oppression and hardship experienced by the exilic community in Babylon are not depicted in the book of Ezekiel.[40]

Fourth, the book of Ezekiel seems to be a first-hand account of 'the moral, political, and military conditions in Judah', and its themes seem to parallel the themes found in the oracles of Jeremiah, a Jerusalemite prophet. Furthermore, Ezekiel seems to know the disposition of the people in Jerusalem (11.15; 12.21-28; 20.32; 33.23-29), and he seems to give an eyewitness account of Zedekiah's failure to escape and his subsequent blinding (12.3-12). Also, the elaborate vision of the temple and the intimate knowledge of the worship in the temple, particularly the plight of Pelatiah, point to Ezekiel being present in Jerusalem during the time of his ministry.[41]

The purpose of this study is not to present a comprehensive examination of the strength and weaknesses of the differing arguments of the historical-critical debate. Moreover, the scope of opinions show that there is no general scholarly consensus among historical-critical scholars, and so it seems most advantageous to refer the reader to the works already cited for a more detailed analysis of the historical-critical questions. Having evaluated the range of opinions put forth by historical-critical scholars, it seems fitting to end this section with Eichrodt's conclusion. He asserts that 'these widely divergent theories serve to illustrate the danger of throwing away what this book testifies to in regards to itself, because it only leads to fleeting speculations, which in spite of all their cleverness, cannot arouse any confidence in the results'.[42]

Literary/Rhetorical Approach

A current survey of Ezekielian scholarship indicates a shift from the historical-critical methods to the literary/rhetorical approach (or synchronic approach).[43] Scholars who prefer to study the text in its present form rather than attend to the historical formation of the text

---

[40] Renz, *The Rhetorical Function of the Book of Ezekiel*, pp. 32-33; William H. Brownlee, 'Ezekiel', *International Standard Bible Encyclopedia* (Reprinted as the introduction to his commentary repr.; Grand Rapids, MI: Eerdmans, 1982), p. xxiv.

[41] Renz, *The Rhetorical Function of the Book of Ezekiel*, pp. 32-33; Brownlee, 'Ezekiel', p. xxiv.

[42] Eichrodt, *Ezekiel*, p. 11.

[43] Johan Lust, *Ezekiel and His Book: Textual and Literary Criticism and Their Interrelation* (BETL, 74; Leuven: Leuven University Press, 1986), p. 2.

stand in sharp contrast to the historical-critical method and its adherents. This shift by no means indicates a 'flight to naïve conservatism',[44] but, instead, signals a preference for other critical methods such as literary approaches, structural analysis, and rhetorical criticism.

The persuasion that the final form of the book of Ezekiel is a unique literary unit and a consistent whole has long been recognized. Well into the twentieth century, it was a forgone conclusion that the book was a coherent whole with a distinctive literary style and the work of a single author.[45] In 1880, R. Smend states that the book of Ezekiel was the product of a very meticulous design with a highly organized structure that would crumble if a single piece of the structure was removed: 'The whole book is … the logical development of a series of ideas in accordance with a well thought-out, and in part quite schematic, plan. We cannot remove any part without disturbing the whole structure.'[46] The literary cohesiveness of the book of Ezekiel was so convincing that at the end of the nineteenth century S.R. Driver declared: 'No critical question arises in connection with the authorship of the book, the whole from beginning to end bearing unmistakably the stamp of a single mind'.[47]

This scholarly consensus, however, came to an end when the book of Ezekiel drew the attention of source and literary critics. As stated above, since the application of the various diachronic approaches to Ezekiel, there has been little agreement on the literary unity and integrity of the book.[48] G.A. Cooke confessed, 'the study of Ezekiel has undergone something like a revolution [and] it is not possible to treat the Book [*sic*] as the product of a single mind and a simple age'.[49]

---

[44] Joyce, *Divine Initiative*, p. 30.

[45] Childs, *Introduction*, p. 357.

[46] R. Smend, *Der Prophet Ezechiel* (Leipzig: S. Hirzel, 1880), p. xxi. Gunkel and Gray were also confident of the book's literary coherence. H. Gunkel, 'Die Israelitische Literatur', in P. Hinneberg (ed.), *Die Kultur Der Gegenwart* (Berlin & Leipzig: B.G. Teubner, 1906), p. 82; and G.B. Gray, *A Critical Introduction to the Old Testament* (London: Duckworth, 1913), p. 198. Joyce notes that Gunkel was convinced that Ezekiel was 'the first prophet who wrote a book', Joyce, *Divine Initiative*, p. 21. G.B. Gray wrote that 'No other book of the Old Testament is distinguished by such decisive marks of unity of authorship and integrity as this', Gray, *A Critical Introduction to the Old Testament*, p. 198.

[47] S.R. Driver, *Introduction to the Literature of the Old Testament* (New York: Scribner, 1913), p. 279.

[48] Peterson, *Ezekiel in Context*, p. 77.

[49] Cooke, *A Critical and Exegetical Commentary on the Book of Ezekiel*, p. v.

This critical crisis has led to the recent and increased interest in analyzing the book of Ezekiel in its present, final form. Avoiding prejudicial conclusions that are anchored in uncertain historical reconstructions, these literary studies dare to follow wherever the text leads, even though the world of Ezekiel may be entirely strange and foreign to a modern audience.

In the past fifty years, scholars from divergent perspectives have changed the direction of Old Testament studies by challenging the traditional paradigms of biblical hermeneutics. The beginnings of a scholarly challenge to the prevailing diachronic methodologies can be traced back to James Muilenburg's precedent-setting address to the Society of Biblical Literature in 1968, and his ensuing article, 'Form-Criticism and Beyond' in 1969.[50] While Muilenburg did not oppose historical-critical methods, he did recognize that the limitations and deficiencies of these methods left the reader with more questions than answers. Therefore, he invited critics to go beyond form criticism and other historical methods and focus upon the literary distinctiveness of a text.[51] Since Muilenburg's decisive call to go beyond the entrenched template of biblical studies, literary/rhetorical criticisms have proliferated, and the result has been to unfasten Ezekiel from the tight hold of historical-critical methods.[52]

Another major advance was made by Brevard Childs who pioneered the canonical approach with the publication of his *Introduction to the Old Testament as Scripture*.[53] The canonical approach is a hermeneutical method that focuses on the text in its final form in order to

---

[50] Joe M. Sprinkle, 'Literary Approaches to the Old Testament: A Survey of Recent Scholarship', *JETS* 32.3 (Sept 1989), pp. 299-310.

[51] J. Muilenburg, 'Form Criticism and Beyond', *JBL 88* (1969), pp. 1-18.

[52] While Muilenburg's address was a turning-point in the legitimization of the literary/rhetorical methods, he was not the first to introduce these methods. Before Muilenberg, a few biblical scholars such as Joseph Blenkinsopp and J.P.U. Lilley, had already begun to utilize literary/rhetorical methods in their study in the book of Judges. Joseph Blenkinsopp, 'Structure and Style in Judges 13-16', *JBL* 82 (1963), pp. 65-76; and J.P.U. Lilley, 'A Literary Appreciation of the Book of Judges', *Tyndale Bulletin* 18 (1967), pp. 94-102.

[53] Although the term 'Canonical Criticism' is closely related to Childs, the term was formally presented by James Sanders in *Torah and Canon* in 1972, as indicated by Rolf Rendtorff, 'Canonical Reading of the Old Testament in the Context of Critical Scholarship', *The Asbury Theological Journal* 54.1 (1999), p. 6. Childs rejected the term. He explains:

It implies that the concern with canon is viewed as another historical-critical technique which can take its place alongside of source criticism, form criticism,

discern its meaning for the community of faith. Child states that the canon 'not only serves to establish the outer boundaries of authoritative Scripture but forms a prism through which light from the different aspects of the Christian life is refracted'.[54] The cumulative effect of Child's canonical approach on the studies of Ezekiel was to metamorphose the way in which critics examined the book of Ezekiel and the entire Old Testament. Several scholars began to analyze the book of Ezekiel in its final canonical form. Even scholars such as Karl-Friedrich Pohlmann, who still embraced the methods of historical criticism, acknowledged the advantages of studying the book of Ezekiel in its final form. He admits that the book of Ezekiel in its present form is undoubtedly an elaborate composition.[55]

Still, it was Moshe Greenberg's 'Holistic Interpretation', an approach that focuses on the literary structure and thematic developments of the book of Ezekiel, that contributed most decisively to the study of the prophetic message in its final form. Greenberg produced a two-volume commentary on Ezekiel and numerous essays that systematically outlined and justified his 'holistic' methodology.[56] He was of the persuasion that in order for scholars to recognize the full implications of the text of Ezekiel they had to listen to the final form of the book: 'There is only one way that gives hope of eliciting

rhetorical criticism, and the like. I do not envision the approach to canon in this light. Rather, the issue at stake in canon turns on establishing a stance from which the Bible is to read as Sacred Scripture.

(Brevard Childs, 'The Canonical Shape of the Prophetic Literature', *Interpretation* 32 [1978], p. 54.)

[54] Brevard S. Childs, *Biblical Theology of the Old and New Testaments* (Minneapolis: Augsburg Fortress, 1993), p. 672.

[55] Karl-Friedrich Pohlmann, *Das Buch des Propheten Hezekiel (Ezechiel) Kapitel 1-19* (Göttingen: Vandenhoeck & Ruprecht, 1996), p. 25.

[56] Moshe Greenberg, *Ezekiel 1-20: A New Translation with Introduction and Commentary* (AB; New York: Doubleday, 1983); idem, *Ezekiel 21-37: A New Translation and Commentary* (AB; New York: Doubleday, 1997); idem, 'The Vision of Jerusalem in Ezekiel 8-11: A Holistic Interpretation', in J.L. Crenshaw and S. Sandmel (eds.), *The Divine Helmsman: Studies on God's Control of Human Events* (New York: KTAV, 1980), pp. 143-64; idem, 'Ezekiel's Vision: Literary and Iconographic Aspects', in Hayim Tadmor and Moshe Weinfeld (eds.), *History, Historiography and Interpretation: Studies in Biblical and Cuneiform Literatures* (Leiden: Brill, 1983), pp. 159-68; idem, 'The Design and Themes of Ezekiel's Program and Restoration', *Int* 38 (1984), pp. 181-208; and idem, 'What Are Valid Criteria for Determining Inauthentic Matter in Ezekiel?', in Johan Lust (ed.), *Ezekiel and His Book: Textual and Literary Criticism and Their Interrelation* (BETL, 74: Leuven: Leuven University Press, 1986), pp. 123-35.

the innate conventions and literary formations of a piece of ancient literature, and that is by listening to it patiently and humbly. The critic must curb all temptations to impose his antecedent judgments on the text.'[57] Greenberg further submits that the book 'is the product of art and intelligent design [because] a consistent trend of thought expressed in a distinctive style has emerged, giving the impression of an individual mind of powerful and passionate proclivities'.[58] Greenberg discerned the canonical text of Ezekiel as a deliberate and well-planned literary product. Therefore, he studied Ezekiel's structure, themes, literary techniques, and patterns to indicate the literary and conceptual coherence of the book.

The influence of Greenberg's 'holistic' approach to Ezekiel is indisputable. Since the 1980s, there has been an upsurge in the number of publications with a synchronic approach. The synchronic approach has created an open and fertile field for diverse voices (literary, feminist, psychological, *et al.*) to interact with the text of Ezekiel. These various literary/rhetorical voices can be heard in the works of Lawrence Boadt,[59] Susan Niditch,[60] Ellen Davis,[61] Gordon H. Matties,[62] Julie Galambush,[63] Daniel Bodi,[64] John F. Kutsko,[65]

---

[57] Greenberg, *Ezekiel 1-20*, p. 21.

[58] Greenberg, *Ezekiel 1-20*, p. 26.

[59] Lawrence Boadt, 'Textual Analysis in Ezekiel and Poetic Analysis of Paired Words', *JBL* 97 (1978), pp. 489-99; *idem*, 'Rhetorical Strategies in Ezekiel's Oracles of Judgment', in Johan Lust (ed.), *Ezekiel and His Book: Textual and Literary Criticism and Their Interrelation* (BETL, 74; Leuven: Leuven University Press, 1986), pp. 182-200; *idem*, 'The Function of the Salvation Oracles in Ezekiel 33-37', *HAR* 12 (1990), pp. 1-21; *idem*, 'A New Look at the Book of Ezekiel', *TBT* 37 (1994), pp. 4-9; and *idem*, 'Mythological Themes and the Unity of Ezekiel', in L.J. Regt *et al.* (eds.), *Literary Structure and Rhetorical Strategies in the Hebrew Bible* (Winona Lake, IN: Eisenbrauns, 1996).

[60] Susan Niditch, 'Ezekiel 40-48 in a Visionary Context', *CBQ* 48 (1986), pp. 208-24.

[61] Davis, *Swallowing the Scroll*; *idem*, 'Swallowing Hard: Reflections on Ezekiel's Dumbness', in J.C. Exum (ed.), *Signs and Wonders: Biblical Texts in Literary Focus* (SBLSS; Atlanta: Scholars Press, 1989), pp. 217-37.

[62] Gordon H. Matties, *Ezekiel 18 and the Rhetoric of Moral Discourse* (SBLDS 126; Atlanta: Scholars Press, 1990).

[63] Julie Galambush, *Jerusalem in the Book of Ezekiel: The City as Yahweh's Wife* (SBLDS 130; Atlanta: Scholars Press, 1992).

[64] Daniel Bodi, *The Book of Ezekiel and the Poem of Erra* (OBO 104; Freiburg: Universitatsverlag, 1991).

[65] Kutsko, *Between Heaven and Earth*.

Thomas Renz,[66] Kalinda Rose Stevenson,[67] Risa Levitt Kohn,[68] James Robson,[69] and, more recently, Brian Neil Peterson.[70]

Lawrence Boadt, for example, espoused the synchronic method by showing that the occurrence of stylistic devices such as repetition, word pairs, and redundancy were rhetorical techniques employed by the author, and inasmuch confirms the literary unity of Ezekiel.[71]

Likewise, Niditch's work provides another example of the literary/rhetorical trend. She focuses on the themes of creation and recreation in chs. 40-48, and she notes that the creation mythology motif strongly binds chs. 38-39 and 40-48 together. The frequent recurrence of similar language and themes throughout the book of Ezekiel convinces Niditch that the same author who wrote chs. 40-48 composed chs. 1-39. [72]

Perhaps one of the most resourceful literary studies in the book of Ezekiel was presented by Ellen Davis in 1989.[73] She designed a theoretical framework to support her assertion that Ezekiel is a written composition of the prophet himself and not the outcome of oral prophetic speech. Davis was not the first to propose that the book of Ezekiel substantiates a movement from orality to literature. H. Ewald in 1841 said that 'writing became a spiritual renewal and fresh creation of oral discourse'.[74] Conrad Orelli also argued, in 1896, that the stylistic features of the book of Ezekiel are unmistakable proofs of the literary activity of the prophet.[75] Davis pursues the course set by Ewald and Orelli and explores how the social situation of the prophet's exile might have impacted the literary style of his prophecy. She argues that the Babylonian exile was the catalyst for organizing

---

[66] Renz, *The Rhetorical Function of the Book of Ezekiel.*

[67] Kalinda Rose Stevenson, *The Vision of Transformation: The Territorial Rhetoric of Ezekiel 40-48* (SBLDS 154; Atlanta: Scholars Press, 1996).

[68] Levitt Kohn, 'Ezekiel at the Turn of the Century', pp. 9-31; *idem, A New Heart and a New Soul: Ezekiel, the Exile, and the Torah* (JSOTSup 358; London: Sheffield Academic, 2002).

[69] James Robson, *Word and Spirit in Ezekiel* (LHB/OTS 447; New York: T. & T. Clark, 2006).

[70] Peterson, *Ezekiel in Context.*

[71] Boadt, 'Rhetorical Strategies', pp. 182-200.

[72] Niditch, 'Ezekiel 40-48 in a Visionary Context', pp. 208-24.

[73] Davis, *Swallowing the Scroll.*

[74] H. Ewald, *Commentary on the Prophets of the Old Testament* (London: William & Norgate, 1880), 4.13.

[75] Conrad von Orelli, *Das Buch Ezechiel* (Munich: Ch. Beck, 1896).

Israel's religious practices and interpretation of current events from oral discourse to a written record.[76]

Matties' published dissertation in 1990 employs the tools of a literary–rhetorical methodology to investigate the ethics of Ezekiel, particularly the ethics of Ezekiel 18. Although his exegesis of ch. 18 uses form-critical and traditional historical approaches, he acknowledges that because of 'recent literary approaches to biblical literature, we may be in a position to recognize the integral function of moral discourse in prophetic literature'.[77] Accordingly, he studies the literary structure, rhetoric, and theology of ch. 18 in order to determine the shape of moral discourse in the book of Ezekiel.

Galambush's study is a feminist, philosophical, and psychological analysis of the book of Ezekiel, and it utilizes both literary and historical-critical methods in her analysis of the text. Influenced by Greenberg's 'holistic interpretation' she submits that the city of Jerusalem is Yahweh's wife. She methodically examines the female metaphor of chs. 16 and 23, and she applies the metaphor to the rest of the book, chiefly to chs. 1-24. Galambush's work has helped elucidate the function of metaphor in the present and final shape of the text.[78]

Moreover, the synchronic approach has enabled several comparative studies in the book of Ezekiel. These comparative studies examine the biblical text in its final form and analyze the impact of the ancient Near Eastern (ANE) culture, mainly Mesopotamia, on the literary framework of Ezekiel and the ways this Mesopotamian influence discloses the rhetorical intent of Ezekiel. Scholars who adopt this kind of approach to the book of Ezekiel include Bodi, Kutsko, and Peterson.[79]

Bodi contends that the message of Ezekiel is lost unless the book is interpreted in the light of an ancient Akkadian song, *The Poem of Erra*. After investigating the literary and thematic parallels between

---

[76] Davis, *Swallowing the Scroll*.

[77] Matties, *Ezekiel 18 and the Rhetoric of Moral Discourse*, p. 2.

[78] Galambush, *Jerusalem in the Book of Ezekiel*.

[79] Bodi, *The Book of Ezekiel and the Poem of Erra*; Kutsko, *Between Heaven and Earth*; and Peterson, *Ezekiel in Context*. See also the essays by Daniel Block, John T. Strong, and Steven Tuell in an SBL conference collection: Margaret S. and John T. Strong Odell, *The Book of Ezekiel: Theological and Anthropological Perspectives* (SBLSymS 9; Atlanta: SBL, 2000), respectively pp. 15-42, 69-95, and 97-166; Launderville, *Spirit and Reason*; Donna Lee Petter, *The Book of Ezekiel and Mesopotamian City Laments* (OBO 246; Fribourg: Academic Press, 2011).

the two works, Bodi concludes that these two oeuvres share twelve motifs that categorically corroborate Ezekiel's dependence on the *Poem of Erra*. Bodi claims:

> Without exhausting all the parallels between the two works, we were able to trace and examine over twelve features shared by both works. This significant correlation excludes the possibility of explaining between these two works as mere coincidence ... The fact that we were able to point out not only formal parallelism between the two works (e.g. the narrative structure of both works follows the departure and the return of the deity to its shrine), but also similarities in content is particularly revealing. These similarities make it probable that the author or redactor of the book of Ezekiel was acquainted with the *Poem of Erra* and used it as one of his sources in the composition and formulation of a number of motifs including one major theme.[80]

Kutsko's study (a revision of his PhD dissertation) is a series of 'case studies' that aim to view the book of Ezekiel through the interpretive lens of its larger, cultural context. He draws upon various Assyrian-Babylonian texts to help identify the images and themes used by Ezekiel. He posits Ezekiel's rhetoric was an adaptation of the political vernacular of the ANE culture, and proposes that the ANE accounts of temple abandonment, exile, the return, and reinstitution of the gods to their restored temples had become the prototype of Ezekiel's prophecy.[81]

Like Kutsko, Peterson maintains that the book of Ezekiel is a coherent text that plainly reflects its ancient milieu. He states that Ezekiel's prophetic message replicates the covenant and curse treatises of the Hittites, Mesopotamians, and Assyrians. The peculiar symbolism, imagery, and metaphors of Ezekiel confirm that 'Ezekiel was a prophet of the exile who had ample opportunity to avail himself of Mesopotamian literature, art, and culture in general'.[82] Additionally, 'Ezekiel's use of the curse motif, coupled with [the] two metaphors [of chs. 16 and 23] and the visionary framework, enabled the prophet

---

[80] Bodi, *The Book of Ezekiel and the Poem of Erra*, p. 306.
[81] Kutsko, *Between Heaven and Earth*.
[82] Peterson, *Ezekiel in Context*, p. 96.

to link present realities in the exile with known ANE and Old Testament punishments for treaty/covenant violations'.[83]

The synchronic method has also made it possible for Renz to argue that the final form of the book of Ezekiel is a rhetorical unit that addresses a specific rhetorical situation: 'the exilic community is to define itself not by the past but by the future promised by Yahweh'.[84] Renz contends that the book is designed to perform several functions: (1) to persuade the second-generation exiles that the fall of Jerusalem was a direct result of Israel's unfaithfulness to Yahweh; (2) to 'call his community to repentance and to warn his people that disaster is always the consequence of rebellion against Yahweh';[85] (3) to sever ties with a 'communal vision in which Yahweh is not central';[86] (4) to identify with a community that recognizes the kingship of Yahweh; and (5) 'to find their identity neither in Babylon nor in Jerusalem of the past, [but as] a nation centered on Yahweh's sanctuary'.[87] Thus, according to Renz, the rhetorical function of the book of Ezekiel demonstrates that Israel can only be transformed by Yahweh and aims 'to encourage faith in Yahweh and his work, and by its nature this faith was not meant to be only a way of a particular situation, but a faith which is valid for all times'.[88]

Stevenson also follows a rhetorical approach in her analysis of Ezekiel 40-48. Stevenson views these chapters through the interpretive lens of human geography, arguing that the extended vision of the temple in chs. 40-48 is not a precise layout for the reconstructed temple but rather a rhetoric for 'spaces' that separated the holy from the profane. The intricate details of the vision are not merely extraneous material but are included in order to offer 'hope to a community in exile'. The 'vision of a future restructured society, a society centered around the temple of YHWH in which Yahweh is the only king engenders hope for the community in exile'.[89]

Levitt Kohn's interest in the book of Ezekiel motivated her to study the lexicographical and homogeneities between Ezekiel and the priestly and Deuteronomist materials. She presents 97 terms that are

---

83 Peterson, *Ezekiel in Context*, p. 334.
84 Renz, *The Rhetorical Function of the Book of Ezekiel*, p. 249.
85 Renz, *The Rhetorical Function of the Book of Ezekiel*, p. 249.
86 Renz, *The Rhetorical Function of the Book of Ezekiel*, p. 229.
87 Renz, *The Rhetorical Function of the Book of Ezekiel*, p. 229.
88 Renz, *The Rhetorical Function of the Book of Ezekiel*, p. 247.
89 Stevenson, *Vision of Transformation*, p. 163.

found in the text of Ezekiel, the P source and the Deuteronomist source, and investigates their connections to one another. The results of Levitt Kohn's investigation reveal that Ezekiel is not just educated in priestly traditions but used vocabulary and terminology from the Pentateuchal materials. Ezekiel's adoption of priestly and Deuteronomistic language is evident in ch. 20. However, the text of Ezekiel is not a facsimile of antecedent traditions, but is rather a 'twisted, poeticized, disarticulated and reconstituted'[90] use of material. Additionally, 'the prophet appropriates terminology and content but situates it in new, different and even contradictory contexts ... [H]e adjusts the material to suit his personal prophetic agenda and the contemporary circumstance of his audience'.[91]

Finally, Robson's revised doctoral thesis argues cogently that the 'word' of Yahweh and the 'spirit' of Yahweh are so strongly linked together that encounter with Yahweh's word and his spirit are the paramount motifs of Ezekiel's prophetic message. Although he confesses to the 'intentional ... redactional unity'[92] of the book of Ezekiel, he embraces the synchronic methodology as he pays attention to the 'communicative intent'[93] of the book: 'I am approaching Ezekiel not simply as a collection of the words of a prophet, but as a book written with a purpose, to a set of addressees'.[94] Consequently, Robson's work follows in the footsteps of Davis, Renz, and Stevenson. In an attempt to ascertain the 'communicative intent' of the book of Ezekiel, Robson meticulously analyzes the relationship between the spirit of Yahweh and the prophetic word in Ezekiel and the rest of the Old Testament. The spirit of Yahweh, according to Robson, is best understood apropos the transformation of the prophecy's audience. Ezekiel's encounter with Yahweh's spirit and his obedient response to Yahweh's word is a graphic contrast to the disobedience and unfaithfulness of the addressees. Yahweh's spirit, therefore, effects an obedient response to his word.[95]

This brief survey of the significant literary/rhetorical approaches to the book of Ezekiel reveals a plurality of methods, which scholars

---

[90] Levitt Kohn, *A New Heart and a New Soul*, pp. 84-85.
[91] Levitt Kohn, *A New Heart and a New Soul*.
[92] Robson, *Word and Spirit in Ezekiel*, p. 6.
[93] Robson, *Word and Spirit in Ezekiel*, p. 10.
[94] Robson, *Word and Spirit in Ezekiel*.
[95] Robson, *Word and Spirit in Ezekiel*.

can now employ to interpret the text. Although my survey considered those publications that facilitated the shift from the diachronic to the synchronic approaches to the book of Ezekiel, recent discussions on Ezekiel show that scholars prefer to study the text in its final form rather than analyze the text's history of development. These scholars include Jurrien Mol, Tyler D. Mayfield, and Elizabeth Keck. Mol extensively studied the philology, grammar, and structure of chs. 18 and 20 in pursuance of redefining the relationship between individual and corporate responsibility motifs in Ezekiel.[96] Mayfield focuses on the synchronic approach to describe how the literary distinctiveness of the prophetic text can help identify the literary structure and literary setting of the book of Ezekiel.[97] Keck's doctoral thesis utilized a synchronic approach to promote the idea that Yahweh's glory in Ezekiel is radically different from his earthly presence when understood in relation to the Deuteronomistic Name theology.[98]

Conclusion

This brief survey of the significant approaches to the book of Ezekiel reveals a movement from the paradigms of historical-critical methods to the literary/rhetorical studies in the book of Ezekiel. Although contemporary Ezekielian scholarship in North America favors a synchronic approach, some scholars believe that the diachronic methods are still appropriate for analyzing the book of Ezekiel.[99] Paul M. Joyce believes that

> the book of Ezekiel has its integrity as a work of literature read synchronically, and an approach to the book which fails to do justice to this and to learn from the wealth of recent studies of this kind would be sadly impoverished. And yet we must take seriously the evidence of redactional activity which is to be discerned within the book of Ezekiel.[100]

---

[96] Mol, *Collective and Individual Responsibility*.

[97] Mayfield, *Literary Structure and Setting in Ezekiel*.

[98] Keck, *Beside the Chebar River*.

[99] Cf. Matties, *Ezekiel 18 and the Rhetoric of Moral Discourse*; and Robson, *Word and Spirit in Ezekiel*.

[100] Paul M. Joyce, 'Synchronic and Diachronic Perspectives in Ezekiel', in Johannes C. De Moor (ed.), *Synchronic or Diachronic?: A Debate on Method in Old Testament Exegesis* (New York: Brill, 1995), p. 125.

Nevertheless, the development of synchronic readings of the book of Ezekiel has allowed present-day Ezekielian scholarship to be more inclusive, acknowledge numerous methods of study, and be more receptive to the various voices of interpretation. There is now an extensive field of studies in Ezekiel from literary, psychological, feminist, and other emerging angles of interpretation, which make room for this thesis that employs a Pentecostal literary/theological approach.

The labyrinth of visions, symbolic acts, images and motifs, along with the historical, ethical, social, moral, political, psychological, gender, cultural, geographical, religious, rhetorical, literary, and theological issues observed in the text validate various methods and approaches to the book of Ezekiel. Ergo, considering the growth, implementation and favorable reception of these multifarious methodologies, Pentecostals should be permitted to explore those elements of Ezekiel's prophecy that are pivotal to the community's disposition, convictions, and traditions. Furthermore, Pentecostal scholarship is now recognized globally by the academic community as an authentic and distinctive academic discipline that produces a comprehensive and systematic theology of Scripture by paying attention to the current critical methods of interpretation. Therefore, a Pentecostal exploration of the text of Ezekiel will only add to the heterogeneous voices of biblical studies.

A literary and theological examination of the text of Ezekiel from a Pentecostal perspective is useful in three ways. First, a Pentecostal approach that utilizes a literary and theological methodology in Ezekiel will enable a fresh hearing and innovative look at the text. A literary analysis forces us to hear the text and to be conscientious of the hermeneutical milieu that is formed by the Pentecostal worshiping community. If we neglect to hear the text, we will be at risk of egregiously ignoring the significance and meaning of the text. Second, this method allows the hermeneut to establish an interrelationship between the glory of Yahweh and the holiness of Yahweh within the visionary framework of the text, and in so doing offer a unique contribution to the theological discussion of Ezekiel. Third, Pentecostals have not paid sufficient attention to the book of Ezekiel. To this date, there is no monograph on the book of Ezekiel from a Pentecostal perspective. Therefore, this research will serve to stimulate and sustain the Pentecostal community.

Taking into consideration the shift from the diachronic methodologies to the literary/rhetorical analysis of the present and final form of the text, my approach to the book of Ezekiel stands with mainstream scholarship. It seems most advantageous to examine the relationship between YHWH's glory and YHWH's holiness in the present literary context of the book of Ezekiel.

3

SEEING AND HEARING: A PARADIGM FOR A PENTECOSTAL INTERPRETATION OF EZEKIEL

INTRODUCTION

To review, I indicated in Chapter 1 that I would be using a literary and theological approach to the book of Ezekiel, which includes exegesis and a close reading of the text. I will utilize this approach to explore the interrelationship between the glory of YHWH and the holiness of YHWH in the book of Ezekiel. I argued in Chapter 2 that the field of biblical hermeneutics in North America has experienced a seismic methodological shift from the long standing diachronic approaches to more recent synchronic approaches that analyze the text in its final form. This change in the methodological contours of biblical hermeneutics has allowed various voices, including the Pentecostal voice, to enter the critical discussions of the Old Testament. Thus, as I pointed out in Chapter 1, my literary-theological seeing and hearing of the book of Ezekiel in its final form from a Pentecostal perspective allows me to appreciate Ezekiel's portrayal of the glory and holiness of YHWH in the narrative. This approach provides new insights to the story and, in turn, contributes to a fresh perspective of Ezekiel. In this chapter, therefore, I will define and articulate the goals of a Pentecostal hermeneutic that emerge from seeing and hearing the word of YHWH.

Although I acknowledge the legitimacy and the immense contribution of the various historical-critical methodologies, my strategy

enables the hermeneut to struggle with the challenging texts of Ezekiel, to engage the literary features of the text in its final form, and
to discern the diverse voices within the text.[1] As I navigate my way
through the book of Ezekiel, I bear in mind the three worlds of the
text: the world behind the text, the world in the text, and the world
in front of the text.[2] Furthermore, a Pentecostal approach recognizes
the transformative power of Scripture. That is, the reading and hearing of Scripture not only convey information about God, but also
transform the hearer. Scripture, therefore, is the living, active, relevant, and powerful word of God that has the ability to affect and
transform lives, challenge our ecclesial doctrines, confront our political agendas, and to speak to us anew in every generation. Additionally, as Kevin J. Vanhoozer argues, Scripture 'is the agent by which
God promises, commands, warns, guides, and yes, reveals'.[3] Thus, in
the words of Rickie D. Moore, I aspire and yearn to 'enter the world
of the living, dynamic, charismatic word of God, a world that is man-
ifested through encounter with the God who is, around, above, be-
low, and in front of every text'.[4] Accordingly, my approach does not
perceive Scripture as object, an object that can be dissected and analyzed by my methodological tools. Rather, my approach recognizes
Scripture as subject – the living and dynamic word of God that interprets, probes, examines, and scrutinizes the intentions and motivations of the heart.[5]

Moreover, such an encounter with Scripture is not done in ab-
stract isolation, but in dialogue with the community of faith.[6] The
unique characteristics of Pentecostalism create the matrix in which I
interpret Scripture. Hence, my Pentecostal context and theological
convictions undeniably affect, shape, and inform my interpretation
of the text of Ezekiel.

---

[1] Cf. Martin, *The Unheard Voice of God*, p. 52.

[2] W. Randolph Tate, *Biblical Interpretation: An Integrated Approach* (Peabody, MA: Hendrickson Publishers, 1991).

[3] Kevin J. Vanhoozer, 'Word of God', in Kevin J. Vanhoozer, Craig G. Bartholomew, Daniel J. Treier, and N.T. Wright (eds.), *DTIB* (Grand Rapids: Baker Publishing Group, 2005), p. 854.

[4] Rickie D. Moore, 'A Pentecostal Approach to Scripture', in Lee Roy Martin (ed.), *Pentecostal Hermeneutics: A Reader* (Leiden/Boston: Brill, 2013), p. 11.

[5] Lee Roy Martin, 'Hearing the Voice of God', in Martin (ed.), *Pentecostal Hermeneutics*, p. 205.

[6] J.C. Thomas, 'Women, Pentecostalism, and the Bible: An Experiment in Pentecostal Hermeneutics', in Martin (ed.), *Pentecostal Hermeneutics*, pp. 81-94.

The highly figurative and bizarre visions of Ezekiel present interpretive challenges for the Ezekielian hermeneut. More than any other Old Testament prophetic book, the book of Ezekiel is a blend of literary genres, which includes narrative and prophetic, prosaic and poetic, visions and symbolism.[7] The plethora of these genres found in one text is without precedent. The various types of literary genres encountered in the book of Ezekiel demand a legitimate and distinctive hermeneutical strategy to the text. Thus, my Pentecostal approach of seeing and hearing the word of YHWH in Ezekiel will provide insights into the relationship between the glory of YHWH and the holiness of YHWH in the book of Ezekiel. Additionally, hearing the voice of YHWH will evoke visualization of the word of YHWH. As I read the visions of Ezekiel, I hear the phrase דבר יהוה (the word of the Lord), which, as Moore has pointed out, is not limited to the oral or recorded words of YHWH, but is 'an event that is encountered, experienced, or seen,'[8] in this case, through the visions of Ezekiel.

Since YHWH's word is portrayed as something to be seen and heard in the book of Ezekiel, the recipients of the prophecy must dare to see and hear alongside Ezekiel. As we see and hear with Ezekiel, the ancient words of YHWH emerge from the past to become relevant, dynamic, and present.[9]

Motivation for a Pentecostal Approach to Ezekiel

Although a distinctive Pentecostal approach to text interpretation is not a new concept, some biblical scholars are still reticent to accept that Pentecostal hermeneutics is a singular, practical, reliable, and suitable method of interpretation.[10] There are difficulties with delin-

---

[7] Cf. Mayfield, *Literary Structure and Setting in Ezekiel*, p. 36.

[8] Rickie D. Moore, 'The Prophetic Calling: An Old Testament Profile and Its Relevance for Today', in *idem*, *The Spirit of the Old Testament* (JPTSup 35; Blandford Forum: Deo Publishing, 2011), p. 58, which I will cite in this monograph. The article was first published in *JEPTA* 24 (2004), pp. 16-29.

[9] Walter Brueggemann, *Texts That Linger, Words That Explode* (Minneapolis: Fortress Press, 2000), pp. 1-3.

[10] Marius Nel, '"Pentecostals" Reading of the Old Testament', *Verbum et Ecclesia* 28.2 (2007), pp. 524-25; Andrew Davies, 'What Does It Mean to Read the Bible as a Pentecostal?', in Lee Roy Martin (ed.), *Pentecostal Hermeneutics*, p. 256, describes

eating a Pentecostal hermeneutic, but given the volume of scholarship that has utilized a Pentecostal method of interpretation since 1992,[11] certain distinctive features have emerged as representative of the commitments and ethos of the Pentecostal community.[12] This does not imply that there is only one Pentecostal approach to interpreting Scripture. Rickie D. Moore and Lee Roy Martin,[13] for example, employ a literary-theological method, Kenneth Archer advocates a semiotic approach,[14] and Robby Waddell recommends intertextuality as an interpretive framework.[15]

As I indicated in Chapter 2, synchronic approaches to biblical and theological studies have unlocked the prolific diversity of interpretive methods. This movement from a historical-critical focus to a focus on the final and finished form of the text has evinced 'that any text is rich and open toward a breadth of interpretive inferences as well as that readers and audiences have much to do with what is heard from the text'.[16] Interpreters of Scripture come to the text guided by their own context, insights, imagination, presumptions, and clearly defined interests,[17] and so discern distinct but cogent interpretations of a text. Thus, as a member of the Pentecostal community, I confess that I interpret Scripture from my own religious and cultural frame of reference. This *pro nobis* reading of Scripture is not a self-centered or an arrogant understanding of the text nor does it permit erroneous, misguided, and faulty interpretations of Scripture.[18] The task of

---

Pentecostals' method of interpreting Scripture as a 'Pentecostal culture of Bible reading' rather than a noteworthy principle of interpretation.

[11] Rickie D. Moore, 'Canon and Charisma in the Book of Deuteronomy', *JPT* 1 (1992), pp. 75-92, was the first publication to utilize a Pentecostal approach to Scripture.

[12] J.C. Thomas, 'Pentecostal Interpretation', in Steven L. McKenzie (ed.), *OEBI* (New York, NY: Oxford University Press, 2013), 2, pp. 89-97.

[13] Moore, 'Canon and Charisma', pp. 75-92. See also Rickie D. Moore, 'Deuteronomy and the Fire of God: A Critical Charismatic Interpretation', *JPT* 7 (1995), pp. 11-16; Martin, *The Unheard Voice of God;* Baker, 'Pentecostal Bible Reading', pp. 41-42, and Archer, *A Pentecostal Hermeneutic*, pp. 4, 5, 166, also approve literary approaches to Scripture. Archer, *'I Was in the Spirit on the Lord's Day'* utilizes a narrative reading of the text of Revelation to construct a Pentecostal theology of worship.

[14] Archer, *A Pentecostal Hermeneutic*.

[15] Waddell, *The Spirit of the Book of Revelation*.

[16] Patrick D. Miller, 'Popularizing the Bible', *ThT* 53 (1997), p. 437.

[17] Daniel Patte, *Ethics of Biblical Interpretation: A Reevaluation* (Louisville, KY: Westminster John Knox, 1995), p. 28.

[18] Waddell, *The Spirit of the Book of Revelation*, p. 98.

hermeneutics is not to bend, distort, exaggerate, or pervert the meaning of the text, but rather, for Pentecostals, the task of hermeneutics is to hear what God is saying through the text.[19] Thus, all critical explanations of Scripture must originate from the text and all interpreters should be required to justify their interpretations of the text.[20] Hence, a Pentecostal hermeneutic is not exempt from the rigorous exercises of academic biblical studies. Although the context of the interpreter will affect the interpretation of the text, it is not legitimate for the interpreter to import her/his presuppositions and ideas into the text.

The narrative of Pentecostal scholarship is chronicled by four generations of Pentecostal scholars.[21] The first generation of Pentecostal scholars achieved their graduate theological degrees in scholastic environments that did not allow an integration of their Pentecostal faith with their academic studies. The second generation of Pentecostal scholars were able to explore Pentecostal concerns but their investigations were regulated by historical and social-science perspectives.[22] The third generation of Pentecostal scholars, equipped with the tools of postmodernity,[23] were able to construct Pentecostal her-

---

[19] For the ways in which Scripture have been erroneously interpreted see, Jim Hill and Rand Cheadle, *The Bible Tells Me So: Uses and Abuses of Holy Scripture* (New York: Anchor Books/Doubleday, 1996).

[20] William W. Klein, Craig L. Blomberg, Robert L. Hubbard Jr., *Introduction to Biblical Interpretation* (Nashville: Thomas Nelson, Inc., 2004), p. 136; Archer, *A Pentecostal Hermeneutic*, pp. 127-91.

[21] R.D. Moore, J.C. Thomas, S.J. Land, 'Editorial', *JPT* 1 (1992), p. 3. See also J.C. Thomas' SPS Presidential Address, 'Pentecostal Theology in the Twenty-First Century', *Pneuma* 20.1 (1998), pp. 3-19; Thomas, *The Spirit of the New Testament*, pp. 3-6.

[22] See for example, V. Synan, *The Holiness-Pentecostal Movement in the United States* (Grand Rapids: Eerdmans, 1971).

[23] Timothy B. Cargal, 'Beyond the Fundamentalist-Modernist Controversy: Pentecostals and Hermeneutics in Post-Modern Age', *Pneuma* 15.2 (1993), p. 187 states:

> As a Postmodern paradigm increasingly illuminates the thinking of our culture in general, any hermeneutic which does not account for its loci of meanings within that Postmodern paradigm will become nonsensical and irrelevant. If for no other reason than that, we must move beyond the Fundamentalist-Modernist controversy to explore the possibilities of a Pentecostal hermeneutic in a Postmodern age.

Mark McLean, 'Toward a Pentecostal Hermeneutic', *Pneuma* 6.2 (1984), p. 37 argues that

meneutical paradigms that faithfully reflect the ethos of the Pentecostal community.[24] This generation of Pentecostal scholars defined
a unique Pentecostal hermeneutic for biblical studies. The emergence
of a distinctly Pentecostal method to interpreting Scripture began
with the publications of Pentecostal scholars such as Rickie D.
Moore,[25] John W. McKay,[26] and John Christopher Thomas.[27]

The ongoing influence of postmodernism will allow the fourth
generation of Pentecostal scholars to (1) occupy a seat at the academic table, (2) analyze, evaluate, and interact with previous and current Pentecostal scholarship, (3) complete their academic theological
programs in Pentecostal institutions, and have (4) 'the courage to
construct Pentecostal theological paradigms from the ground up;

---

[a] strict adherence to traditional evangelical/fundamentalist hermeneutic principles leads to a position which, in its most positive forms, suggests the distinc-
tives of the twentieth century Pentecostal movement are perhaps nice but not
necessary; important but not vital to the life of the Church in the twentieth
century. In its more negative forms, it leads to a total rejection of Pentecostal
phenomena.

Finally, Jackie David Johns, 'Pentecostalism and the Postmodern Worldview',
JPT 7 (1995), p. 85 says, 'Pentecostalism is more an impetus than a consequence of
an emerging dominant worldview. Pentecostalism should then be viewed as a part
of the mainstream that is forging the postmodern era.'

[24] Among the earliest attempts at a Pentecostal hermeneutic were G.T.
Sheppard, 'Word and Spirit: Scripture in the Pentecostal Tradition – Part One',
Agora 1.4 (1978), pp. 4-5, 17-22; *idem*, 'Word and Spirit: Scripture in the Pentecostal
Tradition – Part Two', *Agora* 2.1 (1978), pp. 14-19; McLean, 'Toward a Pentecostal
Hermeneutic', pp. 35-56; H.D. Hunter, *Spirit Baptism: A Pentecostal Alternative*
(Lanham, MD: University Press of America, 1983); R.A.N. Kydd, *Charismatic Gifts
in the Early Church* (Peabody, MA: Hendrickson, 1984); and Roger Stronstad, *The
Charismatic Theology of St. Luke* (Peabody, MA: Hendrickson, 1984). Thomas,
'Pentecostal Interpretation', pp. 89-97, chronicles the history of Pentecostal her-
meneutics.

[25] Rickie D. Moore, 'A Pentecostal Approach to Scripture', *Seminary Viewpoint*
8.1 (1987), pp. 4-5, 11, which was later published in Lee Roy Martin, *Pentecostal
Hermeneutics: A Reader* (Leiden/Boston: Brill, 2013), pp. 11-13, which I will cite in
this monograph; Moore, 'Canon and Charisma', pp. 75-92; Moore, 'Deuteronomy
and the Fire of God', pp. 11-33. The last two articles were also published in Moore,
The Spirit of the Old Testament, pp. 19-34 and 35-55, respectively, and later published
in Martin, *Pentecostal Hermeneutics*, pp. 15-32 and 109-30, respectively.

[26] John McKay, 'When the Veil Is Taken Away: The Impact of Prophetic
Experience on Biblical Interpretation', *JPT* 5 (1994), pp. 17-40.

[27] Thomas, 'Women, Pentecostals and the Bible', pp. 81-94.

paradigms that are faithful to the ethos and world view of the tradition'.[28] The scholars who launched the fourth generation of Pentecostal scholarship include Larry McQueen,[29] Kenneth J. Archer,[30] Robby Waddell,[31] and Lee Roy Martin.[32] In his published thesis, Martin claims that from 1992 to 2008 there were more than forty published articles and books devoted to a Pentecostal approach to Scripture.[33] Currently (eight years since Martin's publication), there are over 130 published articles and books that have utilized a Pentecostal strategy to biblical studies.[34] Considering the vast number of studies committed to a Pentecostal hermeneutics, Pentecostal scholars have certainly earned their seat around the academic table. Therefore, it is no longer necessary to defend the legitimacy of a distinctive Pentecostal hermeneutic.

Nevertheless, since hermeneutics is the process of interpreting Scripture[35] Pentecostals are compelled to devise hermeneutical paradigms that are faithful to the ethos of the tradition,[36] an ethos that views Scripture as the powerful, dynamic and living 'Spirit-Word'.[37] At the core of a Pentecostal hermeneutic is the 'god so near',[38] as Ezekiel himself describes (1.3; 2.2; 3.22; 8.3; 37.1, 40.1). Moore claims that the 'ongoing revelatory manifestation of divine nearness' is the root of prophecy in the book of Deuteronomy.[39] Accordingly,

---

[28] Thomas, *The Spirit of the New Testament*, p. 5. Cf. Veli-Matti Kärkkäinen, 'Pentecostal Hermeneutics in the Making: On the Way from Fundamentalism to Postmodernism', *JEPTA 18* (1998), pp. 31-34.

[29] Larry McQueen, *Joel and the Spirit: The Cry of a Prophetic Hermeneutic* (JPTSup 8; Sheffield: Sheffield Academic Press, 1995), later published as L. McQueen, *Joel and the Spirit: The Cry of a Prophetic Hermeneutic* (Cleveland, TN: CPT Press, 2009).

[30] Archer, *A Pentecostal Hermeneutic*.

[31] Waddell, *The Spirit of the Book of Revelation*, pp. 108-18.

[32] Martin, *The Unheard Voice of God*. For a collection of articles that have significantly contributed to the discussion of Pentecostal biblical hermeneutics since 1987, see Martin, *Pentecostal Hermeneutics*.

[33] Martin, *The Unheard Voice of God*, p. 56.

[34] See Martin, *Pentecostal Hermeneutics*, pp. 285-90.

[35] Cf. Marius Nel, 'Attempting to Define a Pentecostal Hermeneutics', *Scriptura* 114.1 (2015), pp. 1-21; Walter Brueggemann, 'The Legitimacy of a Sectarian Hermeneutic: 2 Kings 18-19', *Interpretation and Obedience: From Faithful Reading to Faithful Living* (Minneapolis, MN: Fortress Press, 1989), p. 62 states that 'a hermeneutic is not only necessary but inevitable. There are no uninterpreted events.'

[36] C.E.W. Green, *Toward a Pentecostal Theology of the Lord's Supper*, p. 183, lists eight general areas of consensus among Pentecostals.

[37] Land, *Pentecostal Spirituality*, p. 100.

[38] Moore, 'Canon and Charisma', pp. 15-32.

[39] Moore, 'Canon and Charisma', p. 23.

I propose that it is the continued revelatory experience of God that creates and sustains a distinctive Pentecostal hermeneutic. This divine revelatory experience inspires a fresh interpretation of the biblical text for the Pentecostal hermeneut who must now hear, see (discern), speak, taste, touch, and obey the word of God. The prophetic encounter of the Pentecostal hermeneut corresponds to the Old Testament prophets' experiences of YHWH. These divine encounters upended and pulverized the prophets' antecedent presumptions and beliefs and created a new theological reality and worldview.[40] The Pentecostal hermeneut, therefore, functions as a prophetic voice to the Pentecostal community.[41] This prophetic encounter with God guards against erroneous and evil misinterpretation of Scripture. For the Pentecostal hermeneut, 'every part of the process of interpretation is performed in the presence of God, who is Lord of past, present, and future. Prayer and worship fuse all the elements together into one pursuit, the pursuit of God himself'.[42]

By proposing a Pentecostal hermeneutic to the biblical text, I am not discrediting other approaches to Scripture. Clearly, it is possible for Pentecostals and non-Pentecostals to appropriately interpret Scripture without employing a Pentecostal strategy. As Willie Wessels argues, 'There is more than one correct method of interpretation and this is to the benefit of the believing community who should realize that interpretation is a dynamic, open-ended, and ongoing process'.[43] However, as a lifelong and practicing member of the Pentecostal community, it is my intention to apply a Pentecostal hermeneutical strategy as I interpret the interrelationship between the glory and holiness of YHWH in the book of Ezekiel. It is my belief that the themes of *seeing* and *hearing* serve as a suitable biblical model for a Pentecostal approach to Ezekiel.

---

[40] Moore, 'The Prophetic Calling', pp. 56-85; Martin, *Pentecostal Hermeneutics*, p. 2

[41] I suggest that Pentecostals must first experience God in order to hear, see, speak, taste, and obey his word. In other words, a divine revelatory encounter stimulates all of the human senses, a transformative experience that compels obedience to the voice of God.

[42] Martin, *The Unheard Voice of God*, p. 58.

[43] Willie J. Wessels, 'Biblical Hermeneutics', in Adrio and S.S. Maimela König (eds.), *Initiation into Theology: The Rich Variety of Theology and Hermeneutics* (Pretoria: Van Schaik, 1998), p. 272.

Seeing and *Hearing* in the Old Testament context

The biblical notion of hearing the word of YHWH as a significant and appropriate paradigm for Pentecostals was highlighted by Martin. Martin argues that the term *hearing* (שָׁמַע) is a conducive way to approach Scripture because: (1) שָׁמַע is a biblical term; (2) it correlates with the oral character of both the biblical and Pentecostal contexts; (3) it is a relational term that implies the 'existence of a "person" who is speaking the Word'; (4) it conveys 'a faithful adherence to the Word, since in Scripture to hear often means to obey'; (5) it prompts 'transformation' as one hears and heeds the Word; (6) it 'demands humility because, unlike the process of "reading" Scripture, "hearing" entails submission to the authority of the word of God'.[44] Although Martin is correct to suggest that Scripture must be heard,[45] I would add that Scripture, particularly the book of Ezekiel, should be both seen and heard.[46]

The stunningly graphic inaugural vision of Ezekiel begins with the prophet seeing the word of YHWH (1.1-3) and then hearing the word of YHWH (2.3). Thus, seeing and hearing is Ezekiel's distinct way of experiencing the word of YHWH. According to Abraham Even-Shoshan, the Hebrew verb רָאה in all its forms is found 1303 times in the Old Testament[47] and 73 times in the book of Ezekiel.[48] The verb means 'to see', 'look at', 'inspect with the eyes',[49] and the extended meaning of the verb includes 'to discern', 'to discover', 'to encounter', 'to know', 'to perceive', 'to provide', 'to understand'.[50] These extended meanings show that the verb רָאה denotes more than the literal usage of seeing with the eyes. The verb expresses the total

---

[44] Martin, *The Unheard Voice of God*, p. 53.

[45] Martin, *The Unheard Voice of God*, pp. 52-79.

[46] Historical critics such as Gunkel viewed the book of Ezekiel as the beginning of the decline of prophecy in ancient Israel. For more on this point see M.H. Floyd, 'Prophecy and Writing in Habakkuk 2, 1-5', *ZAW* 105 (1993), pp. 462-65.

[47] Abraham Even-Shoshan, *A New Concordance of the Old Testament: Using the Hebrew and Aramaic Text* (Jerusalem: Kiryat-Sefer, 2nd edn, 1989), pp. 1041-45. See also Hans F. Fuhs, 'רָאה', in *TDOT*, XIII, p. 212.

[48] Abraham Even-Shoshan, *A New Concordance of the Old Testament*, pp. 1041-45.

[49] Robert D. Culver, 'רָאה', in *TWOT*, II, p. 823; *BDB*, pp. 906-909; William L. Holladay, *A Concise Hebrew and Aramaic Lexicon of the Old Testament* (Grand Rapids, MI: Eerdmans, corrected 10th edn, 1988), pp. 327-28.

[50] Culver, *TWOT*, p. 823; *BDB*, pp. 906-909; Holladay, *A Concise Hebrew and Aramaic Lexicon of the Old Testament*, pp. 327-28.

experience of seeing in which visual and noetic apperceptions fuse.[51] Thus, ראה covers a complex and broad range of meanings.

The theological use of ראה in the Old Testament indicates the wide range of circumstances in which individuals personally experience or encounter God. In this encounter, God emerges from obscurity and reveals himself to humanity. 'Thus [ראה] denotes the act of revelation itself, God's self-manifestation in person and in action'.[52] To see God's face is to encounter God, an encounter that highlights the direct and immediate involvement with God and the individual. The act of ראה establishes a personal relationship, an intimate communion between the one being revealed and the one who sees (Exod. 16.6-7; Job 19.27, 33.36, 42.5; Isa. 17.7, 33.17; Ezek. 1.1.-3).[53]

Additionally, the verb ראה denotes the merging of seeing, observation, reflection, and knowledge. The combination of these various elements of perception convey the totality of seeing expressed by the verb ראה. This synthesis is depicted by the frequent parallel use of ראה and ידע in the Old Testament (Gen. 8.6-13; Num. 24.16-17; Deut. 11.2; 1 Sam. 25.17; Isa. 29.15; 41.20; 44.9, 18; 58.3; 61.9; Jer. 2.23; 5.1; 12.3; Ps. 138.6; Job 11.11; Eccl. 6.5; Neh. 4.5). Therefore, ראה conveys a more substantial meaning of 'knowing'.[54] In other words, the verb may signify to see in such a way as to know (Cf. Deut. 33.9). In Ezekiel, the divine recognition formula ('And they/you will *know* that I am Yahweh') occurs 72 times. It appears 54 times in the third person and 18 times in the second person. However, apart from these 72 occurrences, the verb ראה appears twice in the divine recognition formula: 21.4[20.48][55] and 39.21.[56] The occurrence of the verb ראה in the formula aims to guide the hearer to complete recognition and personal, experiential, and relational knowledge of YHWH's character. Thus, Ezekiel's hearers do not make objective and detached observations of YHWH but arrive at an intimate understanding of

---

51 Fuhs, *TDOT*, pp. 214-15.
52 Fuhs, *TDOT*, p. 229.
53 Fuhs, *TDOT*, p. 229.
54 Fuhs, *TDOT*, pp. 214-39.
55 [20.48] is the English text.
56 Block, *The Book of Ezekiel 1-24*, p. 39. Per Zimmerli, *Ezekiel 1-24*, p. 38, the expression occurs 78 times with slight variations.

who YHWH is through an encounter with his actions in the narrative.[57] To see YHWH is to know YHWH. To know YHWH is to be in a close, dynamic relationship with him. A direct knowledge of YHWH requires a response of loving obedience to him. In Hebrew, knowledge of YHWH is synonymous with love for YHWH (Cf. Ps. 91.14).[58]

To see God also means to experience God's power and his divine presence.[59] When the Hebrews complained of hunger in the wilderness, Moses said, 'This evening you shall know that it was YHWH who brought you out of the land of Egypt, and in the morning you shall see the glory of YHWH' (Exod. 16.6-7). For Pentecostals, to see God's face and to encounter God's divine presence is to experience God's glory and holiness. To sense God's presence during times of worship is vital because it reminds them of the nearness of God. Without the presence of God's glory, Pentecostals believe that worship is ritualistic and lifeless.

Experiencing YHWH's presence creates an awareness and understanding of sinful behaviors, and so prompts repentance and transformation (Deut. 9.16, 29.16; Judg. 19.32; 2 Kgs 23.24; Neh. 13.15; Job 42.5; Ezek. 14.22).[60] The individual/community who *sees* will discern their wickedness, turn from their evil ways, and escape calamity (Ezek. 18.23). Thus, the prophets implored the people not to close their eyes to the realities of their sin (Jer. 2.23, 3.2). However, the community of Israel would rather worship idols manufactured by human hands, which can neither see nor hear (Ps. 115.5-6; 135.16-17). The people's resistance to see YHWH debars the hope of insight (Isa. 5.12; 42.18; Jer. 5.21; Ezek. 12.2). Their persistent disinclination to see and hear the word of YHWH ultimately leads to his judgment, which renders them unable to see and hear (cf. Isa. 6.9-10).[61]

---

[57] Cf. Jackie David Johns and Cheryl Bridges Johns, 'Yielding to the Spirit: A Pentecostal Approach to Group Bible Study', in Martin (ed.), *Pentecostal Hermeneutics*, pp. 33-56. This article was first published as Jackie David Johns and Cheryl Bridges Johns, 'Yielding to the Spirit: A Pentecostal Approach to Group Bible Study', *JPT* 1 (1992), pp. 109-34. This research will continue to cite the more recent publication.

[58] Gregory Mobley, 'Know, Knowledge', in David Noel Freedman, Allen C. Meyers, and Astrid B. Beck (eds.), *Eerdmans Dictionary of the Bible* (Grand Rapids, MI/Cambridge, UK: Eerdmans, 2000), p. 777.

[59] Fuhs, *TDOT*, p. 231.

[60] Fuhs, *TDOT*, p. 232.

[61] Fuhs, *TDOT*, p. 233.

Moreover, prophetic texts such as Ezekiel use ראה to describe a prophetic visionary experience of the prophet.[62] YHWH's self-revelation is the subject of prophetic visions. Joel 3.1 (2.28) indicates that the spirit of YHWH will make all people prophets, and so there is immediate access to YHWH through visions and dreams. This nearness of God rescinds all inequalities and differences amidst humanity.[63]

According to Martin, the person who hears will live because the Hebrew word שמע suggests obedience to the word of YHWH.[64] However, in light of the foregoing discussion, I propose that the one who *sees* and *hears* the word of YHWH will have life. A failure to *see* and *hear* the word of YHWH is symptomatic of a rebellious state (Ezek. 12.2).

Seeing and *Hearing* in Ezekiel

A parallel relationship between the themes of seeing and hearing emerges in the book of Ezekiel. Undisputedly, there are biblical texts that depict hearing the word of YHWH as the governing theme. However, according to Hebrew tradition, when ראה and שמע occur together, the biblical texts either describe a single experience of perception (Deut. 29.3; Isa. 6.9-14; Jer. 5.21; Prov. 20.12; Eccl. 1.8) or they indicate that the act of seeing takes precedence over the act of hearing (Gen. 45.27; 1 Kgs 10.7; Ps. 48. 8; Job 42.5). The idea is that without the act of ראה that which is heard continues to be sterile knowledge. The act of ראה makes what is heard a dynamic and enriching experience.[65] The following discussion will show that there are times in the book of Ezekiel when the act of seeing takes precedence over the act of hearing, as well as times when seeing and hearing function as a unitary act of perception.[66]

The primacy of ראה over שמע in Ezekiel is evident in the first chapter of Ezekiel. From the outset, YHWH's word that occurred to

---

[62] Fuhs, *TDOT*, p. 237.
[63] Fuhs, *TDOT*, p. 239.
[64] Martin, *The Unheard Voice of God*, pp. 68-71.
[65] Fuhs, *TDOT*, p. 216.
[66] While seeing and hearing were the two dominant senses Ezekiel utilized to encounter the word of YHWH, he also tasted the word of YHWH (3.1-3), felt the hand of YHWH upon him.

Ezekiel is saturated with visual language (1.1-28). The prophet Eze-kiel is confronted with a riveting sight. The heavens open and he *sees* 'visions of God' (1.1). As he describes his visionary experience in technicolor detail, he limns a sequence of images of what he sees and hears by using the various forms of the verbs ראה and שׁמע. The verb וארא occurs three times in 1.4, 1.15, and 1.27. ואשמע appears once in v. 24, and ראיתי occurs in v. 27. The visionary experience ends in v. 28 with ואראה and ואשמע.[67] Furthermore, Ezekiel uses the re-lated noun מראה 15 times in the first chapter to signal what he sees, and as he narrates what he sees, he uses the word קול seven times to describe what he hears.[68]

Like other Old Testament prophets, Ezekiel hears the word of YHWH, but for him the visualization of YHWH's revelation is par-ticularly significant.[69] Thus, ch. 1 can be structured around the vari-ous forms of the verb ראה:

1. Preamble: I saw visions of God (vv. 1-3)
2. Vision of storm cloud and fire (v. 4)
3. Vision of the four living creatures (vv. 5-14)
4. Vision of the wheels and their movement (vv. 15-26)
5. The sound of the four living creatures' wings (v. 24)
6. The sound of a voice from above (v. 25)
7. Vision of the chariot throne (vv. 27-28)[70]

Naturally, Ezekiel is simultaneously seeing and hearing the dra-matic spectacle unfolding around him, but he does not simultane-ously recount what he sees and hears. Rather, he delineates the visual details first and then narrates the audio aspects of the vision. The frequency of the phrase 'I saw' in the first chapter compels the hearer to see over and over again with Ezekiel. The phrase 'I saw' occurs six times in ch. 1: 'I saw visions of God' (v. 1); 'I saw ... a storm cloud' (v. 4); 'I saw the living creatures' (v. 15); 'I saw ... the color of amber' (v. 27); I saw ... the appearance of fire' (v. 27); and '... I saw and fell on my face ...' (v. 28). The repetition of the phrase 'I saw' enables

---

[67] Ellen Van Wolde, 'The God Ezekiel 1 Envisions', in Paul M. Joyce and Dalit Rom-Shiloni (eds.), *The God Ezekiel Creates* (London: Bloomsbury T&T Clark, 2015), p. 88.
[68] Wolde, 'The God Ezekiel 1 Envisions', p. 89.
[69] Duguid, *Ezekiel*, p. 47.
[70] Cf. Wolde, 'The God Ezekiel 1 Envisions', p. 89.

the hearer to gain the full impact of what Ezekiel sees because Ezekiel does not interrupt his visual description with what he hears.[71] Ezekiel's hearers imagine visually what he describes. Ezekiel persuades the hearers of his prophecy to look or envision with him as he encounters the glory of YHWH. By introducing his vision as the 'word of YHWH' (1.3), Ezekiel not only invites his hearers to see what he sees, but he urges them to anticipate the revelation of God's word. Furthermore, the impact of what Ezekiel sees is so prominent in the book of Ezekiel that not only can the first chapter be structured around the various forms of the verb ראה, but the entire book of Ezekiel can be structured around the visions of YHWH's glory: chs. 1-8, 8-11, and 40-48. Chapter 1, therefore, establishes the relationship between the motifs of seeing and hearing in the book of Ezekiel.

The intrinsic nature of Judah's offense was their rebellion against YHWH, and their state of rebellion is closely associated with the acts of seeing and hearing (12.2). Fourteen times Ezekiel describes the Israelites as a 'rebellious house' (בית מרי) (2.5-6, 8; 3-9, 26, 27; 12.2-3, 9, 25; 17.12; 24.3), and the term מרי without בית is found twice (2.7 and 44.6).[72] The recurrence of the expression 'rebellious house' and the word 'rebellious' characterize the house of Israel's attitude toward YHWH.[73]

The state of rebellion is so prevalent among the house of Israel that even Ezekiel is tempted to defy what he sees and hears. Why must the Spirit enter Ezekiel before he can hear the word of YHWH (2.1-2)? YHWH warns him in 2.8 not to be rebellious like the rest of the people. YHWH feeds Ezekiel the scroll after commanding him three times to eat it (2.8 – 3.3). After seeing the glory of YHWH, Ezekiel leaves bitter and full of rage in his spirit (3.14), and sits in silence, resisting his call for an entire week (3.15). Following the week of silence, Ezekiel is given a grave warning about disregarding his prophetic call (3.16-21). All of these events suggest that Ezekiel is also susceptible to the spiritual disease that plagued the house of Israel.[74] Clearly, in the book of Ezekiel, to see with the eyes is to hear and obey the words of YHWH, and a refusal to see and hear the

---

[71] From conversations with Lee Roy Martin.
[72] Duguid, *Ezekiel*, p. 313; Block, *The Book of Ezekiel 1-24*, p. 120.
[73] See Block, p. 51
[74] Cf. Block, *The Book of Ezekiel 1-24*, p. 12.

word of YHWH is to revolt against him. Thus, seeing and hearing function as a unitary act of perception.

Based on the foregoing discussion, seeing and hearing the word of YHWH is unequivocally a biblically well-founded, suitable, and legitimate paradigm for Pentecostals to approach Scripture. Several significant elements make seeing and hearing the word of YHWH an appropriate paradigm for a Pentecostal approach to the Bible. Seeing and hearing (1) indicates distinctive ways individuals experienced the word of YHWH in the Old Testament; (2) portrays an intimate relationship between the God who reveals himself and the person/community who sees and hears this revelation; (3) depicts an encounter with God and his divine presence; (4) reveals a close, relational knowledge of YHWH;[75] (5) produces repentance and transformation because an encounter with God gives awareness to sinful behaviors; and (6) signifies steadfast obedience since failing to see and hear the word of God results in rebellion against God.

Thus, the call to see and hear the word of YHWH is a theological commitment of a Pentecostal hermeneutic. Since my goal as a Pentecostal hermeneut is to see and hear the prophetic word of YHWH in Ezekiel, it is essential that I approach the book of Ezekiel equipped with exegetical, literary, narrative, and theological methods. These techniques will enable the Pentecostal interpreter to see and hear the prophetic voice of the text.

Seeing and *Hearing* God in the Community

The Pentecostal communal context presents opportunities for seeing and hearing God through Scripture. Since ראה and שמע denote an encounter with God that leads to repentance, transformation, hearing, and obeying God,[76] these terms are appropriate biblical terms for the Pentecostal community, which stresses an intimate encounter with God, yearns to see God's face, desires to hear God's voice, and espouses sanctification and holiness. For Pentecostals, to see God's face does not imply gawking at his physical countenance, but rather, it represents a direct and personal encounter with the dynamic and

---

[75] Per discussion in previous section.
[76] Cf. Martin, *The Unheard Voice of God*, pp. 52-79; Fuhs, *TDOT*, pp. 208-42.

powerful presence of the living God within the community of faith.[77] It is in the community of faith that we hear God's voice, see God reveal himself through the biblical texts, 'in signs and wonders, in worship and prayer, in very real and powerful ways',[78] and witness the Holy Spirit's creative and transformative work in the lives of the community.

The Pentecostal community provides a safe setting for discerning, enquiring, exploring, interpreting, and studying Scripture.[79] Ergo, the Pentecostal scholar must be a participating member of the Pentecostal worshiping community. The community (1) provides insights and helps form the meaning of the text,[80] (2) applies the meaning of Scripture to our contemporary context,[81] (3) shields from a 'stridently dogmatic, divisive and thus ultimately and fundamentally flawed' interpretation,[82] (4) provides accountability,[83] (5) tests and discerns the interpretation of Scripture, and (6) 'facilitates the uniting of a myriad of contrasting, individualized, contextualized applications of meaning in an arena of mutual coherence and significance'.[84]

Since the interpretation of Scripture is not the solitary endeavor of an individual scholar, the Pentecostal community is a critical member in the interpretive process.[85] This process of hermeneutics is dependent on the leadership of the Holy Spirit to discern the meaning

---

[77] Scott A. Ellington, 'Pentecostalism and the Authority of Scripture', *JPT* 9 (1996), later published as Scott A. Ellington, 'Pentecostalism and the Authority of Scripture', in Martin (ed.), *Pentecostal Hermeneutics*, p. 149-70, which I will cite in this study.

[78] Ellington, 'Pentecostalism and the Authority of Scripture', p. 151.

[79] Keith Warrington, *Pentecostal Theology: A Theology of Encounter* (London: T&T Clard, 2008), p. 198; Archer, *A Pentecostal Hermeneutic*; Dale M. Coulter, 'What Meaneth This? Pentecostals and Theological Inquiry', *JPT* 10.1 (2001), pp. 62-63; Clark H. Pinnock, 'The Work of the Holy Spirit in Hermeneutics', *JPT* 2 (1993), pp. 16-17; Ellington, 'Pentecostalism and the Authority of Scripture', p. 162; Richard D. Israel, Daniel E. Albrecht, and Randall G. McNally, 'Pentecostals and Hermeneutics: Texts, Rituals and Community', *Pneuma* 15.1 (1993), pp. 154-61; Simon Chan, *Pentecostal Theology and the Christian Spiritual Tradition* (JPTSup 21; London: Sheffield Academic Press, 2003), p. 44.

[80] Martin, *The Unheard Voice of God*, p. 61.

[81] Archer, *'I Was in the Spirit on the Lord's Day'*, p. 48.

[82] Warrington, *Pentecostal Theology*, p. 198.

[83] Martin, *The Unheard Voice of God*, p. 79.

[84] Davies, 'What Does It Mean to Read the Bible as a Pentecostal?', p. 260.

[85] Archer, *'I Was in the Spirit on the Lord's Day'*, p. 48; Archer, *A Pentecostal Hermeneutic*, p. 180; J.C. Thomas, '"What the Spirit Is Saying to the Church"– The Testimony of a Pentecostal in New Testament Studies', in K.L. Spawn and A.T. Wright (eds.), *Spirit and Scripture: Exploring a Pneumatic Hermeneutic* (London:

of Scripture in our present day context. The encounter and experiences with God in the community produce fresh and enriched insights and understanding of the text. The Pentecostal communal milieu 'is the place of formation for those who would hear the biblical text ... with Pentecostal ears',[86] who would see by faith the promises that Scripture speaks to us, and by the Spirit 'see beyond our own worldview ... to catch a glimpse of the world as God sees it'.[87]

Seeing, Hearing, and the Holy Spirit

Unless the Holy Spirit opens the eyes and ears of individuals, Pentecostals believe that it is impossible to discern God's lively presence, experience a personal relationship with him, see his mighty acts, and hear his voice. We must have eyes to see and understand, and ears to hear and obey if we are to encounter God's self-disclosure that gives rise to an intimate relationship with him, an awareness of sinful behaviors, transformation, and obedience. This type of seeing and hearing only comes from the Holy Spirit.

Pentecostals willingly concede that there is an active role for the Holy Spirit in the process of hermeneutics. The role of the Spirit in biblical hermeneutics defies rigid, authoritarian, intolerant, and doctrinaire interpretation of Scripture.[88] Since a valid interpretation of Scripture is impossible without the Holy Spirit, Pentecostals invite the Spirit to participate actively in the hermeneutical task.[89] Unlike

---

Bloomsbury T&T Clard, 2012), p. 116; Cheryl Bridges Johns, *Pentecostal Formation: A Pedagogy among the Oppressed* (JPTSup 2; Sheffield: Sheffield Academic Press, 1993), pp. 2, 125.

[86] Thomas, '"What the Spirit Is Saying to the Church"', p. 116.

[87] Ellington, 'Pentecostalism and the Authority of Scripture', p. 168.

[88] Clark H. Pinnock, 'The Work of the Spirit in the Interpretation of Holy Scripture from the Perspective of a Charismatic Biblical Theologian', *JPT* 18.2 (2009), pp. 157-71, later published as, 'The Work of the Spirit in the Interpretation of Holy Scripture from the Perspective of a Charismatic Biblical Theologian', in Martin (ed.), *Pentecostal Hermeneutics*, pp. 233-48, which will be cited in this study.

[89] Archer, *A Pentecostal Hermeneutic*, pp. 185-86. See also Howard M. Ervin, 'Hermeneutics: A Pentecostal Option', *Pneuma* 3.1 (1981), pp. 11-25; French L. Arrington, 'Historical Perspectives on Pentecostal and Charismatic Hermeneutics', in S.M. Burgess and G.B. McGee (eds.), *Dictionary of Pentecostal and Charismatic Movements* (Grand Rapids: Regency Reference Library/Zondervan, 1988), pp. 376-89; Johns and Bridges Johns, 'Yielding to the Spirit'; Pinnock, 'The Work of the Spirit'; K.L. Spawn and Archie T. Wright, *Spirit and Scripture: Exploring a Pneumatic Hermeneutic* (London: Bloomsbury T&T Clark, 2012).

other approaches that do not seek the guidance of the Holy Spirit in the interpretive process, 'the Spirit's role in a Pentecostal biblical hermeneutic is deemed to be concrete and discernible at most every step in the hermeneutical process'.[90] Pentecostal theology must seek to see and hear what the Spirit is saying through Scripture.

The Spirit inspires new insight to Scripture.[91] If we hear Scripture only from a historical perspective, we will keep the biblical texts safely ensconced as a relic in history.[92] The Holy Spirit renders an ancient text alive and contemporary to the present community of faith. Scripture thus becomes relevant and meaningful to our modern context. The original intent of the text is not the only possible meaning of the text.[93] The role of the Spirit in hermeneutics contextualizes Scripture in modern culture and creates fresh understanding and meaning in new circumstances.[94] The Spirit is vital for the interpretation of Scripture to be effective, meaningful, and valid. The Spirit's continuous acts of inspiration prevent Scripture from becoming ossified, frozen, and static. The Spirit allows the historical word of God to be interpreted in a new light. Thus, the biblical texts remain the fresh, dynamic, and timeless voice of God for each new generation. Pentecostals believe that the Holy Spirit is necessary to render an effective and modern expression of Scripture. Moreover, if the Pentecostal hermeneut is to be a prophetic voice to the community, then s/he must be empowered and guided by the Spirit.

Pentecostals and Prophetic Visionary Experiences

Ezekiel's outlandish visions of YHWH, of strange creatures, of wheels with eyes that moved through the air, his eccentric sign acts such as his muteness, his recumbent body bound and naked, and his

[90] Thomas, 'Pentecostal Interpretation', p. 94.
[91] Pinnock, 'The Work of the Spirit', p. 238.
[92] Clark H. Pinnock, *The Scripture Principle* (Eugene, OR: Wipf and Stock Publishers, 1998), p. 156.
[93] M.J. Cartledge, 'Text-Community-Spirit: The Challenges Posed by Pentecostal Theological Method to Evangelical Theology', in Kevin L. Spawn and Archie T. Wright (eds.), *Spirit and Scripture: Exploring a Pneumatic Hermeneutic* (London: London: Bloomsbury T&T Clark, 2012), p. 140.
[94] D.J. Bosch, *Transforming Mission: Paradigm Shifts in the Theology of Mission* (Maryknoll: Orbis, 1991), pp. 113-15.

absence of grief when his wife died, his alarming use of sexual metaphors in chs. 16 and 23, and his hearing of voices have long fasci-
nated and inspired curiosity into the mental/emotional state of the
historical figure of Ezekiel. The prophet, therefore, has been the pa-
tient of many psychoanalytical examinations, which have led to several medical diagnoses that attempt to explain Ezekiel's peculiar visionary experiences and deviant behaviors.[95] Scholars who anatomize
the personality of Ezekiel conclude that the prophet's visionary encounters, his ability to hear voices, and his odd ecstatic experiences
were caused by hallucinations that resulted from acute paranoid
schizophrenia.[96] Other diagnoses include catalepsy,[97] post-traumatic
stress syndrome,[98] and excessive rage toward women.[99]

A few scholars have decried the psychoanalytical approach to Ezekiel.[100] While the psychoanalytical approach may provide thought-
provoking and interesting information, it is based on speculations
and conjectures of the prophet's upbringing and the effects of his
early life on his emotional state – details that are not found in the
final form of the text. Additionally, this approach disregards
YHWH's role, character, speeches, and actions in the book of Ezekiel. YWHH is no longer the sovereign God who reveals himself to

---

[95] David G. Garber, 'Traumatizing Ezekiel, the Exilic Prophet', in J. Harold
Ellens and Wayne G. Rollins (eds.), *Psychology and the Bible: From Genesis to Apocalyptic
Vision* (Westport, CT: Praeger, 2004), pp. 215-36.

[96] E.C. Broome, 'Ezekiel's Abnormal Personality', *JBL* 65 (1946), pp. 277-92.
Broome also believed that Ezekiel displayed symptoms of catanoia, psychosis, and
paranoia.

[97] This diagnosis is accredited to August Klostermann after his publication in
1877. Cf. Mortimer Ostow, *Ultimate Intimacy: The Psychodynamics of Jewish Mysticism*
(London: Karnac Books, 1995), p. 90.

[98] Johanna Stubert, *The Exile and the Prophet's Wife: Historic Events and Marginal
Perspectives* (Collgeville, MN: Liturgical Press, 1998), pp. 87-108.

[99] David J. Halperin, *Seeking Ezekiel: Text and Psychology* (University Park, PA:
The Pennsylvania State University Press, 1993).

[100] These scholars include Zimmerli, *Ezekiel 1-24*, pp. 17-18; Davis, *Swallowing
the Scroll: Textuality and the Dynamics of Discourse in Ezekiel's Prophecy*, p. 66. For psy-
chiatrists who oppose this approach see B. Bron, 'Zur Psychopathologie und
Verkündigung des Propheten Ezechiel: Zum Phänomen der prophetischen
Ekstase', *Schweizer Archiv fürNeurologie, Neurochirugie und Psychiatrie* 128 (1981), pp.
21-31; H. Tellenbach, 'Ezechiel: Wetterleuchten einer 'Schizophrenie' (Jaspers)
oder prophetische Erfahrung des Ganz-Anderen', *Daseinsanalyse* 4 (1987), pp. 227-
36.

Ezekiel; rather he becomes a figment of Ezekiel's very creative imagination.[101] Thus, Ezekiel's striking depiction of unmerited love is reduced to mental illness that is attributed to his uncontrollable rage toward women and a subliminal anger toward men created by unsubstantiated claims of childhood abuse.[102]

While psychologists might find the visions of Ezekiel problematic, Pentecostals, due to their spirituality and mystical inclination, do not question the authenticity of Ezekiel's prophetic experience. In fact, the auditory visions of Ezekiel resonate with the Pentecostal experience. Moreover, Pentecostals accept that visions are prophetic revelations that come from an encounter with God – an encounter that radically alters and destroys the prophet's current perception of reality.[103] Thus, the prophetic seer sees a reality that moves beyond the borders of traditional concept and sees the world through God's perspective.

As discussed in Chapter 1, Pentecostals affirm visions as a legitimate vehicle for divine revelation. The birth of Pentecostalism in North America occurred with the fresh outpouring of the Holy Spirit upon Christian believers who believed that this encounter with the Spirit was very much like the experience of the early church in Acts 2, and a fulfillment of Joel 2.28. Along with glossolalia and prophecy, visions and dreams have always been recognized as a significant experience of the outpouring of God's Spirit in both the Old and New Testaments (Num. 12.6; Joel 2.28; Acts 2.16-18). Pentecostals recognize individuals such as Ezekiel who experienced auditory and visual revelations to be prophets of the Spirit. The Spirit plays a prominent role in the book of Ezekiel. From the very beginning we see the Spirit as the agent and stimulus of Ezekiel's prophetic experience. The phrase, 'the hand of the Lord', occurs frequently in the book of Ezekiel (1.3; 3.14, 22; 8.1; 33.22; 40.1), and this phrase is homologous with the activity of the Spirit in relation to divine revelation and the prophetic word. The hand of the Lord first comes upon Ezekiel in 1.3, and from that time forward the hand of YHWH moves Ezekiel

---

[101] Halperin, *Seeking Ezekiel*, claims that YHWH is 'a creation of Ezekiel's own brain' (p. 223).

[102] Halperin, *Seeking Ezekiel*, pp. 207-8.

[103] Moore, 'The Prophetic Calling', pp. 55-68; Lee Roy Martin, 'Towards a Biblical Model of Pentecostal Prophetic Preaching', *Verbum et Ecclesia* 37.1 (2016), pp. 1-9.

to see, act, and speak the word of the Lord to the exilic community. The diverse activities of the Spirit throughout the book of Ezekiel illustrate that Ezekiel's entire prophetic experience is initiated and steered by the Spirit of YHWH. It was by the Spirit that Ezekiel received his visions, was moved and transported, and given the ability to speak the word of the Lord.[104]

Since the Spirit's presence is prevalent in the prophetic experience of Ezekiel, the prophet's startling ecstatic behaviors are related to the influence of the Spirit. The *ruach* of YHWH is the 'untamable energy and dynamic controlled only by God … It is a force that can come upon persons, seize them, and cause them to get beside themselves in prophetic ecstasy … unnatural, abnormal, and even crazy to civilized society – something to be kept out of bounds'.[105] It is no wonder that some people believe Ezekiel's outré behavior to be symptomatic of psychosis, paranoia, and schizophrenia. However, Ezekiel was not deranged, but radically altered, and completely captivated by the word of YHWH. Consequently, his visionary experiences, theatrical actions, and speech appear to be crazy in the eyes of those who do not comprehend the workings of the Spirit of prophecy.

It is not unusual, therefore, for Pentecostals to integrate visionary experiences in their worship. Visions and dreams have played a significant role in defining the worship of early Pentecostalism. The early Pentecostals' worship was a combination of spontaneity and prophetic proclamation. 'Communication by means of hymns, dreams, [visions], and charismatic messages helped to build community and fellowship without losing sight of its Christian focus'.[106] Like their spiritual ancestors, present-day Pentecostals understand that visions and dreams are manifestations of the prophetic disposition and eschatological gifts of the Spirit.[107]

---

[104] Hildebrandt, *An Old Testament Theology of the Spirit of God*, pp. 187-89; Montague, *The Holy Spirit*, pp. 45-49; Horton, *What the Bible Says About the Holy Spirit*, 66-67; and J.J.M. Roberts, *The Hand of the Lord* (Baltimore: John Hopkins University Press, 1977).

[105] Moore, 'The Prophetic Calling', p. 64.

[106] Jean-Daniel Plüss, *Therapeutic and Prophetic Narratives in Worship: A Hermeneutic Study of Testimonies and Visions* (Bern: Verlag P. Lang, 1988), p. 320.

[107] Stronstad, *The Prophethood of All Believers*.

Conclusion

In this chapter, I have proposed that seeing and hearing the word of YHWH – the goal of my Pentecostal hermeneutic – is an appropriate paradigm for encountering the book of Ezekiel. This Pentecostal approach of seeing and hearing the word of YHWH in Ezekiel provides new insights into the relationship between the glory of YHWH and the holiness of YHWH in the book of Ezekiel. The recurring parallelism of ראה and שמע in the Old Testament suggests that knowledge imparted by hearing the word of YHWH is flat and lifeless until accompanied by the act of seeing. Seeing and hearing are common biblical methods of encountering YHWH, and they provide access to the dynamic and continuous revelatory word of the 'God so near'.

I have demonstrated that an analogous relationship between seeing and hearing unfolds in the book of Ezekiel. Since Ezekiel encounters YHWH and YHWH's word through the acts of seeing and hearing, the modern recipients of this prophecy must be so bold as to see and hear YHWH's word together with Ezekiel. Failing to see and hear the word of YHWH is rebellion against YHWH. Therefore, seeing and hearing the word of YHWH is a theological responsibility of the Pentecostal community.

I further contend that the Pentecostal community is the most suitable context to see and hear God through Scripture. Since the verbs ראה and שמע signify an encounter with God that leads to repentance, transformation, hearing, and obedience, they are biblical terms that correlate with the holiness and sanctification theology of the Pentecostal community. Furthermore, it is the community who offers accountability, is alert and attentive to the appropriate meaning of Scripture, and discerns, validates, and testifies to the radical transformation that results from seeing and hearing the word of God. This type of seeing and hearing that leads to obedience and transformation comes only from the Holy Spirit. Unless the Spirit opens our eyes and ears we will cease to see God's work, hear God's word, and be transformed. We cease to be a community with a prophetic voice. Indeed, we must have eyes to see and ears to hear what the Spirit is saying to the church.

4

LITERARY STRUCTURE, OVERVIEW, AND THEOLOGICAL THEMES OF EZEKIEL

Introduction

This chapter will set Ezekiel's visions of the glory of YHWH in their literary context in terms of the book's literary structure and major theological themes. I will first show that Ezekiel's sequential visions of YHWH's glory provide the basic framework for the book's literary structure, and thus function as an interpretive guide to those who see and hear Ezekiel. Next, a brief overview of the book will serve to familiarize the reader of this study with the basic contents of the book of Ezekiel, and finally, the theological motifs will help outline the message of Ezekiel.

Structure

Although the text of Ezekiel contains alarming images and eccentric content, the book has a clear and well-defined literary structure.[1] A

---

[1] Freedman and others observe that Ezekiel exhibits a more clearly organized structure than other prophetic books such as Jeremiah and Isaiah. See David Noel Freedman, 'The Book of Ezekiel', *Int* 8 (1954), p. 446, 'outlining the Book of Ezekiel is a relatively easy process'. Zimmerli, *Ezekiel 1-24*, p. 2, writes that 'one is struck by the impression of great order in the book of Ezekiel'. Similarly, Boadt, 'Rhetorical Strategies in Ezekiel's Oracles of Judgment', p. 185, acknowledges, 'I suspect the text is highly structured, but am not convinced that we can recover the order by strictly rational and analytical arguments'. Finally, James L. Crenshaw, *Story*

close narrative reading of the final form of the text reveals an impressive display of literary characteristics and devices that contribute to the book's overall coherent structure. When discussing the unity and well-organized structure of Ezekiel, commentators agree that features such as the three vision reports of YHWH's glory, the autobiographical narrative style, the various formulaic expressions, the repetition of key phrases such as 'then they (you) will know that I am YHWH' (found more than seventy times in its various forms), and the book's theological themes add to the text's systematized structure.[2]

While the book may boast a deliberate and logical structure, Ezekielian experts differ on the structure's actual appearance.[3] This disagreement among scholars concerning the book's structure does not imply that the numerous proposed structures of Ezekiel are inaccurate, but rather demonstrate each scholar's methodology, interpretive aims, and theological perspectives. Given the book's intricate design, it is also important to note that there are various organizational features (such as the chronological formulas, the location of the vision reports, and the theological themes) that can be employed to create the book's literary structure. Hence, there is no strict blueprint for the literary structure of Ezekiel. For example, while the chronological formulas can be used to construct the structure of Ezekiel,[4] it is clearly not the only way to organize the book of Ezekiel. The book

---

and Faith: A Guide to the Old Testament (New York: Macmillan, 1986), p. 212, appropriately states: 'In contrast to the imagery within the book, which is often confused and at times even weird, the book's structure is clear and simple'.

[2] Block, *The Book of Ezekiel 1-24*, pp. 17-41. Cf. Paul M. Joyce, *Ezekiel: A Commentary* (T&T Clark International; New York, 2009), pp. 8-17.

[3] A quick review of any commentary on Ezekiel will show that commentators have divided the book into two (1-33 and 34-48), three (1-24; 25-32; 33-48), four (1-24; 25-32; 33-39; 40-48), and even thirteen (1-7; 8-19; 20-23; 24-25; 26-28; 29.1-16; 29.17-30.19; 30.20-26; 31.1-18; 32.1-16; 32.17-33.20; 33.21-39.29; 40-48) sections. See Mayfield, *Literary Structure and Setting in Ezekiel*, pp. 17-28, for a more detailed overview of the history of scholarship concerning the structure of Ezekiel.

[4] Mayfield, *Literary Structure and Setting in Ezekiel*, argues that the chronological formulas are the primary structural devices in the book of Ezekiel, and these formulas divide the book into thirteen distinct literary units. Marvin Sweeney, *Reading Ezekiel: A Literary and Theological Commentary* (Reading the Old Testament; Macon, GA: Smith & Helwys 2013), pp. 4-9, also asserts that the thirteen chronological formulas in Ezekiel form the thirteen-part literary structure of the book.

can also be divided or linked together by the three major vision re-ports of YHWH's glory, repeated phrases, and shared theological themes. Considering the elaborate imagery and complex nature of the text, it is not surprising that each reading of Ezekiel yields fresh discoveries of theological meaning and literary nuances that may have been previously overlooked.

Inasmuch as the act of seeing is a predominant motif in Ezekiel,[5] the book can be organized around the three visions of YHWH's glory (1-3; 8-11; 40-48). These three visions provide the book's struc-tural framework that unifies the entire prophecy of Ezekiel. Terence Collins, following the work of Van Dyke Parunak,[6] also asserts that throughout Ezekiel the three visions continue to be the book's back-bone around which the final literary form of the text assembled. Both Collins and Parunak observe that the visions give the book its cohesive organization.[7] Structuring the book around the three major visions depicts the glorious and holy character of YHWH, YHWH's response to the people's rebellion, YHWH's restoration of the people to himself, and YHWH's return to dwell among his people. Further-more, as discussed in Chapter 3, the visions replete with imagery, symbolism, and sensory details were used as visual aids to proclaim the prophet's message effectively. Throughout the book of Ezekiel, the visions frequently remind the hearers to see, encounter, and know YHWH's glory and holiness. The visions, therefore, create a canvas for the prophet to portray the interrelationship between the glory and holiness of YHWH in the book of Ezekiel.

It is clear that several literary features connect the three visions of YHWH's glory together. (1) The phrase 'visions of God' is found in all three visions (1.1; 8.3; 40.2); (2) the formulaic expression, 'the hand of YHWH was upon me' occurs in all three visions (1.3; 3.14, 22; 8.1; 40.1); and (3) all three visions share the theme of Ezekiel's

---

[5] In Chapter 3, I discuss in detail the significance of the act of seeing in Ezekiel.
[6] Henry Van Dyke Parunak, 'Structural Studies in Ezekiel' (PhD, Harvard University, 1978), pp. 2-24.
[7] Terence Collins, *The Mantle of Elijah: The Redactional Criticism of the Prophetical Books* (The Biblical Seminar 20; Sheffield: JSOT Press, 1993), pp. 88-89. Yehezkel Kaufmann, *The Religion of Israel: From Its Beginnings to the Babylonian Exile* (trans. Moshe Greenberg; Chicago: University of Chicago Press, 1960), p. 437, also ob-serves that the visions of YHWH's glory function as 'a framework for the revela-tion of the divine message'.

encounter with YHWH's glory.[8] In addition to these three features, several other characteristics of the literary structure become apparent after a meticulous study of the text. Each vision is introduced by a chronological statement that indicates the year, month, and day (1.1; 8.1; 40.1). Previous scholars acknowledge that the chronological formulas are primary literary markers in Ezekiel that aid in the structuring of the book, provide a logical and cogent flow to the text, as well as mark the progression of time within the text.[9] It is important to keep in mind that the chronological formulas assist in developing the book's structure and are not exclusively responsible for its literary arrangement. The chronological formulas are embedded and intricately woven into the vision structure of the book.

Another aspect of the book's structure is the narrative unit found in each of the visions. The text of Ezekiel consists of narrative elements such as *wayyiqtols*[10] and the particles את and אשר.[11] Most text linguistics experts such as R.E. Longacre, acknowledge that the *wayyiqtol* is the 'backbone or storyline tense of Biblical Hebrew narrative discourse'.[12] Furthermore, the first two visions of YHWH's glory

---

[8] Joyce, *Ezekiel*, p. 97; Steven Tuell, *Ezekiel* (Old Testament Series: New International Biblical Commentary; Peabody, MA: Hendrickson Publishers, 2009), pp. 4-5.

[9] Childs, *Introduction*, p. 365, for example, observes 'the backbone of the structure is provided by a chronological framework which extends throughout the book and joins the sections together'. Block, *The Book of Ezekiel 1-24*, p. 26, claims that the precise dates of some of the oracles construct a 'chronological framework' for the prophet's ministry. Other scholars such as Robert R. Wilson, 'Ezekiel', in James L. May (ed.), *Harper Collins Bible Commentary* (San Francisco: HarperSan Francisco, 2000), pp. 586-87, and Blenkinsopp, *Ezekiel*, p. 3, view the dates as literary features and structural markers within the book of Ezekiel. Finally, Katheryn Pfisterer Darr, 'The Book of Ezekiel: Introduction, Commentary and Reflections', in Leander E. Keck, *et al.* (eds.), *The New Interpreter's Bible: A Commentary in Twelve Volumes* (Nashville: Abingdon Press, 2001), 6, p. 1089, asserts that the dates give the book its coherent form and contribute to the book's chronological progression.

[10] Cf. H.F.W. Gesenius, *Gesenius' Hebrew Grammar* (trans. A.E. Cowley; New York: Oxford University Press, 1910), § 111a; and Roy L. Heller, *Narrative Structure and Discourse Constellations: An Analysis of Clause Function in Hebrew Prose* (Winona Lake, IN: Eisenbrauns, 2004), pp. 26-27, who point out that the *wayyiqtol* verbal form is the governing verbal form used in Biblical Hebrew (BH) narrative. The *wayyiqtol* clause signifies the logical progression of events or actions in the narrative.

[11] When אשר introduces a perfect verb, in BH narrative, it normally signifies what we would call in English the pluperfect tense.

[12] R.E. Longacre, 'Discourse Perspective on the Hebrew Verb: Affirmation and Restatement', in W. Bodine (ed.), *Linguistics and Biblical Hebrew* (Winona Lake, IN: Eisenbrauns, 1992), pp. 177-89.

begin with the *wayyiqtol* verb וַיְהִי, which is often used in BH narrative literature. According to Edgar W. Conrad, other biblical narrative books such as Joshua, Judges, 1 and 2 Samuel, Jonah, Ruth, and Esther also begin with the verb וַיְהִי, and so like these books, the book of Ezekiel is presented as a narrative.[13]

Each narrative unit (with the exception of the last vision)[14] is then followed by at least one oracle.[15] At the beginning of each oracle is the prophetic word formula, 'The word of the Lord came to me'. This formulaic expression not only marks the beginning of each oracle but functions as a subdivision within the literary unit. In other words, the prophetic word formula does not introduce a new literary unit, only a new division within the narrative unit. The oracles, therefore, do not exist separately from the narrative; instead they are an essential part of Ezekiel's narrative framework.[16]

Since (1) seeing is a significant motif in the book of Ezekiel, (2) the visions repeatedly remind the hearers of YHWH's glory and holiness, (3) the visions are used by the prophet to deliver his message to the people, and (4) the visions depict the interrelationship between the glory and holiness of YHWH, it is appropriate to structure the book of Ezekiel around the three visions of YHWH's glory (1-3; 8-11; 40-48). The three major visions begin with a chronological formula that link each vision to a specific day, month, and year. Each vision contains a narrative, and each narrative unit is followed by one or a series of prophetic oracles.[17] Based on the aforementioned literary features and structural markers, I suggest that the book be divided into the following three major sections: (1) Ezekiel's inaugural vision of YHWH's glory, Ezekiel's call, and Ezekiel's message to Israel (1.1–

---

[13] Edgar W. Conrad, *Reading the Latter Prophets: Toward a New Canonical Criticism* (JSOTSup 376; New York: T & T Clark International, 2003), pp. 63-91. Mayfield, *Literary Structure and Setting in Ezekiel*, p. 94, also agrees that 'the book of Ezekiel can be viewed as one long narrative'.

[14] The last vision report of YHWH's glory (chaps. 40-48) does not contain a prophetic oracle. Various scholars suggest that the absence of one or more oracles indicate that chs. 40-48 were not written by the prophet himself. However, in keeping with the literary themes of restoration and YHWH's return to dwell among his people, it seems more likely that the time for prophecies concerning doom and judgment has ended.

[15] Mayfield, *Literary Structure and Setting in Ezekiel*, pp. 84-124.

[16] Mayfield, *Literary Structure and Setting in Ezekiel*, p. 94.

[17] Cf. Mayfield, *Literary Structure and Setting in Ezekiel*.

7.27); (2) Ezekiel's vision of YHWH's glory departing the temple because of the people's sins, prophecies of judgment against Jerusalem
and other nations, and prophecies of Israel's restoration because of
God's holy name (8.1–39.29); (3) Ezekiel's vision of the return of
YHWH's glory to the new temple (40.1-48.35).

Overview of the Book of Ezekiel

Since this study primarily focuses on Ezekiel's sequential visions of
YHWH's glory (chs. 1-3; 8-11; and 40-48), it is necessary to provide
a brief overview of Ezekiel's book. The subsequent overview uses
the book's major structural divisions to introduce the reader of this
monograph to the content of the book of Ezekiel.

Ezekiel's Inaugural Vision of YHWH's Glory (1.1–7.27)

This first literary section of Ezekiel falls into two parts. The first part,
chs. 1-3, begins with a dated enigmatic vision of YHWH's glory that
leads to the sending and commissioning of Ezekiel. At the conclusion of his initial encounter with YHWH's glory and YHWH's word,
the Spirit returns Ezekiel to the River Chebar, where he sits in silence
for seven days among the exiles (1.1–3.15). After seven days of Ezekiel's silence, the urgency of Ezekiel's prophetic role is made clear by
the watchman imagery (3.16-21). During a fresh encounter with
YHWH's glory, Ezekiel is housebound and made silent by YHWH
(3.22-27).

In the second part, chs. 4-7, Ezekiel performs a series of symbolic
actions that illustrate the siege of Jerusalem and the impending exile
(4.1-8), the significant suffering of the people who are both in Jerusalem and in the exile (4.9-17), and the imminent doom and eventual
fate of the remnants (5.1-4). Apart from Ezekiel's symbolic acts, he
proclaims YHWH's judgment on the mountains and land of Israel
(6.1-14). Once these places are utterly destroyed, Ezekiel announces
the end (7.1-27).

Ezekiel's Vision of YHWH's Glory Departing the Temple (8.1–39.29)

The second literary section may be further divided into four parts.
The first part, 8.1-11.25, begins with a new dated visionary experience, which describes the abominations habitually performed in the
temple. Israel's repeated moral and spiritual revulsions have defiled

YHWH's holiness, and consequently have prompted YHWH's wrath, judgment, and eventual departure from the temple and the city.

The second part, chs. 12-24, restates the formal accusation against Israel and the calamitous judgment that ensues from such blatant rebellion against YHWH. The judgment of YHWH climaxes in ch. 24 with the siege of Jerusalem (24.1-2). The unexpected death of Ezekiel's beloved wife, 'the delight of [his] eyes' (24.16), and the subsequent prohibition to express any signs of mourning would be the final announcement of the end of Jerusalem and the temple.

The third part, chs. 25-32, is a proclamation of doom for seven foreign nations: Ammon (25.1-7), Moab (25.8-11), Edom (25.12-14), Philistia (25.15-17), Tyre (26.1–28.19), Sidon (28.20-24), and Egypt (29.1–32.32), highlighting YHWH's cosmic sovereignty.

The fourth part, chs. 33-39, is the prophetic anticipation[18] of Israel's restoration and renewal. When previous forceful images of the end merge with the actual realization of the end, 'The city has fallen' (33.21), hearers are not prepared for the promises of hope and redemption. These chapters, however, establish a counterpoint to the declarations of judgment in chs. 1-24.[19] Perhaps, Ezekiel's vision of the valley of the dry bones (ch. 37) best illustrates the future of Israel. This vision bespeaks YHWH as the only one who has the power to give life. It must be noted, however, that YHWH's commitment to restoring Israel is rooted in YHWH's desire to vindicate his name (Cf. 36.22, 32).[20]

Ezekiel's Vision of the Return of YHWH's Glory (40.1–48.35)
The final dramatic vision of YHWH's glory returning to the restored temple concludes the book of Ezekiel. The return of YHWH's glorious presence is the ultimate resolution to the departure of YHWH's glory in chs. 9 and 10. In this final vision, hearers are given a personal tour of the new temple that is not built by hands (40.5–42.20)[21], front row seats to the grand return of YHWH's glory (43.1-11), an elaborate description of Israel's renewed worship (43.13–46.24), a breathtaking view of the life-giving, healing river (47.1-12), a journey through the land and its tribal divisions (47.13–48.14, 21-29), and the

---

[18] Walter Brueggemann, *An Introduction to the Old Testament: The Canon and Christian Imagination* (Louisville, KY: John Knox Press, 2003), p. 196.

[19] Brueggemann, *Introduction to the Old Testament*, p. 197.

[20] Joyce, *Divine Initiativ*, p. 103.

[21] Cf. Ezek. 37.26.

name of the new city, 'YHWH is there' (48.35), underscoring the theme of YHWH's presence among his people.

Theological Themes in Ezekiel

The literary structure of the book of Ezekiel demonstrates 'a distinctive emphasis on the absolute centrality of YHWH and his self-manifestation, a radical theocentricity which is of an order difficult to parallel anywhere in the Hebrew Bible'.[22] Thus, several of Ezekiel's theological themes are housed within its literary framework. For reasons of space, it is impossible to discuss in detail the theology of Ezekiel. Nevertheless, I will provide Ezekiel's prominent theological ideas that will familiarize the reader of this study with the book of Ezekiel, as well as serve as a guide for further exploration of these motifs.

A major theme that is apparent from the literary structure of Ezekiel is YHWH' glory. The glory of YHWH is the main thread that weaves together the entire book that bears Ezekiel's name. From the start, Ezekiel's prophetic ministry is commissioned and shaped by his vision of YHWH's glory. From beginning to end, the hearers of Ezekiel are confronted with the divine beauty and majesty of YHWH. The book opens with an elaborate and colorful vision of the transcendent glory of YHWH in Babylon and YHWH's sovereignty over all the earth. YHWH is enthroned above the earth as cosmic king, and his infinitely mobile throne spreads his rule throughout all corners of the earth (1.1-28). YHWH's sovereignty is further emphasized in the prophecies against the nations in chs. 25-32.[23] Chapters 8-11 show that the radiance, beauty, and majesty of YHWH's presence cannot coexist with sin. Thus, because of the abominations in the temple, YHWH willfully departs from it. Chapters 40-48 narrate YHWH's return to the temple to dwell among his people whom he has saved and restored from sin and judgment (40-48).

YHWH's departure and return indicate that his presence is not stationary, paralyzed, confined, or restricted by geographical borders. Rather, the departure and return of YHWH's glory point to YHWH's mobility. YHWH moves freely and independently of any human aid.

---

[22] Joyce, 'Ezekiel and Moral Transformation', p. 150.
[23] Cf. Block, *The Book of Ezekiel 1-24*, p. 47.

Moreover, when he departs from the temple in Jerusalem, he moves to be with his people who are in exile. Although YHWH is responsible for sending Israel into exile, YHWH does not abandon them there (notice that Ezekiel's inaugural vision of YHWH's glory is at the River Chebar in Babylon). YHWH is present wherever his people are. The forcefulness of this theme is explicit in the final phrase of the book, יהוה שמה ('YHWH is there'). YHWH returns to dwell among his people forever.[24]

Significantly, the theme of YHWH's glory gains remarkable force as it interrelates with the theme of YHWH's holiness in Ezekiel.[25] YHWH's glory is the grand and awe-inspiring display of YHWH's holiness.[26] The holiness of YHWH is palpably revealed in the majestic, sublime, awesome, and astounding splendor of YHWH's glory. Accordingly, YHWH is not only majestic and sovereign but YHWH is also holy. YHWH does not merely possess holiness; holiness is the quintessence of YHWH.[27] Holiness is 'God's selfhood, the very Godness of God'.[28] That is to say, holiness is the fundamental, distinguishing, unique, and unchangeable nature of YHWH. Expressed another way, holiness is YHWH's 'DNA', and YHWH's glory is the face of YHWH's holiness. Thus, YHWH exists, functions, and acts as holy.

Although Ezekiel does not use the appellation 'Holy One of Israel' that is so frequently found in Isaiah,[29] the message of Ezekiel is certainly preoccupied with the holiness of YHWH. Since Ezekiel employs the language of holiness and purity more than any of his counterparts, he undoubtedly has a profound awareness of YHWH's holiness.[30] According to Abraham Even-Shoshan, the word קדש is

[24] Cf. Joyce, *Ezekiel*, p. 31.
[25] The interrelation of these themes – YHWH's glory and YHWH's holiness – will be developed further as I closely study the texts relating to Ezekiel's visions of YHWH's glory.
[26] John Goldingay, *Old Testament Theology: Israel's Faith* (Downers Grove, IL: InterVarsity Press, 2006), II, p. 24.
[27] Cf. Taylor, *Ezekiel*, p. 41.
[28] Stephen A. Seamands, 'An Inclusive Vision of the Holy Life', *The Asbury Theological Journal* 42.2 (1987), p. 85.
[29] Cf. Block, *The Book of Ezekiel 1-24*, p. 47; and John N. Oswalt, *The Book of Isaiah: Chapters 1-39* (The New International Commentary on the Old Testament; Grand Rapids, MI: Eerdmans, 1986), p. 33.
[30] J. Muilenburg, 'Ezekiel', in M. Black and H.H. Rowley (eds.), *Peake's Commentary on the Bible* (London: Routledge, 1999), p. 569, claims that 'Ezekiel's

found approximately 38 times in Ezekiel, 23 times in Isaiah, and 6 times in Jeremiah.[31] Furthermore, קדשׁ (both the noun and verb forms) is used in close relation with YHWH's 'holy name' (for example, 20.39; 36.20, 21; 39.7, 25; 43.7, 8). Thus, the use of קדשׁ in its various forms has a strong theocentric focus in Ezekiel.[32]

Accordingly, it was Israel's sins that caused YHWH's glory – the tangible expression of YHWH's holiness – to depart from the temple and from among them. Their abominations had defiled the holiness of YHWH to the extent that he could no longer dwell among them. Furthermore, YHWH's concern for YHWH's holy name is the chief reason for YHWH's judgment, salvation, and restoration of the people of Israel. Since Israel's constant apostasy violated YHWH's holy name, the exile was orchestrated by YHWH to judge Israel for their spiritual degeneracy and moral depravity:[33]

וטמאו את־שם קדשי בתועבותם אשר עשו ואכל אתם באפי
(Ezek. 43.8. See also 36.20-21)[34]

Nevertheless, it is because of YHWH's holy name that YHWH saves and restores Israel:

אשיב את־שבית יעקב ורחמתי כל־בית ישראל וקנאתי לשם קדשי:
בשובבי אותם מן־העמים וקבצתי אתם מארצות איביהם ונקדשתי
בם לעיני הגוים רבים (Ezek. 39.25, 27)[35]

The significance of YHWH restoring Israel because of YHWH's holy name is made plain in Ezek. 36.22:

כה אמר אדני יהוה לא למענכם אני עשה בית ישראל

---

awareness of the divine holiness is more awesome, more sublime, and majestic, more cosmic and "tremendous" than that of his prophetic predecessors'.

[31] Even-Shoshan, *A New Concordance of the Old Testament*, pp. 1003-1005.

[32] Cf. Joyce, 'Ezekiel and Moral Transformation', pp. 153-54.

[33] Cf. Luc, 'A Theology of Ezekiel', pp. 137-43.

[34] 'And they defiled my holy name with their abominable deeds that they committed, and I consumed them in my anger.' Unless noted otherwise, all English translations of the Hebrew text will be my own translation.

[35] 'I will cause Jacob to return from captivity, and I will show love to all the house of Israel. I will be jealous for my holy name … When I have restored them from the people and gathered them from the lands of their enemies, I will show myself holy among them in the sight of many nations.'

³⁶:‏כי אם־לשם־קדשי אשר חללתם בגוים אשר־באתם שם

The holiness of YHWH provides the foundation for understanding the message of Ezekiel. YHWH's holiness explains the departure of YHWH's glory from the temple, justifies the exile, and is the motive for YHWH's love, salvation, and restoration of Israel.

The utter depravity of Israel is another theme that is visible in the literary structure of Ezekiel. Not only does the sinfulness of Israel contrast sharply with YHWH's glory and holiness, it is also connected to the foregoing two motifs. Encountering YHWH's glory, which is the splendid display of YHWH's holiness, made Ezekiel acutely aware of Israel's heinous sins. In chs. 16, 20, and 23, Ezekiel presents an extensive history of Israel's sins to prove their recurring wickedness and rebellion against YHWH. From the beginning, Israel persisted in their unfaithfulness to YHWH. Moreover, their abominations were more reprehensible than Sodom (16.46-48).[37] Their idolatry, adultery, murder, rape, stealing, lying, and oppression permeated each level of society – kings, princes, priests, prophets, and the general public (ch. 22). The comprehensive survey of Israel's sins explains why YHWH's glory departs from the temple: YHWH's holy presence could no longer co-exist with the moral and spiritual filth of unholy Israel. Thus, the exile was a just and appropriate punishment[38] for 'the rebellious house of Israel'.

'Then they (you) will know that I am YHWH', a prophetic formula,[39] is another theme that persists throughout the book of Ezekiel. This phrase occurs 72 times in the book of Ezekiel (54 times in

---

[36] 'Thus said the Lord Yahweh: It is not for your sake I am going to act, O house of Israel, but rather for *the sake of* my holy name, which you have profaned among the nations when you went there.'

[37] Cf. Duguid, *Ezekiel*, p. 36; and Luc, 'Theology of Ezekiel', pp. 137-43.

[38] Joyce, *Ezekiel*, p. 18.

[39] 'Then they (you) will know that I am YHWH' is one of several formulaic expressions found in the book of Ezekiel. Other formulaic phrases found in the book of Ezekiel include, but are not limited to: (1) 'Thus says the Lord YHWH', occurring approximately 120 times in Ezekiel; (2) 'the declarations of the Lord YHWH', found 85 times in Ezekiel; (3) 'the word of YHWH came to me', appearing about 50 times in the book; (4) 'the hand of YHWH was upon me there', which occurs seven times in Ezekiel; and (5) 'I am YHWH'. See Block, *The Book of Ezekiel 1-24*, pp. 32-39, for further discussion on the various formulaic expressions found in the book of Ezekiel. On 'the declarations of the Lord YHWH' see also Rolf Rendtorff, 'Zum Gebrauch der Formel *ne'um jahwe im* Jeremiabuch', *ZAW* 66 (1954), pp. 27-37; and Friedrich Baumgärtel, 'Die Formel n*e'um Jahwe*', *ZAW* 73 (1961), pp. 277-90. For a definitive analysis of the expression, 'I am YHWH', see

the third person and 18 times in the second person).[40] A careful analysis of this expression reveals that the formula is directly connected to YHWH's actions of judgment and restoration (see for example 5.13; 6.7, 10, 13, 14; 7.4, 9, 27; 11.10, 12; 12.15-16, 20; 15.7; 20.9, 26, 38, 42, 44; 22.16; 23.49; 24.24, 27; 28.26; 29.16, 21; 33.29; 34.27, 30; 36.11, 38; 37.6, 14, 28; 39.7, 21-22, 28).[41] The refrain indicates that YHWH will be made known to Israel and to the nations through YHWH's actions. The formula is a purpose statement, which declares that YHWH's acts of judgment and restoration are not capricious and random, but rather YHWH's actions are deliberately designed to compel a rebellious people to encounter and acknowledge his existence, divine presence, character, and claims on their lives.[42] The tautological phrase leaves no doubt in the minds of Ezekiel's hearers that (1) YHWH alone is sovereign and holy; and (2) it is YHWH who acts to bring judgment and destruction, as well as salvation and restoration. 'In short, YHWH acts because he is YHWH and must be known to be YHWH'.[43]

The final theme grows out of the theme of YHWH's holiness: YHWH's promise of restoration. Because of YHWH's holiness, YHWH restores Israel and does not leave them in exile. YHWH promises to bring them back to their homeland, give them a renewed heart and spirit (36.24-28), and to return to dwell permanently in their midst (40.1-48.35). Ezekiel's message of restoration culminates in the final phrase of the book: 'YHWH is there' (48.35). The defiled city and temple that were once abandoned in chs. 10 and 11 are now made holy and serve as an appropriate dwelling place for a holy God. The book that begins with the awesome sight of YHWH's glory in Babylon, concludes with YHWH's glory dwelling in the restored city and temple. Significantly, Israel's restoration does not depend on their repentance. 'The promise of a future is unilateral and unconditional; YHWH does not any longer wait for Israel's repentance. Instead, what is offered is an act of radical grace ... that is rooted in and

---

Walther Zimmerli, 'I Am Yahweh', in *I Am Yahweh* (trans. D.W. Scott; Atlanta: John Knox, 1982), pp. 1-28; and *idem*, 'Knowledge of God According to the Book of Ezekiel', in *I am Yahweh* (trans. D.W. Scott; Atlanta: John Knox, 1982), pp. 29-98.

[40] Cf. Block, *The Book of Ezekiel 1-24*, p. 39; and Mayfield, *Literary Structure and Setting in Ezekiel*, p. 84.

[41] Luc, 'Theology of Ezekiel', pp. 137-43.

[42] Block, *The Book of Ezekiel 1-24*, p. 211.

[43] Joyce, 'Ezekiel and Moral Transformation', p. 156.

motivated by YHWH's own self-regard'.[44] The salvation and restoration of Israel demonstrates YHWH's love for Israel, as well as YHWH's commitment to his covenant.

Summary

It is suitable to structure the book of Ezekiel around the three visions of YHWH's glory because (1) seeing is a significant theme in the book of Ezekiel, (2) the visions repeatedly remind the hearers of YHWH's glory and holiness, (3) the visions are used by the prophet to deliver his message to the people, and (4) the visions depict the interrelationship between the glory and holiness of YHWH (1-3; 8-11; 40-48).

The multiple themes that permeate the book reveal the theocentric message of Ezekiel, as well as explain how YHWH's glory and holiness relate to one another in the text. (1) YHWH's glory is the tangible self-manifestation of YHWH's holiness. (2) Since holiness is the fundamental and immutable nature of YHWH, YHWH refuses to dwell among a people who is morally feculent and spiritually contaminated. (3) Israel's utter depravity galvanized the departure of YHWH's glory from the temple. The heinous sins of Israel scandalized YHWH's holy name, and so the exile is a fitting punishment for YHHW's rebellious children. Because of YHWH's holiness, YHWH judges and restores Israel. (4) Through YHWH's acts of judgments and restoration, both Israel and the nations will come to an intimate and authentic knowledge of YHWH: 'Then they (you) will know that I am YHWH'. (5) Because of YHWH's concern for his holy reputation, YHWH promises to save, restore, and return to tabernacle permanently in the midst of his people.

---

[44] Brueggemann, *Introduction to the Old Testament*, p. 207.

5

SEEING AND HEARING YHWH'S GLORY AND HOLINESS

Introduction

A picture of the interrelationship between the glory of YHWH and the holiness of YHWH in Ezekiel will begin to emerge in this chapter as I enter into the biblical text to see and hear with Ezekiel. In this chapter, I will explore how the motifs of YHWH's glory and holiness interrelate in the book of Ezekiel by carefully examining the first major vision narrative of YHWH's glory recorded in Ezekiel 1-3. In order to organize the chapter and to guide the reader through the first vision of YHWH's glory, I begin with some general observations about chs. 1-3, move to a thorough study of the vision, paying particular attention to the themes of seeing and hearing, and then I provide a summary of the interrelationship between the glory of YHWH and the holiness of YHWH in the first vision.

'The heavens were opened and I saw visions of God': Who, When, and Where (1.1–3.27)

Before I begin in earnest the study of Ezekiel's opening vision, it is appropriate to mention a few overall comments about the initial vision of YHWH's glory. First, Ezekiel's inaugural vision of YHWH's glory serves as a prologue to the entire book of Ezekiel. As a prologue, ch. 1 sets the stage for the rest of the book, provides the date, time, and setting of the narrative, establishes the main characters, and introduces the themes of YHWH's glory and holiness. Second, the verb ואראּ ('and I saw') is a prominent and distinctive feature of ch. 1, which underscores Ezekiel's personal and direct encounter with YHWH. Thus, Ezekiel's vision is presented as a reliable experience of YHWH's glory and not mere fantasy.[1]

Third, the vision employs ambiguous and analogical words and phrases such as 'something like', 'appearance', 'like', and 'looked like' (see for example 1.26-27),[2] signaling Ezekiel's difficulty to describe in human language what he sees. Ezekiel uses the words דמות fifteen times (ten of the fifteen instances occur in ch. 1 alone: 1.5 (twice), 10, 13, 16, 22, 26 (three times), 28; 8.2; 10.1, 10, 21, 22) and מראה twenty-three times (1.5, 13 (twice), 14, 16 (twice), 26 (twice), 27 (four times), 28 (three times); 8.2 (three times), 4; 10.1, 9, 10, 22) to describe the living creatures, the wheels, YHWH's throne, and YHWH's glory.[3] It is no wonder that Ezekiel's opening vision is obscure, complicated, and puzzling.[4] Ezekiel is striving to describe something that is essentially indescribable.[5]

Fourth, the copious use of the *wayyiqtol* verbal form presents the narrative sequence of Ezekiel's first vision, and therefore advances the narrative from one action or event to the next.[6] At first, the narrative progresses slowly because after each *wayyiqtol* verb in vv. 4, 15, and 24, the narrative pauses to describe in detail the subsequent visual and auditory experiences of Ezekiel. That is to say, after the *wayyiqtol* verbs ואראּ in vv. 4 and 15, and ואשמע in v. 24, the following statements report precisely what Ezekiel sees and hears, and the narrative

---

[1] Wolde, 'The God Ezekiel 1 Envisions', p. 87.

[2] Nancy R. Bowen, *Ezekiel* (AOTC; Nashville, TN: Abingdon Press, 2010), p. 3; and Millard C. Lind, *Ezekiel* (Believers Church Bible Commentary; Scottdale, PA: Hearald Press, 1996), p. 29.

[3] de Vries, *The Kabôd of YHWH*, p. 250.

[4] See further Margaret S. Odell, 'Ezekiel Saw What He Said He Saw: Genres, Forms, and the Vision of Ezekiel 1', in Marvin Sweeney and Ehud Ben Zvi (eds.), *The Changing Face of Form Criticism for the Twenty-First Century* (Grand Rapids: Eerdmans, 2003), pp. 168-76, for the various uses of דמות and מראה.

[5] Bowen, *Ezekiel*, p. 6.

[6] Roy L. Heller, 'Hebrew Language', in Bill T. Arnold and H.G.M. Williamson (eds.), *Dictionary of the Old Testament Historical Books: A Compendium of Contemporary Biblical Scholarship* (Downers Grove, IL: Intervarsity Press, 2005), p. 284.

does not proceed until Ezekiel recounts fully the details of each sensory experience.[7] Thus, in the first chapter, Ezekiel describes in a sequential order what he sees and hears at each stage of the vision.

'I saw visions of God' (1.1-3)

The first three verses of the prologue contain narrative background information to Ezekiel's inaugural vision.[8] Before anything else, the hearers of Ezekiel are informed of the precise calendrical date of Ezekiel's visions: 'in the thirtieth year, on the fifth day of the fourth month' (1.1); and, as if to leave no doubt about the date, v. 2 correlates the 'thirtieth year' to the 'fifth year of the exile of King Jehoiachin'.[9] The setting is 'the land of the Chaldeans by the River Chebar' (1.1), where Ezekiel is living 'among the exiles' (1.1). Verse one makes clear to the hearers that the exile is the social scene of Ezekiel's inaugural vision of YHWH's glory. Ezekiel and his fellow compatriots are driven from their homeland and forced to live in exile far away from Jerusalem and the temple, the place of YHWH's residence. Significantly, it is during the exile in a foreign land, on the fifth day of the fourth month of the thirtieth year, that the heavens open and 'I saw visions of God', ואראה מראות אלהים (1.1)[10]. The appearance of

---

[7] Christopher R. Bechtel, 'Ezekiel and the Politics of Yahweh: A Study in the Kingship of God' (PhD, The University of Edinburgh, 2011), p. 48.

[8] Cf. Kirsten Nielsen, 'Ezekiel's Visionary Call as Prologue: From Complexity and Changeability to Order and Stability', *JSOT* 33.1 (2008), p. 100.

[9] For a discussion concerning the two dates, see George Ricker Berry, 'The Title of Ezekiel (1.1-3)', *JBL* 52 (1932), pp. 54-57; and C.F. Whitley, 'The "Thirtieth" Year in Ezekiel', *VT* 9 (1959), pp. 326-30.

[10] The Hebrew phrase מראות אלהים is ambiguous and varies in translation. While the phrase is frequently translated as 'visions of God', Block, *The Book of Ezekiel 1-24*, p. 84, argues that the phrase should be translated in the singular: 'a divine vision' because אלהים is an appellative and not a proper noun. He further contends that the translation of the phrase as 'a divine vision' is consistent with the translations found in 8.3 and 40.2. Certainly, the phrase points to the divine or supernatural nature of the inaugural vision, but the singular translation of the phrase restricts the interpretation of the phrase to only what is seen and not heard (which is noted by Lind, *Ezekiel*, p. 27), dismisses that YHWH chose to reveal himself to the prophet in exile, and disregards the prophet's personal encounter with God. As established in Chapter 3, one of the various uses of the verb ראה in the Old Testament is to indicate a direct and personal encounter with God. Thus, God steps out from obscurity and reveals himself to humanity. Accordingly, 'visions of God' is an appropriate and legitimate interpretation of מראות אלהים. The phrase 'visions of God' not only expresses the divine nature of the inaugural vision, but it also signifies that everything that follows is a revelatory experience that originated with an intimate encounter with God.

YHWH in a foreign land no doubt testifies to the mobility of YHWH's presence.[11] YHWH is neither locked nor left behind in the temple in Jerusalem. YHWH moves at will to be present with the exiles in a distant and alien land.

Moreover, v. 3 identifies the *visions* as 'the word of YHWH [that] surely came to Ezekiel'. Thus, the *visions of God* mentioned in v. 1 is *the word of YHWH* occurring to Ezekiel in v. 3.[12] By directly relating the visions to the *word of YHWH*, the narrator underscores the reliability of the visions to the hearers. The דבר of YHWH in prophetic literature does not simply refer to the spoken word of YHWH, but also points to an event that is seen or heard.[13] Thus, *the word of YHWH* includes all of the visual, aural, and oral aspects of the visionary experiences.

Additionally, in v. 3, Ezekiel is identified for the first time as the recipient of the visions and the narrator of the book. Ezekiel, whose name means 'God is strong', 'God strengthens' or 'May God strengthen',[14] is further described as a priest and the son of Buzi. As the narrator of the book, all of the events in the book are presented from Ezekiel's point of view.

Verse three begins with the word of YHWH occurring to Ezekiel and concludes with the hand of YHWH on Ezekiel. The phrase 'the hand of YHWH' is found seven times in the book of Ezekiel (1.3; 3.14, 22; 8.1; 33.22; 37.1; 40.1) and is closely associated with Ezekiel's visionary experiences and the activities of the spirit of YHWH.[15] In prophetic texts such as Ezekiel, YHWH's hand is a symbol of YHWH's power, and is often used to describe YHWH's possession, commission, and empowering of an individual.[16] In addition to the prevailing understanding of the expression, I would suggest that the hand of YHWH also signifies the nearness of YHWH to the individual. The hand of YHWH assures Ezekiel that even in exile YHWH is near him. YHWH's hand on Ezekiel also accentuates Ezekiel's close, direct, and intimate encounter with YHWH, which un-

---

[11] Brueggemann, *Introduction to the Old Testament*, p. 192.
[12] Taylor, *Ezekiel*, p. 53.
[13] Moore, 'The Prophetic Calling', p. 59.
[14] Block, *The Book of Ezekiel 1-24*, p. 9; Joyce, *Ezekiel*, p. 67.
[15] Hildebrandt, *An Old Testament Theology of the Spirit of God*, p. 190.
[16] Hildebrandt, *An Old Testament Theology of the Spirit of God*, pp. 190-91.

derscores the legitimacy of Ezekiel's prophetic message. Further-more, as Rickie D. Moore notes, 'it is precisely this matter of divine nearness that ... characterize[s] the nature and origin of prophetic revelation'.[17] The prophetic role of Ezekiel, therefore, is initiated by the word of YHWH and the hand of YHWH.[18]

'I looked and I saw a windstorm' (1.4-14).

With the introduction complete (vv. 1-3), Ezekiel's account of the inaugural vision begins in v. 4. As the heavens open, the first thing Ezekiel sees is a windstorm accompanied by a cloud approaching from the north. With his eyes fixed on the phenomenon, his attention is captivated by the 'great' cloud. The greatness of the cloud does not only refer to its enormous size, but also to its fierce intensity.[19] Eze-kiel describes the cloud as (1) ablaze by rapid, ongoing, and coalesc-ing flashes of fire,[20] (2) encircled by brilliant light, and (3) having the appearance of glowing amber in the middle of the flashing fire.[21] Ezekiel's hearers would immediately understand that this is no ordi-nary storm, but a theophanic encounter with the presence of YHWH (cf. Exod. 19.16; Ps. 18.7-15).[22] Such imagery depicts both the stun-ning and terrifying awe of YHWH's glory and holiness, as well as reinforces YHWH's nearness to Ezekiel.

Moreover, the use of the word רוח to describe the storm further highlights the theophanic nature of the storm. רוח is often translated as 'wind', 'breath', or 'spirit', and these three interpretations of רוח are utilized in the book of Ezekiel. For instance, the storm Ezekiel sees is a 'windstorm' (1.4), the four living creatures and the four wheels are directed by the 'spirit' (1.12, 20), the wheels have the 'spirit' of the living creatures (1.21), the 'spirit' enters Ezekiel and

---

[17] Moore, 'Canon and Charisma', p. 22.

[18] Block, *The Book of Ezekiel 1-24*, p. 9.

[19] Cf. *BDB*, pp. 152-53.

[20] Cf. *BDB*, p. 544, ואש מתלקחת literally means 'a fire taking hold of itself'. The phrase seems to indicate that the flashes of fire occur in such close succession that each flash merges with the one before, and so forming one continuous flash of fire. This same phrase is found only in Exod. 9.24 in connection with a hail-storm. The LXX interprets the phrase as 'fire flashing like lightning'.

[21] Cf. *BDB*, p. 365, the word חשמל is found only in Ezek. 1.4, 27; 8.2, and its precise meaning is unknown. *DCH*, III, p. 333, defines it as 'amber' or perhaps 'bronze'. The LXX translates חשמל with the Greek ἤλεκτρον, which may indicate either amber or a combination of gold and silver (*LS*, p. 768).

[22] Zimmerli, *Ezekiel 1-24*, p. 119; and Odell, *Ezekiel*, pp. 18-19.

positions him on his feet (2.2), and the dead bones live because of YHWH's creative 'breath' (37.5) Since Ezekiel's inaugural vision is a vision of YHWH's glory, then everything Ezekiel sees is concomitant with the presence and activity of YHWH. Furthermore, the fact that the stormy wind (רוח סערה) is the first thing Ezekiel sees after the heavens open underscores the divine origin of the windstorm. Thus, in v. 4, רוח translated as 'wind' is a demonstration of YHWH's mystery and dynamic power[23] that heralds the appearance of YHWH's glory.

The next thing Ezekiel sees is 'something like four living creatures' (1.5), appearing from the fiery cloud. In the Old Testament, fire frequently accompanies storm theophanies and is often a sign of the external demonstration of YHWH (see for example, Exod. 3.2; 19.16, 19; 20.18, 21; Deut. 4.12, 15, 33, 36; 5.4, 22-26; 10.4). Certainly, there is a direct connection between YHWH's כבוד 'glory' and fire in the Old Testament.[24] The emergence of the living creatures from the midst of the fire underscores their close relation to YHWH. The living creatures appear to have a physical human form, but each living creature has four faces, four wings, straight legs with soles that resembled calves' feet, which sparkled like polished bronze, and human hands beneath their wings (1.6-8). This overall description of the four living creatures is followed by Ezekiel's stunning and close-up account of their four faces and wings. He sees the face of a human on the front, the face of a lion on the right, the face of an ox on the left, and the face of an eagle on the back (1.10). Their four faces suggest that they represent various parts of creation (humanity, wild beasts, domesticated animals, and birds).[25] Since the living creatures face all four directions concurrently, they are able to move in any direction without turning their bodies (1.9, 11).[26]

---

[23] John Goldingay, 'The Breath of Yahweh Scorching, Confounding, Anointing: The Message of Isaiah 40-42', *JPT* 11 (1997), p. 13.

[24] M. Weinfeld, 'כבוד', in *TDOT*, VII, pp. 22-38.

[25] Cf. Taylor, *Ezekiel*, p. 55. See also Greenberg, 'Ezekiel's Vision', p. 165. This concept seemed to already exist in Jewish tradition. The Rabbinic commentary on the book of Exodus states the following about the four living creatures: 'Four kinds of proud beings were created in the world: the proudest of all – man; of birds – eagles; of domestic animals – the ox; of wild animals – the lion; and all of them are stationed beneath the chariot of the Holy One' (*Exodus Rabba: 23.13*).

[26] Julie Galambush, 'Ezekiel', in John Barton and John Muddiman (ed.), *The Oxford Bible Commentary* (New York: Oxford University Press, 2001), p. 538.

Next, Ezekiel gives a brief description of the living creatures' four wings. Each living creature had two wings that stretched upward and united with the wings of the other living creature that was on either of its sides, and the other two wings covered their bodies (1.11). Once again, hearers are told that the living creatures moved forward without turning their bodies (1.12), but this time Ezekiel notes that their movement is completely dependent on the spirit: 'Wherever the רוח would go, they would go' (1.12). In other words, the spirit is the powerful and dynamic force of the living creatures.[27] They moved solely when the spirit moved and did not veer from the path of the spirit. Significantly, it is the approaching רוח that brings the living creatures into sight (1.4) and it is the רוח that animates and guides the living creatures (1.12).

After his close-up description of the four living creatures, Ezekiel says that the four living creatures appear to be 'like burning coals of fire or like torches going back and forth between the living creatures' (1.13). Here, Ezekiel seems to struggle for words to express what he sees before him. Thus, he gives not just one, but two striking descriptions of the incense: 'like burning coals ... like torches'. The fiery appearance of the living creatures immediately recalls the great fiery cloud in v. 4 that carried the four living creatures. In fact, the description of the burning appearance of the four living creatures is almost identical to the great cloud afire in v. 4. Here, as in v. 4, 'brightness' (נגה) is produced by fire, and while the great cloud was ablaze by the rapid and continuous flashes of fire in v. 4, in v. 13 'lightning was flashing out of the fire'. Furthermore, the swift movement of the living creatures was described as 'lightning' (1.14). The repetition of such brilliant imagery keeps the windstorm present in the minds of hearers, suggests that a tight connection exists between the 'great cloud' and the four living creatures, and reminds the hearers of the stunning and fiery radiance associated with YHWH's glory.

'I looked and I saw one wheel' (1.15-21)

The phrase 'I looked and I saw' signals a new sight in Ezekiel's vision. Ezekiel now sees 'one wheel on the earth beside each of the four living creatures' (1.15). Like the four living creatures, the description of the wheels is complex, elaborate, and difficult to visualize. This

---

[27] Cf. Hildebrandt, *An Old Testament Theology of the Spirit of God*, p. 188; and Montague, *The Holy Spirit*, p. 45.

convoluted description once again demonstrates Ezekiel's struggle to describe an otherworldly experience using human vocabulary.[28]

All four wheels had the same design. Each wheel sparkled like beryl[29] (1.16), appeared to be 'a wheel within a wheel' (1.16), moved in any of the four directions without turning (1.17), and possessed rims that 'were high and awesome, and … full of eyes all around' (1.18). The wheels seemed to be engineered for quick, effortless, and instantaneous movement in any direction.[30] This concept does not seem contrived when hearers recall that the living creatures' swift movement was described as lightning and then learn that the wheels moved at the same pace as the living creatures (1.19). Moreover, the wheels are imposing, and they inspire admiration as well as fear: 'high and awesome' (1.18),[31] reminding hearers that the sight of YHWH's glory is simultaneously grandiose and fearsome. Further, like the four living creatures who each has eyes at the front, back, right, and left side of their heads, the wheels are 'full of eyes all around' (1.18), which indicates that the living creatures and wheels possess complete and comprehensive vision.[32] Thus, Ezekiel seems to suggest the 'all-seeing [and all-knowing] character of the chariot and its rider'.[33]

---

[28] Cf. Wright, *Message of Ezekiel*, p. 49.

[29] The Hebrew word is 'Tarshish stone', which is a precious stone. However, the precise meaning of the word is uncertain. The term has also been translated as 'topaz', 'beryl', or 'chrysolite'.

[30] Cf. Block, *The Book of Ezekiel 1-24*, p. 100; and Wright, *Message of Ezekiel*, p. 49.

[31] Some scholars believe that the Hebrew word יראה 'fear' or 'awe' (translated as 'awesome' in several versions) in this text is obscure and possibly an error. See, for example, Brownlee, *Ezekiel 1-19*, p. 13. However, the meaning of the word is consistent with the majesty and fearsome experience associated with YHWH's glory.

[32] Some scholars such as Block, *The Book of Ezekiel 1-24*, p. 100, and Odell, *Ezekiel*, p. 28, believe that since the Hebrew word עין 'eye' was translated earlier in vv. 4 and 16 as 'sparkle, gleam', the wheels' עינים refer to precious stones shaped like eyes that add to the brilliance of Ezekiel's vision. While this interpretation corresponds with the luminous quality of Ezekiel's vision, the interpretation of עינים as simply organs of sight also fits with the dynamic and animated character of the wheels. After all, the spirit that was in the living beings is also in the wheels (1.20). Thus, the wheels are not inanimate objects, but are just as 'alive' as the four living creatures. It is possible that the word עינים in v. 18 has a double entendre: the wheels were *full of eyes that sparkled* …

[33] Vawter, *Ezekiel*, p. 28.

Significantly, the same spirit that is in the living creatures is also in the wheels (1.20-21), conveying an extremely close connection between the living creatures and the wheels. Thus, the living creatures and the wheels move with impeccable synchronism, an observation that is mentioned three times in vv. 19, 20, and 21.[34] This threefold repetition emphasizes that the living creatures and the wheels move together in unison. This concept of unity finds further support with the use of the singular רוח החיה in vv. 20, 21, and 22. Three times Ezekiel says, 'spirit of the living creature', not 'spirit of the living creatures'. However, it is also possible for the phrase רוח החיה to mean 'spirit of life'[35] since Ezekiel uses a form of חיה instead of חיים for 'life' in 7.13. While either interpretation can be justified, it is possible that the phrase has a double entendre. The singular use of החיה רוח not only points to the single and unified identity of the living creatures, but also to the unity of the entire phenomenon. Moreover, since the spirit of the living creature, which is also the 'spirit of life' is in the wheels, the wheels that are usually inanimate objects become 'alive' and dynamic just as the living creatures. Additionally, it is the spirit of life that energizes and vivifies Ezekiel's entire phenomenon.[36]

Above the living creatures' heads, Ezekiel sees something like 'a platform, sparkling like awesome crystal' (1.22). The use of the participle ירא 'fear' to describe the platform reinforces the idea that YHWH's glory is at the same time majestic and dreadful. Once again, the living creatures' wings come into focus, and he repeats his initial observation of their wings: two wings are outstretched and joined to the wings of the living creature opposite, while the other two wings covered their bodies (1.23).

---

[34] Block, *The Book of Ezekiel 1-24*, p. 101.

[35] Daniel Block, 'Text and Emotion: A Study in the "Corruptions" in Ezekiel's Inaugural Vision (Ezekiel 1:4-28)', *CBQ* 50 (1988), pp. 418-42, argues that the singular use of רוח החיה demonstrates a stylistic problem that occurs when Ezekiel experiences a heightened and sustained emotional state. He later states in Daniel Block, 'The Prophet of the Spirit: The Use of RWHI in the Book of Ezekiel', *JETS* 32 (1989), pp. 36-37, that the use is 'intentional' and refers to 'the spirit of life', stressing the animating power of the spirit. See also Wright, *Message of Ezekiel*, p. 50.

[36] Block, 'Prophet of the Spirit', pp. 36-37.

'and I heard …' (1.22-27)

For the first time, Ezekiel narrates what he hears, and interestingly, his first description of sound pertains to the sound of the living creatures' wings, not the sound of the windstorm, or the locomotion of the wheels: 'And I heard a sound of their wings, like the sound of many waters, like the sound of the Almighty when they moved, a roaring sound of commotion like an army. When they stood still, they lowered their wings.' (1.24). Just as he had struggled to describe the appearance of the wheels, Ezekiel now grapples to find the appropriate simile to describe the sound of the living creatures' wings. Although Ezekiel wrestles to associate the sound he hears to a familiar sound, he makes clear that the motion of the creatures' wings produced an extremely loud and tumultuous noise. When the living creatures stop moving, they drop their wings and the deafening noise ceases.[37]

The silence yields to a voice from above the platform (1.25). Significantly, Ezekiel does not identify the one who is speaking, neither does he reveal what the voice says nor to whom the voice speaks. The voice directs his gaze from beneath the platform to above the platform, and on the platform he sees 'something like a sapphire stone shaped like a throne', and a form enveloped in fire resembling a man seated on the throne (1.26). It is conceivable that Ezekiel does not identify the voice because the figure on the throne is obscure and mysteriously concealed by the blinding light that is surrounding the form. Thus, unlike his elaborate description of the four living creatures, Ezekiel does not provide any physical details of the man's appearance. Instead, Ezekiel's description takes the form of a dazzling fiery glow. The upper body gleamed like amber and was surrounded by fire; the lower body resembled fire and was surrounded by a brilliant light (1.27). Ezekiel compares the stunning, multicolored radiance to a rainbow in a cloud on a rainy day (1.28). The image of a rainbow in a cloud after a storm would no doubt remind hearers of God's covenant with Noah to never again destroy the earth by means of a flood.[38]

---

[37] Block, *The Book of Ezekiel 1-24*, p. 104.

[38] Cf. J.C. Thomas and Frank D. Macchia, *Revelation* (The Two Horizons New Testament Commentary; Grand Rapids, MI: Eerdmans, 2016), p. 137.

Significantly, v. 4 and vv. 27-28 correlate to each other in language, form, and content.[39] The description of the man seated on the throne matches the description of the 'great cloud' seen by Ezekiel at the beginning of the vision. Mention of the 'glowing amber', 'brilliant light', and the storm phenomena in vv. 27-28 matches in reverse order the description of the storm event in 1.4,[40] indicating a direct connection between the man on the throne and the great cloud.

The dramatic spectacle finally reaches its climax with Ezekiel's twofold declaration: 'It was the appearance of the glory of YHWH' (1.28a). First, Ezekiel's announcement introduces a new character in the narrative – YHWH: 'While vv. 1-28a could pass as a mere record of the prophet's experience, the figure on the throne in v. 28b indicates that the preceding verses are no less than an elaborate technique for introducing the book of Ezekiel's main character, Yhwh'.[41] Second, as is common with the rest of the chapter, the spectacular presence of YHWH's glory is too grand for Ezekiel to describe in words. His only recourse is to use vocabulary framed by analogy to explain that he had just seen the glory of YHWH.

Ezekiel's concluding statement gives hearers a complete and comprehensive understanding of the puzzling and bizarre vision – the entire phenomenon represents the glorious and magnificent presence of YHWH. As Ezekiel narrates his vision, his hearers are invited to see and hear along with him, and accordingly, they also experience a direct and intimate encounter with YHWH's glory that comes from seeing and hearing the word of YHWH. The encounter with YHWH's glory has the same impact on the hearers as on Ezekiel: total awe and reverence. Clearly, YHWH's presence is ambulant. He is not fixed to a stationary throne but enthroned on a chariot that has unrestricted mobility.[42]

'and I saw, and I fell …, and I heard…' (1.28-2.2)
The narrative of Ezekiel's inaugural vision reaches a dramatic conclusion with a rapid succession of *wayyiqtol*s.[43] Ezekiel realizes that he

---

[39] Wolde, 'The God Ezekiel 1 Envisions', p. 89.

[40] H. Van Dyke Parunak, 'The Literary Architecture of Ezekiel's *Mar'ot 'Ĕlōhîm*', *JBL* 99 (1980), pp. 61-74.

[41] Bechtel, 'Ezekiel and the Politics of Yahweh', p. 51.

[42] Cf. Tuell, *Ezekiel*, p. 11.

[43] Janina Maria Hiebel, *Ezekiel's Vision Accounts as Interrelated Narratives: A Redaction-Critical and Theological Study* (Berlin/Boston: Walter de Gruyter GmbH, 2015), p. 86.

had just seen the radiant and striking splendor of YHWH's glory, and therefore the narrative gives way to a series of sudden and abrupt actions: 'And I saw, and I fell …, and I heard …' (1.28). The vision begins and ends with the exact verbal form of וָאֵרֶא (1.1, 28), creating an inclusio around the first chapter of Ezekiel's book.[44] Thus, Ezekiel establishes that everything he sees and hears after the heavens open is no doubt a vision of the glory of YHWH, further establishing that his account is trustworthy and not just wild imaginations.[45]

Completely aware that he is in the divine presence of YHWH, Ezekiel appropriately flings himself with his face toward the ground in worship. Considering his encounter with the awesome, terrifying, and overwhelming reality of YHWH's glory, it is not surprising that Ezekiel's response was that of immediate obeisance. In this single action of falling, Ezekiel moves from being a passive spectator of YHWH's glory to a participator in worship, indicating that an encounter with YHWH's glory results in sincere worship. While in this posture of reverent worship, Ezekiel hears a voice of someone speaking to him (1.28).[46] As before, Ezekiel does not identify the voice.[47] Perhaps there is no need for Ezekiel to reveal the voice's identity. Given that Ezekiel made clear that he had just seen the stunning and breathtaking presence of YHWH's glory, it is possible that Ezekiel expects his hearers to know that the voice is none other than the voice of YHWH.[48] It also seems likely that the initial unidentified voice/sound in v. 25 is the same voice Ezekiel now hears speaking to him in v. 28. Hearers should recall that when Ezekiel first heard the voice/sound coming from above the platform (1.25), he looked above the platform, possibly to identify the voice, and saw a fiery form seated on the throne that seized his attention. Upon recognizing that he had just seen the glory of YHWH, he immediately falls facedown to the ground where he once again hears a voice/sound. This time, while in a state of worship, he hears the voice speaking to him, suggesting that Ezekiel could only hear the voice speak to him while he is in a state of worship.

---

[44] Cf. Leslie C. Allen, 'The Structure and Intention of Ezekiel I', *VT* 43.2 (1993), p. 148.
[45] Wolde, 'The God Ezekiel 1 Envisions', pp. 87-89.
[46] Block, *The Book of Ezekiel 1-24*, p. 115.
[47] Greenberg, *Ezekiel 1-20*, p. 127, observes that the text is 'oddly vague' about the origin of the speech.
[48] Cf. Wright, *Message of Ezekiel*, p. 53.

Up until the point Ezekiel hears the voice of someone speaking to him, the word of YHWH to Ezekiel is dominated by visual images and auditory sounds (1.1-28a). From this point in the narrative, Ezekiel's inaugural vision is governed by YHWH's speech (2.1-3.11),[49] signaling a shift from seeing to hearing.[50] Contrary to those who argue that the visionary portion has come to a close, this shift by no means indicates an end to the visual part of the word of YHWH to Ezekiel.[51] The sight of YHWH's glory is still present because YHWH is speaking to Ezekiel. Chapters two and three are mainly concerned with YHWH's speech because it is YHWH's voice that now holds Ezekiel's attention.

Ezekiel, who is still face down on the ground hears YHWH say to him, 'Son of man, stand on your feet, and I will speak with you' (2.1). Interestingly, YHWH addresses Ezekiel as בן־אדם (son of man), and not by his given name.[52] Whereas this phrase occurs fourteen times outside the book of Ezekiel,[53] it is found ninety-three times in Ezekiel.[54] The phrase continues to remind Ezekiel and Ezekiel's hearers of his feeble human state that is certainly no equal to the stunning and terrifying sovereignty of YHWH.[55] Indicated by the imperative עמד, YHWH commands Ezekiel to stand up in order to speak with

---

[49] Cf. Block, *The Book of Ezekiel 1-24*, p. 111.
[50] Hiebel, *Ezekiel's Vision Accounts*, p. 87.
[51] Contra Achim Behrens, *Prophetische Visionsschilderungen im Alten Testament sprachliche Eigenarten, Funktion und Geschichte einer Gattung* (AOAT; Münster, Germany: Ugarit-Verlag, 2002), pp. 184-86, who believes that there is a clear separation between the visual part in 1.28 and the speech section in 2.1. Hiebel, *Ezekiel's Vision Accounts*, pp. 86-87, argues that there are several textual indicators that point to the conclusion of the visionary part in 1.28c and the speech part beginning in 2.3, with 1.28d-2.2 functioning as a bridge between 1.28c and 2.3. However, I concur with Block, *The Book of Ezekiel 1-24*, p. 111, who calls into question those scholars who assert that an individual cannot have simultaneous visual and auditory experiences.
[52] Throughout the book of Ezekiel, YHWH addresses the prophet as 'son of man', and not by his first name.
[53] Cf. Duguid, *Ezekiel*, p. 69.
[54] Cf. Block, *The Book of Ezekiel 1-24*, p. 30.
[55] John Skinner, *The Book of Ezekiel* (The Expositor's Bible; New York: Armstrong & Son, 1895), who translates בן־אדם as 'member of the human race', states that the phrase 'expresses the infinite contrast between the heavenly and the earthly, between the glorious Being who speaks from the throne and the frail creature who needs to be supernaturally strengthened before he can stand upright in the attitude of service' (p. 44).

him.[56] Astonishingly, Ezekiel who had just encountered the powerful presence of YHWH does not obey YHWH's command. However, Ezekiel's failure to obey YHWH's instruction should not be interpreted as a deliberate act of disobedience by Ezekiel. Rather, Ezekiel's mere human status leaves the prophet impotent and powerless in the presence of YHWH. Indeed, which mortal being can stand in the holy and dreadful presence of YHWH? Thus, unable to stand, Ezekiel requires an agent of YHWH to enable him to stand in YHWH's holy presence:[57] 'And a spirit/wind entered me as he spoke to me, and stood me on my feet, and I heard the one speaking to me' (2.2). Earlier, the spirit mobilizes the living creatures and animates the wheels.[58] Here, the spirit vitalizes Ezekiel and empowers him for his prophetic ministry:

> This extraordinary experience occurs often in Ezekiel and underlines the strong enabling of the prophet by the *rûachi* for his difficult task. The task of Ezekiel as presented in 2.3-8 is clearly a difficult one that will bring much opposition and thus requires much divine help.[59]

Remarkably, not only is Ezekiel able to stand once the spirit enters into him, but he is also able to hear the words of YHWH who is already speaking to him. As pointed out in Chapter 3 of this monograph, the person who sees and hears the word of YHWH experiences transformation and obeys the word of YHWH. Thus, it is essential for Ezekiel, who has already seen the word of YHWH, to hear the word of YHWH. By seeing and hearing the word of YHWH Ezekiel stands in stark contrast to the rebellious house of Israel who refuses to see and hear the words of YHWH.

Hearing the Word of YHWH (2.3–3.11)

Once the spirit enters Ezekiel, he immediately hears what YHWH is saying to him. During YHWH's speech, six series of events propel the narrative forward: (1) the sending of Ezekiel (2.3-7); (2) the vision of the scroll (2.8 – 3.3); (3) the repetition of YHWH's commission

---

[56] Brownlee, *Ezekiel 1-19*, p. 25, states: 'He is bidden to stand upon his feet in preparation for an immediate response to the subsequent commission to go'.
[57] Cf. Hildebrandt, *An Old Testament Theology of the Spirit of God*, p. 189.
[58] Cf. Block, *The Book of Ezekiel 1-24*, p. 115.
[59] Hildebrandt, *An Old Testament Theology of the Spirit of God*, p. 189.

to Ezekiel (3.4-11); (4) the vision ends, and Ezekiel returns 'bitter' (3.12-15); (5) Ezekiel is appointed watchman of Israel (3.16-21); and (6) Ezekiel sees the glory of YHWH again (3.22-27). Several elements are revealed from this sequence of events.

YHWH Sends Ezekiel

For the second time in the narrative, YHWH addresses Ezekiel as בֶּן־אָדָם. The address is followed by a participial phrase, 'I am sending you to the descendants of Israel', a phrase that occurs four times in YHWH's commissioning of Ezekiel (2.3, 4; 3.5, 6).[60] The phrase identifies YHWH as the one who sends Ezekiel,[61] Ezekiel as the one being sent by YHWH, and the 'descendants of Israel' as the people to whom Ezekiel is sent.[62] The fact that YHWH is the one who sends Ezekiel further legitimizes Ezekiel's prophetic ministry. Thus, as the book unfolds, hearers understand that everything Ezekiel sees, hears, speaks, and does proceeds from YHWH.[63]

YHWH's Characterization of Israel

Strikingly, YHWH does not use the covenantal term, 'my people', to refer to the 'descendants of Israel'; but rather calls them rebellious. Israel's rebellion against YHWH governs chs. 2 and 3. Out of the ten verses in ch. 2, YHWH mentions Israel's rebellion seven times (2.3 [three times], 5, 6, 7, 8, 9)! Plus, in v. 3, YHWH uses two different words to express Israel's rebellion three times! The first word, מָרַד, primarily means to 'refuse allegiance to, rise up against a sovereign'.[64] The second word, פֶּשַׁע, conveys 'transgression/revolt against God';[65] and, according to Johannes Pedersen, it is the strongest Hebrew word

---

[60] Lind, *Ezekiel*, p. 33. Cf. the 'sending' of other prophets: Moses in Exod. 3.10, Isaiah in Isa. 6.8, Jeremiah in Jer. 1.7, and Elijah in Mal. 4.5.

[61] See M. Delcor and E. Jenni, 'שׁלח', in E. Jenni and C. Westermann (eds.), *THAT* (2 vols.; Munich: Kaiser, 1976), 2, pp. 909-14, for examples of individuals sent by YHWH.

[62] Cf. Block, *The Book of Ezekiel 1-24*, p. 117.

[63] This phrase by no means indicate that Ezekiel lacks free will or has become YHWH's 'automan' as stated by Robert R. Wilson, 'Prophecy in Crisis: The Call of Ezekiel', *Int* 38.2 (1984), p. 126.

[64] Greenberg, *Ezekiel 1-20*, 63. Cf. Gen. 14.4; 2 Kgs 18.7, 20; 24.1; Jer. 52.3, מרד (antonym to עבד) is used in the context of national rebellions.

[65] Helmer Ringgren and Horst Seebass, 'פּשׁע', in *TDOT*, XII, pp. 133-51.

available for conveying a violation of a covenant.[66] From the beginning, Israel has revolted against YHWH: 'they and their fathers have
transgressed against me until this very day' (2.3).

YHWH continues to illustrate Israel's recalcitrance by using
phrases such as 'stiff of face and hard of heart' (2.4), 'briers and
thorns … and scorpions' (2.6), 'rebellious house'[67] (e.g. 2.5, 7), and
'hard of forehead and stiff of heart' (3.7). YHWH's portrait of Israel's sin is bold and unashamed defiance that is passed down from
one generation to the next: 'These are a people who not only do not
show any feelings toward their God, but also are resolutely determined not to. Their faces are as frozen as their hearts'.[68] Israel's brazen stubbornness and impenitence are caused by their failure to hear
and obey the words of YHWH: 'whether they hear or not hear' (2.5,
7).[69]

Ezekiel Must Speak YHWH's Words

Ezekiel must only speak the words of YHWH to the rebellious people of Israel: '… and you will say to them, "Thus says the Lord
YHWH"' (2.4; cf. 3.1, 4, 10, 11), a directive that is repeated in v. 7:
'you will speak **my** words to them whether they listen or not …'
YHWH's charge to Ezekiel clearly indicates that Ezekiel is not free
to speak anything other than the words of YHWH.[70] The prophet
must only declare YHWH's words regardless of his hearers' hostile
reaction to the word of YHWH.

---

[66] Johannes Pedersen, *Israel: Its Life and Culture* (4 vols; London: Oxford
Univeristy Press, 1926), I, p. 414. The pairing of מרד and פשע occurs twice in the
Old Testament, and both occurrences are found in Ezekiel (2.3; 20.38).

[67] The Hebrew מרי (rebellion) occurs 16 times in Ezekiel. It is used here in
construct ('house of rebellion'). According to Ludger Schweinhorst, 'מרד', in
TDOT, IX, pp. 1-5; and *idem*, 'מרי', in *TDOT*, IX, pp. pp. 5-8, the Hebrew word מרי
conveys a willful, calculated, and deliberate act of decision to disobey, just like the
'rebellious' and impenitent son in Deut. 21.18-21.

[68] Wright, *Message of Ezekiel*, p. 56.

[69] Cf. Block, *The Book of Ezekiel 1-24*, p. 120.

[70] Cf. Hermann Gunkel, *Die Propheten* (Göttingen: Vandenhoeck & Ruprecht,
1917) who began the study of prophetic speech forms; Claus Westermann, *Basic
Forms of Prophetic Speech* (trans. H.C. White; Philadelphia: Westminster Press, 1967),
pp. 98-128; and section 4 of Marvin Sweeney and Ehud Ben Zvi, *The Changing Face
of Form Criticism for the Twenty-First Century* (Grand Rapids, MI: Eerdmans, 2003),
pp. 269-325.

'Do Not Fear'

YHWH warns Ezekiel not to be afraid of the people and 'their words' (2.6). This warning is conveyed by using two different expressions: אל־תירא and אל־תחת.[71] Although these phrases denote prohibitions, they are prohibitions that indicate words of solace, reassurance, and hope.[72] Interestingly, YHWH warns Ezekiel twice in v. 6 not to fear the words of the people, but admonishes him to 'speak my words' in v. 7, implying that in order for Ezekiel to declare the words of YHWH, he must hear the words of YHWH and not the words of the people. This concept is further underscored in v. 8: '... hear what I am speaking to you. Do not be rebellious like the rebellious house ...' Undoubtedly, there is a striking contrast between YHWH's words and 'their words'. The implication is made clear: to hear the words of YHWH is to obey YHWH; to hear the words of the people is to rebel against YHWH.

Although Ezekiel is one of the 'descendants of Israel', he must not be rebellious like the rebellious house of Israel (2.8). This warning (אל־תהי־מרי) is bookended by imperatives, forming an inclusio that serves to underscore the theme of hearing YHWH's words: command-warning-command. Verse 8 opens with YHWH commanding Ezekiel to '*hear* what I am speaking to you'. This command is immediately followed by a warning against rebellion, a state that results from not hearing YHWH. Next, YHWH commands Ezekiel to '*open* your mouth and *eat* whatever I am giving you', an opportunity for Ezekiel to hear and obey the word of YHWH and to differentiate his behavior from that of the rebellious people of Israel.[73]

---

[71] According to Gesenius, *Gesenius' Hebrew Grammar*, § 107o, p. 341, the particle אל followed by the jussive indicates a warning. Cf. Lee Roy Martin, *Introduction to Biblical Hebrew* (Cleveland, TN: CPT Press, 2009), p. 68, who states, 'The jussive preceded by אל expresses warning or a more immediate and urgent prohibition'.

[72] Cf. conversations with Lee Roy Martin. Additionally, אל־תירא and אל־תחת, found here in Ezekiel's call narrative are also found in Jeremiah's call narrative. Like Ezekiel, YHWH uses these prohibitive phrases to provide encouragement and reassurance to Jeremiah (Jer. 1.8, 17).

[73] Cf. Tuell, *Ezekiel*, p. 14.

The Vision of the Scroll

While the theme of hearing YHWH governs the first eight verses of ch. 2, v. 9 reintroduces the theme of seeing YHWH, reminding hearers that seeing and hearing are interrelated themes in the book of Ezekiel.

Given that YHWH had just commanded Ezekiel to 'eat' whatever is given to him, hearers of Ezekiel might expect YHWH to offer the prophet some type of food. Instead, they hear Ezekiel say, 'I saw and behold, a hand was stretched out to me, and in it was a scroll with writing on it' (2.9). The first words, 'I saw' (ואראה is the same Hebrew word found in 1.1, 28), notifies hearers of a new element in Ezekiel's vision. The image of the outstretched hand will no doubt remind hearers of YHWH's hand that is on Ezekiel (1.3). The scroll that Ezekiel sees has 'laments, mourning, and wailing' written on both its front and its back (2.10). Bearing in mind that ancient scrolls usually had writings on one side only,[74] this was conceivably an alarming and unexpected sight for Ezekiel. Also, considering that Ezekiel was previously instructed to proclaim only the words of YHWH, the writings on both sides of the scroll may suggest that the scroll contained the absolute, complete, and definitive word of YHWH, giving Ezekiel no room to alter the message of YHWH.[75] Furthermore, the contents of the scroll suggest that YHWH's message to the rebellious descendants of Israel is a message of judgment, death, and destruction that will result in moaning and wailing – expressions of deep sorrow. That is, when Ezekiel declares the word of YHWH to the rebellious people of Israel, the effect on his hearers will be lamentation, mourning, and wailing.[76]

As Ezekiel reviews the scroll, he is interrupted by the sound of YHWH's voice. Earlier, in 2.8, YHWH's commands were 'hear ... open ... eat'. Here, in 3.1, YHWH's commands are 'eat ... eat ... go,

---

[74] Cf. Peter C. Craigie, *Ezekiel* (Philadelphia: Westminster, 1983), p. 17; Emil G. Kraeling, *The Brooklyn Museum Aramaic Papyri* (New Haven: Yale University Press, 1953), p. 127; and G.R. Driver, *Aramaic Documents of the Fifth Century B.C.* (Oxford: Clarendon, 1954), plates 1-4.

[75] Zimmerli, *Ezekiel 1-24*, p. 135; Lamar Eugene Cooper, *Ezekiel: An Exegetical and Theological Exposition of Holy Scripture* (The New American Commentary; Nashville, TN: B&H Publishing Group, 1994), p. 78; and John T. Bunn, 'Ezekiel', *The Broadman Bible Commentary* (Nashville, TN: Broadman, 1971), p. 241.

[76] Zimmerli, *Ezekiel 1-24*, p. 135; Craigie, *Ezekiel*, p. 17; and Block, *The Book of Ezekiel 1-24*, p. 125.

speak' (3.1). This event of eating the scroll is significant for several reasons. First, the command to eat the scroll is followed by the commands to 'go' and 'speak', representing the commissioning of Ezekiel's prophetic ministry.[77]

Second, while the verb אכל can simply mean 'eat', it can also mean 'devour' or 'consume' in a figurative sense.[78] In this context, Ezekiel must first devour the scroll by ingesting it and absorb its contents for strength and sustenance (cf. 3.3) before proclaiming the word of YHWH.[79] The scroll and its contents must become a part of him.[80] Thus, the one who devours the words of YHWH will be filled, nourished, and strengthened.

Third, the quick succession of the commands, 'eat ... eat ... go, speak' implies an urgency to Ezekiel's message. As soon as he eats the scroll, he must immediately go and speak the word of YHWH to the people of Israel. This idea demonstrates a tight connection between the contents of the scroll and the prophetic ministry of Ezekiel. Before he can declare the word of YHWH, Ezekiel must first eat the scroll that is in the outstretched hand. For this reason, YHWH commands Ezekiel three times to eat the scroll (2.8; twice in 3.1), and in 3.1, the commands to eat the scroll are followed with the commands, 'go' and 'speak'. Therefore, given the exigent nature of the message, devouring the scroll seems to be an appropriate imagery.

Fourth, Ezekiel's obedient response to YHWH's commands (3.2-3), demonstrates that he will not be rebellious like the rebellious house of Israel (cf. 2.8). In so doing, he separates himself from those who have revolted against YHWH.[81] Moreover, the image of YHWH feeding Ezekiel the scroll represents YHWH placing divine words in Ezekiel's mouth.[82] This visual illustrates Ezekiel's message coming directly from YHWH and shows a prophet filled with the word of YHWH. This graphic episode reminds hearers of Jer. 1.9: 'Then

---

[77] Cf. Thomas and Macchia, *Revelation*, p. 196, who see a parallel between Rev. 10.8-11 to Ezek. 2.8 – 3.2. Like Ezekiel, John is commanded to 'take' and 'eat' the book that is in the angel's hand. This 'episode [in Revelation] takes the form of a prophetic commissioning as John is directed to come and take the open scroll, bringing to mind Ezekiel's prophetic commission (cf. esp. Ezek. 2.8-3.2)'.

[78] Jack B. Scott, 'אכל', in *TWOT*, I, pp. 39-40.

[79] Cf. Cooper, *Ezekiel*, 78; and Thomas and Macchia, *Revelation*, p. 196.

[80] Wright, *Message of Ezekiel*, p. 59; Craigie, *Ezekiel*, p. 17.

[81] Zimmerli, *Ezekiel 1-24*, p. 135; Block, *The Book of Ezekiel 1-24*, p. 126; and Tuell, *Ezekiel*, p. 14.

[82] Tuell, *Ezekiel*, p. 14.

YHWH stretched out his hand and touched my mouth and said to me, "Behold, I have put my words in your mouth"'. Since YHWH is the one who feeds Ezekiel, this imagery also depicts YHWH as Ezekiel's source of strength.

Fifth, when Ezekiel devours the scroll, he surprisingly announces that the taste is 'sweet like honey' (3.3). This metaphor might remind hearers of Ps. 19.11 and 119.103, texts that also compare the word of YHWH to the sweetness of honey. Considering that the contents of the scroll effect mourning and woe, the metaphor seems to imply that even YHWH's message of divine judgment can certainly be a pleasant experience to those who embody the word of YHWH.

Israel's Deafness

Once Ezekiel has fully digested the scroll, YHWH recapitulates the sending of Ezekiel (3.4-9). YHWH's speech in vv. 4-9 should not be viewed as simply a repetition of 2.3-7.[83] While there are certainly similarities to the first commission, here YHWH uses more precise language to send Ezekiel and piercing vocabulary to portray another element of Israel's stubbornness. Once again, YHWH sends Ezekiel to the 'house of Israel', but this time YHWH tells him to speak to them *'in/with* my words' (ודברת בדברי 3.4) and not simply to 'speak my words to them' (ודברת את־דברי 2.7). The presence of the preposition in 3.4 explicitly indicates that Ezekiel must repeat verbatim the word of YHWH to the 'house of Israel', reinforcing the idea that Ezekiel is prohibited from amending the words of YHWH.[84]

Furthermore, in these verses, YHWH provides hearers with another dimension of Israel's recalcitrance: their spiritual deafness. Israel is not simply unresponsive to the word of YHWH; they are unresponsive because they have refused to hear the word of YHWH.[85] YHWH, therefore, highlights their deliberate deafness in two ways. First, YHWH compares Israel to other nations with languages that

---

[83] Cooper, Sr., *Ezekiel*, p. 80, states that Ezek. 3.4-9 merely repeats 2.3-7.

[84] Zimmerli, *Ezekiel 1-24*, p. 137; Greenberg, *Ezekiel 1-20*, p. 68; and Block, *The Book of Ezekiel 1-24*, p. 128.

[85] Certain scholars such as Block, *The Book of Ezekiel 1-24*, p. 128; and Bowen, *Ezekiel*, p. 11, characterize YHWH's fresh description of Israel's rebellion as unresponsive. However, I would argue that Israel's unresponsiveness is caused by a failure to hear the word of YHWH.

are incomprehensible to the people of Israel (3.5-6).[86] If YHWH had sent Ezekiel to nations that spoke a foreign language, they undoubtedly would have heard the word of YHWH. However, YHWH is not sending the prophet to speak to a group of people with a strange language; rather, YHWH is sending Ezekiel to his own fellow compatriots who share the same language, culture, and traditions.[87] A language barrier, therefore, is not the reason for Israel's deafness, but their unwillingness to hear YHWH (3.7).[88] Thus, Israel will not hear Ezekiel because they have refused to hear the word of YHWH (cf. 2.3). Second, Israel willfully resists the voice of YHWH because 'all' of Israel have a 'hard forehead and a stiff heart' (3.7). Whereas Ezekiel uses the metaphor 'hard forehead' to describe Israel's stubbornness, in Jer. 3.3 the expression refers to the shameless 'brow of a harlot'. The analogy implies that Israel is flagrantly and unblushingly brazen in their refusal to hear YHWH.[89]

YHWH Hardens Ezekiel

Since YHWH is sending Ezekiel to speak to a hardened group of people who will not hear him, YHWH must also harden Ezekiel against the people's unresponsiveness and reaction to the word of YHWH (3.8-9). Whereas Israel had hardened their brow against YHWH, YHWH will harden Ezekiel's brow against Israel.[90] In so doing, the prophet truly becomes 'Ezekiel' (יחזקאל) 'God strengthens'/ 'God hardens').[91] Thus, YHWH makes Ezekiel's forehead 'harder than flint' (3.9), and once again charges Ezekiel not to fear the rebellious people of Israel (3.9).

While the people of Israel will not hear the word of YHWH, YHWH instructs Ezekiel to 'take in your heart all the words that I speak to you, and hear' (3.10). Interestingly, YHWH uses imperfective verb forms to express his instruction to Ezekiel, implying that

---

[86] Allen, *Ezekiel 1-19*, p. 41, notes that in 2.3-7 there is a 'vertical' comparison of the current house of Israel with their forefathers, but in 3.5-7 there is a 'horizontal' comparison of Israel with the surrounding nations.

[87] Blenkinsopp, *Ezekiel*, p. 26.

[88] A similar account of Israel's disobedience is found in 1 Sam. 8.7.

[89] Greenberg, *Ezekiel 1-20*, p. 69; Bowen, *Ezekiel*, p. 11; Cf. Zimmerli, *Ezekiel 1-24*, p. 138; and Block, *The Book of Ezekiel 1-24*, p. 129.

[90] Zimmerli, *Ezekiel 1-24*, p. 138.

[91] Block, *The Book of Ezekiel 1-24*, pp. 9, 129. Interestingly, the same Hebrew word used to describe Israel's hard faces (חזק) makes up Ezekiel's name (יחזקאל).

Ezekiel must continue to hear and receive the words of YHWH.[92] YHWH concludes his speech by repeating for a third time, the command to 'go' (3.1, 4, 11), emphasizing Ezekiel's prophetic mission. The juxtaposition of the commands 'take, hear' and 'go, speak' (3.10, 11) brings to mind the eating of the scroll.[93] The proximity of these commands underscores the concept that hearing the word of YHWH precedes the speaking the word of YHWH. Keeping in mind the theological implication of the verb שמע, the prophet must first hear and absorb the word of YHWH before he can proclaim the word of YHWH to the exiles. Finally, Ezekiel is reminded to repeat exactly the words of YHWH despite the exiles' response to the message.

Ezekiel's Response to Seeing and Hearing the Word of YHWH (3.12-15)

At the conclusion of YHWH's speech, the רוח that had entered Ezekiel and set him on his feet in 2.2, now takes him to Tel Abib, which is along the River Chebar, where the exiles lived (3.12, 14). As the רוח lifts Ezekiel, he hears a 'great quaking sound' as YHWH's glory rises from the ground (3.12). Likewise, he hears the 'great quaking sound' of the movement of the four living creatures' wings and the four wheels, which are beside the four living creatures (3.13). Interestingly, while ch. one places emphasis on the visual images of YHWH's glory, in 3.12-13, the focus is on the auditory sounds of the vision.

After Ezekiel personally encounters the awesome and stunning vision of YHWH's glory, hears the word of YHWH, and experiences the pleasant taste of YHWH's words, he astonishingly goes away from YHWH's presence 'bitter and angry in … spirit' (3.14). Undoubtedly, Ezekiel's 'bitter and angry' emotions are remarkably surprising and unorthodox for two reasons. First, Ezekiel does not respond verbally, but emotionally, to what he had seen and heard by the River Chebar. Second, hearers might expect Ezekiel to experience comfort and hope by the appearance of YHWH's glory in a foreign land. Instead, Ezekiel's description of his mood after encountering the glory of YHWH conveys strong negative emotions. The Hebrew word מר ('bitter') is the same word used to describe Esau's emotional response when he learned that his brother, Jacob, stole his blessing

---

92 Zimmerli, *Ezekiel 1-24*, p. 138.
93 Cf. Block, *The Book of Ezekiel 1-24*, p. 130.

(Gen. 37.34), to illustrate the effect of the Egyptians' enslavement of the Israelites (Exod. 1.14), and to portray Naomi's reaction to the deaths of her husband and her two sons (Ruth 1.20).[94] In the contexts of Gen. 37.34; Exod. 1.14; and Ruth 1.20, the word מר reflects loss and grief – loss of a blessing, loss of freedom, and loss of loved ones. Later in the book of Ezekiel, מר characterizes the lamentation of Tyre (27.30, 31).

According to Block, the Hebrew word חמה ('angry') occurs eighty-five times in the Old Testament, and thirty-one of those eighty-five occurrences are found in Ezekiel, pointing to the nature and disposition of Ezekiel's prophetic ministry.[95] While the word is used here in 3.14 to describe Ezekiel's mood, elsewhere in Ezekiel it refers to YHWH's wrath (e.g. 5.13, 15). Thus, Ezekiel returned from the presence of YHWH in bitter rage.

Why would Ezekiel be bitter and furious after seeing and hearing YHWH? The text does not explicitly state the reason for his acute negative reaction, but it seems possible that Ezekiel is resistant to his call.[96] This concept does not seem too far-fetched especially considering the description of Ezekiel's antipathetic mood is followed by the phrase, 'and the hand of YHWH was strong upon me' (3.14). The succession of the phrase, 'I went bitter and angry in my spirit' with the phrase, 'and the hand of YHWH was strong upon me' suggests that YHWH will force Ezekiel to fulfil his prophetic mission. That is, as long as YHWH's strong hand is upon Ezekiel, the prophet will not be able to resist the call of YHWH. Ezekiel has no choice but to hear and obey the word of YHWH. This notion gains force when Ezekiel hears the word of the Lord in 3.16. YHWH simply will not allow Ezekiel to reject him.

Furthermore, the fact that Ezekiel returns to the exiles and remains silent for an entire week (3.15), after YHWH had commanded

---

[94] Bowen, *Ezekiel*, p. 12.
[95] Block, *The Book of Ezekiel 1-24*, p. 137.
[96] Cf. Abraham J. Heschel, *The Prophets* (New York: Harper & Row, 1962), pp. 307-22. Allen, *Ezekiel 1-19*, p. 13, argues that מר 'does not fit the context', and therefore believes חמה conveys 'passion' rather than 'anger'. According to Allen, it is unlikely that Ezekiel experienced bitterness and rage, and so he interprets the phrase as, 'I was passionately moved' (p. 4). Zimmerli, *Ezekiel 1-24*, p. 139, asserts that חמה was added by a later editor. G.R. Driver, *Canaanite Myths and Legends* (Edinburgh: T&T Clark, 1956), p. 152, proposes that the verb מרר could also mean 'strengthened'.

him three times to 'go, speak' to the rebellious people of Israel, also reinforces the concept that Ezekiel objected to his prophetic task. It is no wonder that he felt the strong hand of YHWH upon him. Additionally, the Hebrew word חזק, used to describe the hand of YHWH, would not be lost on Ezekiel's hearers because they would recall that it is the same word used to depict the hardened nature of Israel's rebellion, that it illustrates YHWH hardening Ezekiel's forehead against Israel, and that the word forms part of Ezekiel's name, which means 'God strengthens/hardens'. Thus, it is not contrived to think that as Ezekiel sat in silence, resisting the call of YHWH for seven days, the strong hand of YHWH was also strengthening him for his prophetic ministry. Finally, the image of YHWH's strong hand upon Ezekiel brings to mind the hand of YHWH being on Ezekiel at the beginning of the inaugural vision. Thus, 3.14 forms an inclusio with 1.3, emphasizing YHWH's powerful influence on Ezekiel's life.

The Word of the Lord for Ezekiel (3.17-21)

After seven days of silence, 'the word of the Lord came to' Ezekiel (3.16), a phrase that occurs fifty times in Ezekiel, appearing more frequently in Ezekiel than in any other Old Testament prophetic book.[97] On hearing the phrase, 'the word of the Lord came to me' (3.16), hearers might expect to hear a message for the rebellious house of Israel. Instead, they hear YHWH sternly warning the stubborn prophet of the consequences for disobeying his commands to go and speak to the descendants of Israel. Ezekiel has already spent seven days in silence resisting the call of YHWH. So when 'the word of the Lord' comes to Ezekiel, YHWH immediately addresses the urgency of Ezekiel's message to the rebellious house of Israel: 'Son of man, I have appointed you a watchman for the house of Israel' (3.17), signifying that Ezekiel was installed as watchman by YHWH.

The metaphor of Ezekiel as a watchman makes clear Ezekiel's role as a prophet to the house of Israel. The duty of a watchman was to 'keep watch'[98] and to sound the alarm when the enemy was approaching the city.[99] In so doing, the watchman saves lives. Thus, as Israel's watchman, Ezekiel must warn and alert the people of YHWH's imminent judgment. If Ezekiel refuses to warn the people (both the

---

[97] This phrase is found nine times in Jeremiah and twice in Zechariah.
[98] *BDB*, p. 859.
[99] The role of the watchman is described in 2 Sam. 18.24 and 2 Kgs 9.17.

wicked and the righteous person who has turned away from right-eousness) of YHWH's pending judgment, then YHWH will hold him responsible for their deaths (3.18, 20). If, however, he warns them of YHWH's approaching judgment, then Ezekiel would be blameless before YHWH, and his life would be saved (3.19, 21).

A Fresh Encounter with YHWH's Glory (3.23-24)

For a third time, the 'hand of YHWH' comes upon Ezekiel (3.22; see also 1.3; 3.14), and once more he sees the glory of YHWH as he had seen by the River Chebar. Just like in 1.28, he falls face down to the ground in worship after seeing the glory of YHWH (3.23), and once again, the Spirit raises him to his feet so that YHWH could speak to him (3.24; see 2.2).

Under YHWH's instructions, Ezekiel begins his ministry under house arrest and in silence (3.25-27), which is strange given YHWH's repeated commands to the prophet to 'go and speak' to the rebellious house of Israel. Ezekiel is only allowed to speak when YHWH speaks to him, and when he speaks, he must only speak the words of YHWH (3.27). The narrative of Ezekiel's call ends with a familiar refrain: 'Those who hear, let them hear, and the one who refuses [to hear], let that one refuse, for they are a rebellious house' (3.27; see 2.5; 3.11), underscoring, once again, Israel's persistent stubbornness toward YHWH.

Summary

The seeing and hearing of Ezekiel's inaugural vision reveal several striking features of YHWH, YHWH's glory, and YHWH's holiness. First, the stunning multisensory and multicolored vision clearly por-trays the majestic reality of YHWH's glory. From beginning to end, the dazzling radiance of YHWH's presence confronts the one who sees and hears the message of Ezekiel. The fact that the account of YHWH's glory immediately follows the mention of the exile is sig-nificant for two reasons: (1) YHWH is mobile. The imagery of YHWH's chariot throne enhances this theme of YHWH's mobility and thus YHWH's ubiquity.[100] YHWH is not confined to an earthly structure, restricted by boundaries, or dependent on mere mortals for

---

[100] Cf. Frank-Lothar Hossfeld and Erich Zenger, *Die Psalmen I, Psalm 1-50* (NEchtB; Würzburg: Echter Verlag, 1993).

transportation. YHWH is able to move anywhere at any time.[101] (2) YHWH is present with the deportees in exile. Furthermore, the manifestation of YHWH's glory by the River Chebar represents YHWH's personal encounter with Ezekiel in Babylon.

Second, the vision of the glory of YHWH unveils the holiness of YHWH. When Rudolph Otto's approach to holiness[102] is applied to chs. 1-3, YHWH's holiness is apparent from beginning to end: (1) in the storm, lightning, thunder, and the effortless movement of the chariot's wheels (the divine *energicum*);[103] (2) in the brightness of the fiery cloud, the gleaming of the living creatures' bronze legs, the crystalline platform, and the glowing fiery form upon the throne (the divine *maiestas*); (3) in the eyes of the four living creatures and the wheels, which signifies the all-seeing, the all-wise, and the all-knowing nature of YHWH (divine *fascinans*); (4) in the entire vision, which is described as 'the appearance of the glory of YHWH' (1.28; the divine *mysterium*); and (5) in Ezekiel's response to the awesome presence of YHWH's glory and holiness in 1.28 (the divine *tremendum*).[104] The theme of holiness is implicit in the description of the four living creatures who cover their bodies with their wings,[105] and is amplified by YHWH who sits alone, separate, high, and exalted above the earth. YHWH sets himself apart from creation. Thus, the dazzling form of the infinite, holy YHWH can only be seen through the crystal platform.

---

[101] Brandon Frendenburg, *Ezekiel* (The College Press NIV Commentary; Joplin, MO: College Press Publishing Co., 1966), p. 101.

[102] Rudolph Otto, *The Idea of the Holy* (trans. John W. Harvey; Oxford: Oxford University Press, 1928), describes five significant features of the holy or the numinous: (1) the element of '*tremendum*' creates a sense of awful dread and includes the wrath and vengeance of God; (2) the element of 'overpoweringness', which points to the majesty of the numinous and inspires a sense of humility; (3) the element of 'fascination' or compelling attraction; (4) the element of 'energy' or urgency, vitality, force, movement, passion, excitement, which is exemplified in the 'consuming fire' of God; and (5) the element of '*mysterium*', the wholly other, transcendent, beyond the realm of the familiar, different, supernatural.

[103] The Latin *energicum* was not used by Otto, but by Johannes Hänel, *Die Religion der Heiligkeit* (Gütersloh: Der Rufer, 1931), p. 7, a devoted follower of Otto.

[104] John G. Gammie, *Holiness in Israel: Overtures to Biblical Theology* (Minneapolis: Augsburg Fortress Press, 1989), p. 49.

[105] Cf. Isa. 6.2, where the seraphim cover their 'feet' with their wings. There in Isaiah, 'feet' is used euphemistically to refer to genitals. See also Otto Kaiser, *Isaiah 1-12* (Philadelphia: Westminster, 1972), p. 76.

Third, the glory and holiness of YHWH point to YHWH's sovereignty and power. Not only is YHWH set apart from creation, but YHWH is enthroned on high. Like Isaiah, Ezekiel sees YHWH sitting upon a throne. However, unlike Isaiah, the throne Ezekiel sees is mobile, underscoring YHWH's ubiquitous kingship, authority, and power over all the earth.

Fourth, the glory and holiness of YHWH call for seeing and hearing the word of YHWH. In 1.3, Ezekiel's 'visions of God' are closely connected to the word of YHWH, indicating that the word of YHWH does not only refer to the spoken word of YHWH, but also points to an event that is seen or heard. When Ezekiel sees 'the appearance of the glory of YHWH' (1.28), he is completely aware that he is in the presence of YHWH,[106] immediately falls to the ground in worship, and hears YHWH speaking to him. Thus, in the context of Ezekiel, we must see the word of YHWH before we can hear the word of YHWH. If we do not see the word of YHWH, then we cannot hear the word of YHWH, and if we do not hear the word of YHWH, then we join with the rebellious people of Israel in the insurgency against YHWH. A failure to see and hear the word of YHWH results in revolt against YHWH.

Fifth, the role and activity of the Spirit is prominent in chs. 1-3. In these chapters, the רוח initiates the vision of YHWH's glory, guides the four living creatures, animates the four wheels, enters Ezekiel, sets him on his feet, enables him to hear the words of YHWH, and moves him from one place to another. Undoubtedly, the Spirit's role and activity in Ezekiel is closely tied to the glory and holiness of YHWH.

---

[106] Recall that the verb ראה can also denote understanding and knowledge.

6

SEEING AND HEARING THE DEPARTURE OF YHWH'S GLORY FROM THE TEMPLE

Introduction

This chapter examines the glory and holiness of YHWH by applying the themes of seeing and hearing to the narrative of Ezekiel's second major vision (chs. 8-11). The interplay between the visual and auditory images brings into focus the idolatry, wickedness, and bloodshed that have driven YHWH from YHWH's own residence.

YHWH's Glory Departs the Temple and the City (8.1–11.25)

The slow and deliberate departure of YHWH's glory from the temple and the city of Jerusalem presents chs. 8-11 as a literary unit[1] with a chiastic structure,[2] highlighting the theme of YHWH's glory. The

---

[1] David L. Thompson and Eugene Carpenter, *Ezekiel, Daniel* (Cornerstone Biblical Commentary; Downers Grove, IL: Tyndale House, 2010), p. 78; Bowen, *Ezekiel*, p. 43.
[2] Ka Leung Wong, *The Idea of Retribution in the Book of Ezekiel* (VTSup 87; Leiden: Brill, 2001), p. 158. See also Frank-Lothar Hossfeld, 'Die Tempelvision Ez 8-11 im Licht unterschiedlicher methodischer Zugänge', in Johan Lust (ed.), *Ezekiel and His Book: Textual and Literary Criticism and Their Interrelation* (BETL, 74; Leuven: Leuven University Press, 1986), pp. 156-57; and Block, *The Book of Ezekiel 1-24*, p. 272.

repetition of 8.1-3 found in reverse order in 11.22-25 form an inclusio, indicating this unit's literary borders.[3] As with Ezekiel's first vision (chs. 1-3), the second vision (chs. 8-11) is presented as a narrative, with each chapter in this unit having its own narrative plot and style. The visual and aural images of this unit are striking, emphasizing the themes of seeing and hearing in Ezekiel. Throughout this literary unit, Ezekiel uses words, as well as visual and auditory tools to enable his hearers to see and hear along with him. Thus, hearers see the various forms of idolatry in the temple (ch. 8), hear YHWH summon the executioners (9.1), hear YHWH's command to the man in linen (9.3), hear both of Ezekiel's outbursts of horror (9.8; 11.13), see afresh the glory of YHWH (ch. 10), hear the word of YHWH (ch. 11), and see (as well as understand fully the reason for) the complete withdrawal of the glory of YHWH from the temple and the city of Jerusalem (11.23).

Additionally, the opening verses of chs. 8-11 recall several literary features found in the first few verses of chs. 1-3: (1) a precise record of the date, setting, and the audience (8.1); (2) the phrase 'the hand of YHWH' (8.1), which signals YHWH's nearness, empowerment, and divine hold on Ezekiel, the means by which Ezekiel sees visions, and Ezekiel's mode of transportation; and (3) the expression 'I saw ... visions of God' (8.2, 3), emphasizing the visionary nature of Ezekiel's prophetic experience.

The narrative of Ezekiel's second major vision of YHWH's glory (chs. 8-11) may be divided into four parts: (1) the abominations in YHWH's temple (8.1-18); (2) YHWH's response to the abominations in the temple (9.1-11); (3) the movement of the glory of YHWH from the temple to the entrance of the temple's eastern gate (10.1-22); and (4) prophecies against the inhabitants of Jerusalem, promises of restoration, and YHWH's departure from the city (11.1-25). Chapters 8-11 reveal the reason for the exile and justify YHWH's judgment upon the city of Jerusalem and departure from the temple.

---

[3] Block, *The Book of Ezekiel 1-24*, p. 272, includes 8.4 as part of this unit's introduction. However, Moshe Greenberg, 'The Vision of Jerusalem in Ezekiel 8-11: A Holistic Interpretation', in James L. Crenshaw and Samuel Sandmel (eds.), *The Divine Helmsman: Studies on God's Control of Human Events* (New York: KTAV, 1980), p. 150, sees 8.4 as the beginning of the first visionary scene. See also, Hossfeld, 'Die Tempelvision Ez 8-11', pp. 156-57.

Abominations in YHWH's Temple

On the fifth day of the sixth month of the sixth year, Ezekiel is sitting in his Babylonian home with the exiled elders of Judah, and the 'hand of the Lord YHWH' falls upon him there (8.1). With YHWH's hand upon him, Ezekiel immediately sees (וארא והנה) the appearance of a fiery human figure (8.2) resembling the glowing human form in 1.26-27[4] and the figure's outstretched hand seizing him by his hair (8.3). Next, the spirit picks him up and transports him to the temple in Jerusalem by 'visions of God' (8.3). There in Jerusalem, Ezekiel witnesses four different kinds of idolatrous worship occurring in the temple. Each scene is characterized by the various forms of YHWH's question, 'Do you see what they are doing?', and each scene, with the exception of the last, progresses with YHWH's remark, 'You will see greater abominations than these', preparing Ezekiel and his hearers for something worse than the current abomination.[5]

The Statue of Jealousy that Provokes to Jealousy (8.4-6)

Upon his arrival at the northern entrance of the inner court, Ezekiel sees 'the statue of jealousy that provokes jealousy' (8.3). This graven image is a contemptible antithesis to the glory of YHWH.[6] After Ezekiel mentions the idol in v. 3, he immediately recognizes 'the glory of the God of Israel' in the temple (8.4) as he had seen earlier in Babylon, underscoring the theme of YHWH's mobility, as well as presenting hearers with a side-by-side portrait of the lifeless statue of jealousy and the dynamic and stunning presence of YHWH. The effect of this juxtaposition is clear: the idol of jealousy is a repulsive contrast to the brilliance and majesty of YHWH's glory.

Interestingly, Ezekiel uses the expression 'the glory of the God of Israel' in 8.4, rather than the phrase the 'glory of YHWH' as in chs. 1-3. By using the distinct title, 'the God of Israel', Ezekiel identifies YHWH as the only God of Israel who refuses to coexist with or tolerate Israel's idols.[7] YHWH, the sole focus of Israel's worship, 're-quires no physical representations of presence – indeed he forbids

---

[4] Cooper, *Ezekiel*, p. 119, observes that chs. 8-10 echo chs. 1-3 in reverse order.

[5] Zimmerli, *Ezekiel 1-24*, pp. 238-39.

[6] Cf. Block, *The Book of Ezekiel 1-24*, p. 282.

[7] Walther Zimmerli, 'Life before God', in Ben C. Ollenburger (ed.), *Old Testament Theology: Flowering and Future* (Winona Lake, IN: Eisenbrauns, 2003), I, p. 128.

them[8] – choosing, instead, to reveal his tangible and actual presence to his people. Thus, the carved image of jealousy and the subsequent detestable acts of worship described later in the chapter underline Israel's apostasy, rebellion, and ultimate betrayal of YHWH.[9] YHWH will not share Israel's worship with any of Israel's carved images! YHWH alone has redeemed them; YHWH alone has saved them; and YHWH alone has delivered them. YHWH alone deserves all of their worship and adoration. The institution of a carved image evokes YHWH's jealousy, violates YHWH's temple, and pushes YHWH out of his own residence. One of the main ideas of this unit is conveyed in 8.6. YHWH does not leave his sanctuary voluntarily, but is ousted by Israel: 'He said to me, "Son of man, do you see what they are doing, the great abominations that the house of Israel are doing here, to drive me far away from my sanctuary"' (8.6)? As abominable as the statue of jealousy is, YHWH tells Ezekiel that he will see worse abominations than this (8.6).

Worshiping Engraved Images (8.7-13)

Next, Ezekiel is brought to the entrance of the court where he sees a hole in the wall. Upon instruction, Ezekiel enlarges the hole, discovers a doorway, and enters through the door to see 'the evil abominations they are doing' in the room (8.7-9). Once in the room, Ezekiel sees 'every image of creeping thing and beast, detestable things, and every idol of the house of Israel engraved on the wall all around' (8.10). Mention of these engraved images will no doubt remind hearers of Deut. 4.17-18, which catalogs all of the forbidden carved images used as physical representations of YHWH.[10] Still, Ezekiel sees 'seventy of the elders of the house of Israel' (8.11) burning incense 'in the dark' to the loathsome creatures on the wall (8.12).

Ezekiel clearly conveys to his hearers the repulsiveness of this scene. On the walls of YHWH's sacred temple are paintings of abhorrent animals and slithering creatures, which function as gods for seventy of Israel's elders. The use of certain words such as שקץ ('detestable thing') and גלולים ('idols') to describe the images on the wall further underlines the repugnance of this scene. The second term,

---

[8] Daniel Block, *Deuteronomy: From Biblical Text ... To Contemporary Life* (The NIV Application Commentary; Grand Rapids, MI: Zondervan, 2012), p. 313.

[9] Block, *The Book of Ezekiel 1-24*, p. 282.

[10] Cf. Wright, *Message of Ezekiel*, p. 102.

גִּלּוּלִים, which means 'logs, blocks, and shapeless things',[11] appears forty-seven times in the Old Testament, and thirty-eight of those occurrences are found in the book of Ezekiel.[12] Furthermore, a few scholars suggest that גִּלּוּלִים is a derogatory word that refers to the idols as 'dung pellets' or 'droppings of excrement',[13] signaling Ezekiel's withering and scornful critique of Israel's idolatry. Moreover, Ezekiel avoids using the term 'god/gods' to refer to Israel's idols, emphasizing that the worship of these גִּלּוּלִים in YHWH's temple is certainly appalling, disgusting, and detestable! The effect of Israel's spiritual depravity is plain: they have replaced the beauty, magnificence, and grandeur of YHWH's glory with despicable creaturely and reptilian figures made out of logs. What a graphic contrast between the idols of the seventy elders and the beautiful radiance of YHWH's holiness!

Lamenting for Tammuz (8.14-15)

As Ezekiel and his hearers struggle with the inconceivable sight of seventy elders worshiping engraved images of beasts and creeping creatures in a dark and smoke-filled room, they hear YHWH say, 'You will see them committing even greater abominations than these' (8.13). What could be more reprehensible than burning incense to paintings of animals and reptiles? The sight and sound of 'women … lamenting for Tammuz' at 'the entrance of the north gate of the house of YHWH' (8.14)! The only occurrence of the name Tammuz in the Old Testament is found here in Ezekiel. Various scholars are agreed that lamenting for Tammuz was a Babylonian custom that observed the god Dumuzi's death and descent into the underworld.[14] The offense of this ritual is twofold. First, these women of Israel are shedding tears for a dead deity of Babylon, the same country that violently invaded their land and forcibly displaced several of their

---

[11] *BDB*, p. 165.

[12] Bruce K. Waltke, 'גִּלּוּל', in *TWOT*, I, p. 164.

[13] Ludwig Koehler and W. Baumgartner, *Supplementum Ad Lexicon in Veteris Testamenti Libros* (Leiden: Brill, 1958); Block, *The Book of Ezekiel 1-24*, p. 292; and Wright, *Message of Ezekiel*, p. 102.

[14] Thorkild Jacobsen, 'Toward the Image of Tammuz', in W.L. Moran (ed.), *Toward the Image of Tammuz and Other Essays* (Cambridge, MA: Harvard University Press, 1970), p. 100; E.M. Yamauchi, 'Tammuz and the Bible', *JBL* 84 (1965), pp. 283-90; and O.R. Gurney, 'Tammuz Reconsidered: Some Recent Developments', *JSS* 7 (1962), pp. 156-77.

fellow compatriots. Second, in YHWH's own temple, mourning for a dead deity had replaced the worship of YHWH, the living God.[15]

Sun Worship (8.16-17)

In this final scene, Ezekiel sees Israel's greatest abominable act of idolatry occurring in the 'inner court of the house of YHWH' (8.16). Twenty-five men turn their backs on YHWH's temple, face the east, and bow in worship to the sun (8.16). A couple of elements reveal why this last scene is the ultimate affront to YHWH. First, the worship of the sun is occurring in the holiest area of YHWH's temple – the inner court. Only priests were allowed to enter the inner court, implying that the twenty-five male sun worshipers are priests.[16] It was the inner court, the place between the porch and the altar, where Joel assembled the priests to lament before YHWH in repentance (Joel 2.17).[17] Second, with their backs toward the temple and their faces toward the sun, these men of Israel have demonstrated their rejection of YHWH as their God in favor of the sun, a thing created by YHWH.[18]

In these four scenes, Ezekiel describes a comprehensive condemnation of Israel's idolatry. From the northern gate outside the temple to the inner court of the temple, pagan idols occupy YHWH's temple. The people have thrown YHWH out of his own home (cf. 8.6). The multiple atrocities to his glory and holiness are intolerable. The result of their spiritual treachery is a land full of violence (8.17). Here, Ezekiel suggests that there is an inseparable relationship between worship and moral living.[19] Thus, YHWH will deal with them in anger. YHWH will not show pity, will not spare, and will not hear their most deafening and desperate cries for help (8.18).

YHWH's Glory and YHWH's Judgment

The sight of the abominations occurring in the temple concludes with YHWH's announcement of judgment upon the house of Israel (8.18), conveying a sense of finality. Promptly following YHWH's grim declaration in 8.18, Ezekiel hears a loud voice summoning the

---

[15] Duguid, *Ezekiel*, p. 133.
[16] Duguid, *Ezekiel and the Leaders of Israel*, p. 70.
[17] Wright, *Message of Ezekiel*, p. 107.
[18] Block, *The Book of Ezekiel 1-24*, p. 298.
[19] Craigie, *Ezekiel*, p. 65.

'guards'[20] of the city' to come near, 'each with his tool of destruction in his hand' (9.1). Six men appear from the upper gate. Curiously, Ezekiel does not give any details about the appearance of these six men. The only thing hearers learn about these six men is that each of them is carrying his weapon of destruction (9.2). Standing among these six men, Ezekiel sees a seventh figure 'dressed in white linen with a scribe's inkhorn on his hips' (9.2). The seven men enter the temple site and stand next to the 'bronze altar' (9.2).

At this point in the narrative, hearers are anticipating YHWH's command to these seven men, but instead they see along with Ezekiel, 'the glory of the God of Israel lifted up from the Cherub [and moved][21] to the threshold of the house' (9.3). The curious movement of YHWH's glory to the entrance of the temple foreshadows YHWH's departure from the temple,[22] creating suspense and raising questions for Ezekiel's hearers. Why is the glory of YHWH at the door of the temple? Is the God of Israel going somewhere? The intrusion of YHWH's movement at this point in the narrative makes the hearers of Ezekiel sense that something unexpected is going to unfold. Moreover, Ezekiel again uses the expression 'the glory of the God of Israel', highlighting that YHWH alone is Israel's God. Israel's replacement of YHWH with idols does not change the reality that YHWH alone is God. Also, it is noteworthy that here in 9.3, YHWH's temple is simply called 'house', not 'the house of YHWH' as in 8.16. The lack of the possessive signals that the temple is no longer the private residence of YHWH,[23] and therefore, presages the departure of the glory of YHWH from the temple.

Here, at the threshold of the temple, YHWH instructs the scribe in white linen to 'go through the city of Jerusalem and put a mark[24]

---

[20] Cf. Zimmerli, *Ezekiel 1-24*, p. 247, in this context, the expression פקדות העיר points to agents of destruction. Thus, Block's translation, 'executioners of the city', also seems to be an appropriate interpretation of the phrase; Block, *The Book of Ezekiel 1-24*, p. 300.

[21] This author has inserted the words 'and moved' in the translation for clarity.

[22] See S. Fisch, *Ezekiel* (London: Soncino, 1950), pp. 47-48, and Greenberg, *Ezekiel 1-20*, pp. 176, 194-98, for a detailed analysis of the movements of YHWH's glory. See also Taylor, *Ezekiel: An Introduction and Commentary*, p. 102.

[23] Cf. Block, *The Book of Ezekiel 1-24*, p. 326.

[24] The word translated 'mark' is the Hebrew letter *tav* (ת), the last letter of the Hebrew alphabet. Block, *The Book of Ezekiel 1-24*, p. 307, notes that the paleo-Hebrew form of the letter *tav* was an X or a cross. See David Diringer, *The Alphabet:*

on the people who sigh and groan over all the abominations being done in it' (9.4), suggesting that there are people in Jerusalem who grieve, wail, and agonize over the detestable worship described in ch. 8. The words אנח and אנק ('sigh', 'moan') are powerful rhyming words that illustrate loud, emotional, and verbal expressions of grief.[25] The mark serves to protect those who wail over the sins of the city from the massacre about to be unleashed by the six men (cf. 9.6),[26] clearly indicating that YHWH will not destroy the righteous with the unrighteous.

Next, Ezekiel hears YHWH command the six executioners to follow the scribe through the city and exterminate anyone who does not have the mark; old men, young men, maidens, children, and women were to be annihilated (9.5-6). Even the weak, defenseless, and innocent should not be pitied or spared.[27] YHWH intends to carry out a holocaust until all evidence of their existence is wiped out. The comprehensiveness of their destruction forebodes their extinction. YHWH's judgment, which is immediate, swift, and horrendous begins at 'my sanctuary' (9.6) because it is at YHWH's own temple where Israel's spiritual filth is visibly seen (8.5-18). Since YHWH's temple was already desecrated by Israel's idolatry, YHWH was willing to defile it further with the corpses from the carnage (9.7). The scene of YHWH's massacre is so frightful, ghastly, and grisly that once Ezekiel recognizes he is left alone in the terrifying presence of YHWH, he falls to the ground and pleads, 'Alas, Lord YHWH! Will you wipe out the entire remnant of Israel when you pour out your rage upon Jerusalem' (9.8)? YHWH's response justifies the genocide of the house of Israel. YHWH points to Israel's enormities, bloodshed, and perverted justice (9.9). Such violence and lawlessness pervade the land because the people believe that 'YHWH has abandoned the land, YHWH does not see' (9.9). However, unlike the idols to which they burn incense and for which they weep, YHWH does see the extent of Israel's crimes. Thus, YHWH's eye will not show pity or spare the wicked (9.10).

A Key to the History of Mankind (2 vols.; New York: Funk & Wagnalls, 3 edn, 1968), II, pp. 143-55, for illustrations of the ancient Hebrew and Semitic alphabets.

[25] Block, *The Book of Ezekiel 1-24*, p. 307; Wright, *Message of Ezekiel*, p. 112; Bowen, *Ezekiel*, p. 50. In Exod. 2.23 and Lam. 1.11, the moaning indicates physical distress.

[26] Recalls the mark on Cain and the mark on the doorposts in Exodus 12.

[27] Block, *The Book of Ezekiel 1-24*, p. 308; Duguid, *Ezekiel*, p. 134.

The Glory of YHWH Moves through the Temple towards Departure

With the frightening sound of slaughter still reverberating in his ears, Ezekiel becomes aware of YHWH's glory: 'As I looked, I saw above the platform that was over the head of the cherubim something like a sapphire stone, resembling the shape of a throne appearing above them' (10.1). The image of a sapphire throne will bring to mind Ezekiel's inaugural vision of YHWH's glory (1.26). Mention of the glory of YHWH reminds Ezekiel's hearers that YHWH is present and visible during the slaughter of the wicked. This jarring image of the massacre occurring in the presence of the glory of YHWH fully demonstrates that YHWH's judgment of the unrighteous is consonant with YHWH's glory and YHWH's holiness.

Whereas the throne-chariot had transported the glory of YHWH in Ezekiel's initial vision, here, YHWH's chariot appears with fiery coals of divine judgment for the city of Jerusalem and will later leave carrying the glory of YHWH out of the temple and away from the city,[28] underscoring the direct connection between YHWH's glory and judgment. As Ezekiel focuses on the image of YHWH's throne-chariot, he hears YHWH command the man dressed in white linen to 'go between the wheelwork, underneath the cherubim, and fill your hands with coals of fire from among the cherubim and scatter them over the city' (10.2). As the figure dressed in white leaves to fulfill YHWH's command, the stunning radiance of the glory of YHWH captures Ezekiel's attention. Ezekiel sees the cherubim standing on the south side of the temple (10.3), the glory of YHWH moving from above the cherubim to the 'threshold of the temple (10.4), the cloud filling the temple (10.4), and the brightness of the glory of YHWH (10.4). Then, he recalls the impressively sonorous wings of the cherubim that could be 'heard as far away as the outer court, like the sound of God Almighty when he speaks' (10.5). The sight and mention of the glory of YHWH at certain points in the narrative intensify the awareness of YHWH's glory,[29] and thus serve to keep Ezekiel and his hearers cognizant of the discernable and mobile presence of YHWH's glory in the temple.

---

[28] Block, *The Book of Ezekiel 1-24*, p. 317.
[29] Tuell, *Ezekiel*, p. 55.

Ezekiel returns to the narrative of the man dressed in white linen in 10.6-8 by repeating YHWH's command to 'take fiery coals from among the cherubim' (10.6). As the man in white enters YHWH's chariot, Ezekiel sees one of the cherubim stretch out his hands, take some of the coals from the fire, and give it to the man dressed in white, who then exits the chariot and disappears from the scene (10.7). Once the man in white leaves, Ezekiel offers a fresh description of the glory of YHWH (10.9-22) that parallels his inaugural vision of the glory of YHWH in ch. one.[30] While Ezekiel's second report of YHWH's glory in 10.9-22 corresponds to his initial account of YHWH's glory in ch. one, there are several discernible differences.[31] However, it is not necessary for Ezekiel's hearers to be preoccupied with these variations, because three times Ezekiel stresses that his current vision of YHWH's glory in the temple is identical to his previous vision of YHWH's glory, which he had seen by the river Chebar (see 10.15, 20, 22). The main idea of this literary unit (chs. 8-11) is the departure of the glory of YHWH from the temple and the city of Jerusalem on account of Israel's spiritual perversion and moral corruption. Accordingly, over the next two chapters (chs. 10 and 11), Ezekiel and his hearers watch as the glory of YHWH withdraws hesitantly and unhurriedly, giving the impression that YHWH is stalling[32] his departure from the temple and the city of Jerusalem. Not only does Ezekiel's fresh, detailed, and at times redundant description of the glory of YHWH highlight the centrality of YHWH's

---

[30] Cooper, *Ezekiel*, p. 129.

[31] For example, the word גלגל (wheelwork) does not appear in ch. 1; the designation כרבים (cherubim) appears in ch. 10 instead of חיות (living creatures); the four faces of the cherubim differ from the four faces of the living creatures (see 1.10; 10.14); and while in ch. 1 only the wheels were 'full of eyes all around' (1.18), here in ch. 10, it appears that both the wheels and the cherubim were covered with 'eyes' (10.12). See C.B. Houk, 'The Final Redaction of Ezekiel 10', *JBL* 90 (1971), pp. 42-47, for a chart of similarities between chs. 1 and 10. For other analyses of these two chapters (1 and 10), see Daniel Block, 'Text and Emotion: A Study in the "Corruptions" in Ezekiel's Inaugural Vision (Ezekiel 1.4-28)', *CBQ* 50 (1988), p. 440-42; Greenberg, *Ezekiel 1-20*, p. 198-99. In spite of the discrepancies between chs. 1 and 10, there is no evidence that these chapters are the compositions of multiple authors. Due to the parallels and differences between Ezekiel's visions of YHWH's glory, some scholars have chosen either to delete all of ch. 10 or to reduce the current text to a few core verses. For example, H. Schmidt, 'Die grossen Propheten Übersetzt und erklärt', in H. Gressmann (ed.), *SAT* (Göttingen: Vandehoeck und Ruprecht, 1915), II, pp. xi-lxxii; Zimmerli, *Ezekiel 1-24*, retains five verses; and Eichrodt, *Ezekiel*, keeps only two verses.

[32] Greenberg, *Ezekiel 1-20*, p. 191.

glory[33] in this unit, it also serves to develop the tension and suspend the climax of the entire vision.[34]

From the beginning of his arrival at the northern gate's entrance of the temple, Ezekiel and his hearers have been mindful of the intimidating presence of the glory of YHWH in the temple (cf. 8.4).[35] The first movement of the glory of YHWH towards departing the temple is detected in 9.3: 'Now the glory of the God of Israel had gone up from above the cherub, over which it had been, [and moved] to the threshold of the house'. The exact movement of the glory of YHWH recorded in 9.3 is repeated in 10.4, but here (10.4), Ezekiel gives a more comprehensive description of the movement of the glory of YHWH:[36] 'Now the glory of YHWH rose from above the cherub [and moved] to the threshold of the house. The house was filled with the cloud, and the court was filled with the brightness of the glory of YHWH.' By repeating the movement of the glory of YHWH in 10.4, Ezekiel continues to create suspense and prepares his hearers for the glory of YHWH to abandon the temple and the city of Jerusalem.[37]

From the threshold of the temple, the glory of YHWH moves to the south side of the temple, where the cherubim are waiting (cf. 10.3) and rests above the cherubim (10.18). With YHWH in the chariot, presumably sitting on the throne, the cherubim lift from the earth and stop 'at the entrance to the east gate of the house of YHWH' (10.19). Here, Ezekiel sees the glory of YHWH hovering over the cherubim (10.19). YHWH's throne-chariot coming to a standstill at the east gate pauses the narrative of YHWH's movement. This interlude serves to: (1) heighten the narrative's dramatic tension, (2) allow Ezekiel to see a new scene and to hear the word of YHWH, and (3) provide the hearers of Ezekiel with additional information that will not only intensify their curiosity (and thus maintaining their interest

---

[33] Duguid, *Ezekiel*, p. 147.
[34] Craigie, *Ezekiel*, p. 73.
[35] Wright, *Message of Ezekiel*, p. 119.
[36] Brownlee, *Ezekiel 1-19*, p. 150.
[37] Contra Lind, *Ezekiel*, p. 83, who writes, 'There is some confusion about the movement of the glory at this point (cf. 9.3)'.

in the story), but also deepen their understanding of what comes after the interlude[38] – YHWH's departure from the temple and the city
of Jerusalem.

The Interlude before the Climax

In 10.19, Ezekiel sees the throne-chariot carrying YHWH from the
south side of the temple to the entrance of the east gate of the temple. After a final description of the cherubim and two declarations
that assured his hearers that the four cherubim were the same beings
as the four living creatures he had seen by the Chebar River (10.20,
22), the Spirit transports Ezekiel (echoing 8.3) to the eastern gate of
the temple (11.1), allowing him to see and hear what YHWH sees
and hears: a group of twenty-five public officials discussing their future plans (cf. 11.3). Ezekiel spots and recognizes two of these leaders – 'Jaazaniah son of Azzur and Pelatiah son of Benaiah' (11.1).
Other than this brief introduction, Ezekiel gives no additional details
about these two characters.

YHWH accuses these leaders of 'devising[39] wickedness[40] and offering evil counsel' (11.2). The knowledge of their atrocious villainies
and perverted counsel provokes YHWH to declare judgment on
these twenty-five officials. Their premeditated and gruesome crimes
require immediate action from YHWH. Furthermore, YHWH's double commands, 'prophesy … prophesy' express YHWH's extreme
degree of vehemence toward these men and their vicious injustices.[41]
Significantly, before Ezekiel prophesies the words of YHWH, the
Spirit of YHWH falls upon Ezekiel and inspires Ezekiel with the
words of YHWH: 'Say, "Thus says YHWH …"' (v. 5).

---

[38] Cf. Solomon Pasala, *The 'Drama' of the Messiah in Matthew 8 and 9: A Study from a Communicative Perspective* (Bern: Peter Lang 2008), p. 52; and Sternberg, *The Poetics of Biblical Narrative*, p. 287.

[39] According to Block, *The Book of Ezekiel 1-24*, p. 332, n. 25, the verb חשב denotes 'rational, scientific calculation or planning', and it often appears with a negative object.

[40] This usage of און ('wickedness') occurs only in Ezek. 11.2. While the word appears in 30.17, it is translated differently. The word in its current context conveys a religious and ethical abuse of power. See K.H. Bernhardt, 'אָון', in *TDOT*, I, pp. 140-47. Additionally, G. Herbert Livingston, 'אָון', in *TWOT*, p. 1, claims that the primary meaning of און is twofold: (1) it emphasizes trouble that leads to wicked-ness; and (2) it stresses emptiness that leads to idolatry.

[41] Block, *The Book of Ezekiel 1-24*, p. 334.

Not only is YHWH aware of these men's wicked schemes and evil counsel, but YHWH also knows their most secret thoughts and concealed intentions: 'I know the steps of your spirits' (11.5). Then, YHWH indicts them for murder: 'You have killed many in this city and have filled the streets with the slain' (11.6). Thus, for YHWH, the only appropriate punishment for their grievous injustices and ruthless butchery is death (11.7-11). YHWH's sentence is swift and immediate. While Ezekiel is prophesying, Pelatiah son of Benaiah dies (11.13). The sudden death of Pelatiah, whose name means, 'YHWH delivers', ominously signals to Ezekiel and his hearers that there is no hope of deliverance from YHWH's impending doom. Having realized the full significance of Pelatiah's untimely death, Ezekiel reacts with shock and horror by falling down on his face and emitting a loud and distressing cry:[42] 'Alas, Lord YHWH! You are completely annihilating the remnant of Israel' (11.13). Ezekiel's hopeless outburst in 11.13 is similar to his outcry of horror in 9.8. However, while YHWH's response to Ezekiel's cry in 9.9-10 seems to be an affirmative reply, here, YHWH offers a message of hope to those in exile (11.14-21), suggesting that the banished deportees are the remnant of Israel.

Although YHWH orchestrated the exile, 11.14-21 demonstrates that the exile is not the end of Israel's story. YHWH promises to be a 'little' sanctuary for those who are in exile (11.16), to bring them out of the countries of exile and return them to their homeland (11.17), and to remove their stony hearts and implant in them 'one heart and ... a new spirit' (11.19).[43] The effect of this divine surgery[44] is a complete transformation of the people of Israel and a renewed covenant: 'they will be my people, and I will be their God' (11.20).[45]

---

[42] Eichrodt, *Ezekiel*, p. 138.

[43] Ezekiel expands on this subject in ch. 36.

[44] Cf. Block, *The Book of Ezekiel 1-24*, pp. 352-53, who refers to the procedure as a 'heart/mind transplant'.

[45] This expression is known as the 'covenant formula', which conveys the notion of intimate relationship between YHWH and YHWH's people. The formula occurs as a promise to Abraham (Gen. 17.7-8), Moses (Exod. 6.7), and to the nation of Israel (Exod. 29.45). This theme of covenant will be developed more fully in Ezek. 20.5-8; Gordon J. McConville, 'בְּרִית', in Willem Van Gemeren (ed.), *NIDOTTE* (5 vols.; Grand Rapids, MI: Zondervan, 1997), I, p. 753, observes that the notion of 'covenant' was widely known in the ANE, as were the related concepts of the oath and the curse; however YHWH's covenant with the people of Israel is a 'distinctively biblical' theological concept; M. Weinfeld, 'ברית', in *TDOT*,

Previously, YHWH had criticized the people of Israel for being a hard-hearted, rebellious people (2.4; 3.7), but after the exile, they will have a heart that is faithful to YHWH. YHWH's renewed covenant with Israel shows that YHWH's primary desire is to have a personal, intimate, and faithful relationship with the people of Israel. While YHWH yearns to have a covenant relationship with Israel, 11.21 quickly reminds Ezekiel and his hearers that Israel should not have a presumptuous attitude towards YHWH and YHWH's covenant blessings: "'But as for those whose hearts walk after their detestable things and their abominations, I will bring their conduct down upon their heads," declares the Lord YHWH'.

The Climax

At last, Ezekiel's second vision reaches its dramatic and explosive end: the solemn exit of the glory of YHWH from the temple and the city of Jerusalem to the mountain, which is east of the city (11.22-23). The complete withdrawal of the glory of YHWH from the city and its temple highlights a few observations. First, YHWH's departure signals YHWH's averse resistance to share the temple, YHWH's place of residence, with Israel's idols. YHWH's sanctuary was no longer holy, but common, unexceptional, and rendered unfitting for the radiant beauty of YHWH's majesty. Second, YHWH's abandonment indicates the full end and destruction of the city of Jerusalem, the consequence of the people's grievous crimes against YHWH and humanity. Third, YHWH's appearance at the temple, YHWH's movement throughout the temple, and YHWH's exit from the city once again demonstrate the theme of YHWH's mobility. YHWH 'is free to appear anywhere at any time',[46] unlike Israel's lifeless deities that have fixed positions both outside and inside the temple.

II, p. 278, notes: 'The idea of a covenant between a deity and a people is unknown to us from other religions and cultures … the covenant idea was a special feature of the religion of Israel, the only one to demand exclusive loyalty and to preclude the possibility of dual or multiple loyalties such as were permitted in other religions'. See also, M. Weinfeld, 'The Covenant of Grant in the Old Testament and in the Ancient near East', *JAOS* 90.2 (1970), pp. 184-203; *idem*, 'Covenant, Davidic', in Keith R. Crim (ed.), *IDBSup* (Nashville: Abingdon, 1976), pp. 188-92; and *idem*, *The Promise of the Land: The Inheritance of the Land of Canaan by the Israelites* (Berkeley: University of California Press, 1993).

[46] Greenberg, *Ezekiel 1-20*, p. 197.

Summary

While the word 'holy' is not mentioned in chs. 8-11, the theme of holiness pervades the entire literary unit, underscoring the direct relationship between the glory of YHWH and the holiness of YHWH in the book of Ezekiel. From the outset, Ezekiel cleverly employs a high degree of colorful detail to portray and contrast the beauty of YHWH's holy presence with the hideous and unholy images of Israel's gods. Hearers should recall the first thing Ezekiel sees when he arrives at the temple in Jerusalem is the statue of jealousy stationed at the entrance of the temple's northern gate (8.3, 5-6). However, the idol was only the first of Israel's spiritual violations. The first scene of the statue of jealousy is followed by three additional scenes of Israel's abominable acts of worship (72 elders burning incense to idols, 8.7-13; women weeping for Tammuz, 8.14-15; and 25 men worshiping the sun, 8.16-18), and each subsequent scene of Israel's profane worship is worse than the previous act of idolatry (8.6, 13, 15). Israel's spiritual orgies with their repulsive idols have defiled YHWH's holy sanctuary, and so YHWH is forced out of the temple: 'do you see what they are doing, the great abominations that the house of Israel are doing here to drive me far away from **my** sanctuary' (8.6)? Since Israel persistently refuses to separate themselves from the unholy, YHWH must now separate himself from Israel.

The glory and holiness of YHWH require judgment on the violators and demand justice for all of humanity. Israel's spiritual, moral, and social sins justify the judgments of YHWH upon Israel:[47] 'the sin of the house of Israel and Judah is extremely great. The land is full of blood, and the city is full of perverted justice' (9.9). YHWH will hold Israel responsible for its recalcitrant, scandalous, and unfaithful behavior towards YHWH (7.2-4; 11.21).[48] Israel's fidelities to their idols resulted in Israel's moral, political, and social corrosion. The house of Israel is as blind and deaf as the idols they worship, the cause for their spiritual decline. From its origin as a nation, Israel has obstreperously rebelled against YHWH (20.5-31). In other words,

[47] Joyce, *Divine Initiative*, p. 62.
[48] Chapters 16, 18, 22, and 23 give a detailed list of Israel's sins, reasons for YHWH's furious judgments upon them (cf. 22.31).

from their beginning, the people of Israel have deliberately and cal-culatedly defied YHWH.[49] Thus, Israel is like a disobedient child who must be punished for wrongdoing. Furthermore, the judgments of YHWH are designed to bring about justice for the oppressed. YHWH's justice, therefore, is a response to the 'mistreatment of the vulnerable … the deep longing for the removal of oppression',[50] and the yearning for order, peace, and equality. Thus, YHWH is the ulti-mate 'organizer, dispenser, and protector of justice'.[51] Clearly, in Eze-kiel, the judgments and justice of YHWH are fundamental expres-sions of the glory and holiness of YHWH.

The glory and holiness of YHWH compel YHWH to save and restore Israel (cf. 11.16-21).[52] Although the hope of restoration urges Israel to take responsibility for their wrongdoings,[53] restoration is not determined by Israel's spiritual endeavors. In fact, in Ezekiel, restora-tion is solely an act of YHWH's transformative power.

---

[49] Cf. James W. McClendon, *Systematic Theology: Doctrine* (Nashville: Abingdon, 1994), p. 130.

[50] M. Daniel Carrol Rodas, 'Seek Yahweh, Establish Justice: Probing Prophetic Ethics. An Orientation from Amos 5.1-17', in Cynthia Long Westfall and Bryan R. Dyer (eds.), *The Bible and Social Justice: Old Testament and New Testament Foundations for the Church's Urgent Call* (Eugene, OR: Wipf and Stock Publishers, 2015), p. 64.

[51] Cf. Rolf P. Knierim, *The Task of Old Testament Theology: Substance, Method, and Cases* (Grand Rapids, MI: Eerdmans, 1995), p. 106.

[52] This theme of restoration will receive greater attention in the last major vi-sion of the glory of YHWH (chs. 40-48).

[53] Christopher D. Marshall, *Beyond Retribution* (Grand Rapids, MI: Eerdmans, 2001), pp. 132-35.

7

SEEING AND HEARING THE RETURN OF YHWH'S GLORY TO THE TEMPLE

Introduction

This chapter examines Ezekiel's final vision of YHWH's glory and holiness. In this last vision narrative, hearers see YHWH's glory return to the temple. In addition to the analysis of the text, this chapter continues to pay close attention to the visual and auditory terminology and images in chs. 40-48. The intersection between the themes of seeing and hearing in the text reveals a complete portrait of YHWH's glory and holiness in the book of Ezekiel.

YHWH's Glory Returns to the Temple (40.1-48.35)

Whereas the vision's exact date indicates the beginning of this literary unit, references to the city in 40.2 and 48.35 serve as an inclusio that marks the beginning and end of the vision narrative. The themes of YHWH's glory and YHWH's holiness continue to weave together in Ezekiel's final vision of the glory of YHWH (chs. 40-48). The interrelationship between the glory of YHWH and the holiness of YHWH is a unifying characteristic of these last nine chapters of the book of Ezekiel. We have seen that chs. 1-3 describe Ezekiel's first encounter with the glory of YHWH, and chs. 8-11 narrate the departure of the glory of YHWH from the temple and the city of Jerusalem because of the people's sins. Now, we will observe that chs. 40-

48 describe the return of the glory of YHWH to dwell in a holy temple among a restored and holy people.[1] Thus, chs. 40-48 is an inver-
sion of chs. 8-11.[2] Notably, the appearance of the glory of YHWH
in Babylon, YHWH's departure, and YHWH's return provide a literary and theological framework for understanding the entire book of
Ezekiel.

Furthermore, several shared literary features connect Ezekiel's final vision in chs. 40-48 to his earlier visions in chs. 1-3 and 8-11. Each
vision (1) precisely records the year, month, and day of the vision
(1.1; 8.1; 40.1); (2) has the expression 'visions of God' (1.1; 8.3; 40.2);
(3) has the phrase 'the hand of YHWH' (1.3; 3.14, 22; 8.1; 40.1); and
(4) includes the words 'the glory of YHWH' (1.28; 3.12, 23; 10.4, 18;
11.22, 23; 43.4, 5; 44.5).[3]

Also, Ezekiel's final vision confirms that the themes of seeing and
hearing serve as an appropriate biblical approach to the book of Ezekiel. The first words that are spoken to Ezekiel in this final vision
include the commands to 'see ... and hear ...' (40.4), and each subsequent scene visually and audibly depict the events of this drama.
Accordingly, these last chapters of the book of Ezekiel may be divided by the things Ezekiel sees and hears into the following five sections: (1) the new temple (40.1-42.20); (2) the return of the glory of
YHWH (43.1-11); (3) an intricate description of Israel's renewed
worship (43.12-46.24); (4) the temple's healing river (47.1-12); and (5)
the division of the land and the city's name (47.13-48.35).

The City and the New Temple
Ezekiel's final vision of the glory of YHWH begins with the hand of
YHWH placing Ezekiel on a very high mountain in Israel (40.1-2).
Upon his arrival, he is met by a man whose entire appearance looked
like bronze, holding a linen cord and a measuring rod in his hand
(40.3). Interestingly, the man's first words to Ezekiel are a series of
imperatives: 'see with your eyes and hear with your ears. Pay close
attention' (40.4).[4] It is noteworthy that the first speech Ezekiel hears

---

[1] Cf. Pieter de Vries, 'Ezekiel: Prophet of the Name and Glory of YHWH –
the Character of His Book and Several of Its Main Themes', *JBPR* 4 (2012), p. 105.
[2] Bowen, *Ezekiel*, p. 239.
[3] See Steven Tuell, *The Law of the Temple in Ezekiel 40-48* (HSM 49; Atlanta:
Scholars Press, 1992), pp. 35-37, for more details on the unity of chs. 40-48.
[4] The literal translation of the Hebrew phrase is 'see/look with your eyes and
hear with your ears. Set your mind/heart ...'

in his final vision of the return of the glory of YHWH begins with the commands to 'see ... and hear'. Hearers should recall that a failure to see and hear results in rebellion against YHWH (cf. 12.2). Thus, the man's commands not only underscore *seeing* and *hearing* as an appropriate approach to the book of Ezekiel, but his commands also convey the theological significance of seeing and hearing the word of YHWH. It is also necessary for Ezekiel to see, hear, and pay close attention to everything that the bronze man shows him because he must tell the people of Israel everything he sees and hears in this vision (40.4). The sole purpose for relaying all that he sees and hears is made explicit in 43.10: 'so that they may be ashamed of their sins'. By describing the new temple to the house of Israel, YHWH compels Israel to recognize the magnitude of their idolatry and various violations of the glory and holiness of YHWH.[5] This awareness of their sins will produce guilt and shame that lead to repentance.[6]

What Ezekiel sees next is an elaborate series of meticulous and exact measurements completed by the man holding the linen cord and measuring rod in his hand. These last chapters of the book of Ezekiel (40-48) emphasize the themes of holiness and purity.[7] The root קדשׁ occurs 99 times in the book of Ezekiel, and 65 of those occurrences are found in the last nine chapters of the book of Ezekiel.[8] According to Berry, the complex notion of holiness found in chs. 40-48 is more acute than anywhere else in the Old Testament.[9] While at first glance the bronze guide's activities may seem uninteresting and incongruous with the themes of YHWH's glory and YHWH's holiness, the guide's measurements clearly identify and guard the holy areas of the city, the sanctuary, and all persons and things associated with it.[10]

The new temple is a concrete and visible sign of YHWH's holiness. This concept is made clear as hearers follow Ezekiel and his

[5] Cf. Block, *The Book of Ezekiel: Chapters 25-48*, p. 589; Wright, *Message of Ezekiel*, p. 337.
[6] Cf. Walther Zimmerli, *Ezekiel 2: A Commentary on the Book of the Prophet Ezekiel Chapters 25-48* (trans. James D. Martin; Hermeneia; Philadelphia: Fortress Press, 1983), pp. 418-19.
[7] de Vries, 'Prophet of the Name and Glory of YHWH', p. 101; George Ricker Berry, 'The Authorship of Ezekiel 40-48', *JBL* 34.1/4 (1915), p. 18.
[8] Jo Bailey Wells, *God's Holy People: A Theme in Biblical Theology* (JSOTSup 305; Sheffield: Sheffield Academic Press, 2000), p. 165.
[9] Berry, 'The Authorship of Ezekiel 40-48', p. 18.
[10] Bowen, *Ezekiel*, p. 240; Berry, 'The Authorship of Ezekiel 40-48', p. 18.

bronze tour guide through the city and the temple. The expressions of holiness are apparent in the strict measurements, the perfect geometric design of the temple, the accurate numerical symmetries,[11] the entrances and exits,[12] the distinctions between the duties of the Zadokite priests and the Levite priests, the rooms for the priests, the garments of the priests, the engraved cherubim and palm trees that decorate the walls of the temple, the renewed worship of Israel, the social reforms, and the division of the land. Scholars are agreed that increasing degrees of holiness are detected in the architectural details of the temple.[13] The outer court, for example, is seven steps higher than the ground level (40.6, 22, 26); the inner court is on a level that is eight steps higher than the outer court (40.31, 34, 37); and the temple building itself is erected on an elevated platform that is higher than the inner court(41.8).[14] No doubt, the element of height plays a significant role in underscoring the holiness of the new temple.[15] From the beginning of Ezekiel's tour in 40.5 until 41.4, Ezekiel and his guide move from outside to inside and upward to higher levels of holy ground.[16] One of the last things Ezekiel's tour guide measures in ch. 42 is a wall which serves to prevent the holy space from becoming polluted by the profane (42.20), spotlighting once again, the theme of absolute holiness in these final chapters of the book of Ezekiel.

The Return of the Glory of YHWH

With the measurements complete and the new city and temple purified and protected from the abominations and contaminants of Israel's idolatry, the scene is set for the return of the glory of YHWH.

---

[11] Wright, *Message of Ezekiel*, pp. 327-33; de Vries, 'Prophet of the Name and Glory of YHWH', pp. 101-103; *idem*, 'The Relationship between the Glory of Yahweh and the Spirit of Yahweh in Ezekiel 33-48', p. 343.

[12] Stevenson, *Vision of Transformation*, pp. 18-19.

[13] See P. Jenson, *Graded Holiness: A Key to the Priestly Conception of the World* (Sheffield: JSOT Press, 1992); de Vries, 'Prophet of the Name and Glory of YHWH', pp. 101-103; Zimmerli, *Ezekiel 25-48*; Michael Konkel, 'The System of Holiness in Ezekiel's Vision of the New Temple (Ezek 40-48)', in Christian Frevel and Christophe Nihan (eds.), *Purity and the Forming of Religious Traditions in the Ancient Mediterranean World and Ancient Judaism* (Leiden/Boston: Brill, 2013); and Bennett Simon, 'Ezekiel's Geometric Vision of the Restored Temple: From the Rod of His Wrath to the Reed of His Measuring', *HTR* 102.4 (2009), pp. 411-38.

[14] Wright, *Message of Ezekiel*, pp. 330-33; de Vries, 'Prophet of the Name and Glory of YHWH', pp. 101-03.

[15] Cf. Hiebel, *Ezekiel's Vision Accounts*, p. 197.

[16] Hiebel, *Ezekiel's Vision Accounts*, p. 198.

Concern for the holiness of YHWH and the preservation of YHWH's sacred spaces from defilement[17] is the *sine qua non* for the return of the glory of YHWH in Ezekiel. Ezekiel's guide leads him 'to the gate facing east' (43.1); and there, Ezekiel sees the meteoric return of the glory of YHWH from the east (43.2), the same direction in which it had departed the temple in 10.18-19. In contrast to the reluctant and gradual departure of YHWH's glory from the temple in chs. 8-11, the return of YHWH's glory is swift and direct,[18] giving the impression that YHWH is eager to return to the temple, YHWH's 'house'.

As YHWH returns from the east and enters the temple, the whole earth is illuminated by the brightness radiating from the splendor of YHWH's glory (43.2), illustrating that without the glory of YHWH, darkness fills the earth. The astoundingly memorable sight is accompanied by amplified sounds of YHWH's glory: the roaring and deafening sound of 'many waters' (43.2), recalling Ezek. 1.24. In fact, Ezekiel's comment in 43.3, connects his current vision of YHWH's glory to his earlier visions of YHWH's glory: 'The sight of the vision I saw was like the vision I had seen when [YHWH] came to destroy the city, and like the vision I saw by the Chebar River …' The sight and sounds associated with the glory of YHWH not only herald the return of the glory of YHWH, but they also strengthen the view that encountering the presence of God involves seeing and hearing God. Significantly, Ezekiel describes the spectacular sight in the east as the 'glory of the God of Israel' (43.2), a phrase that occurs in 8.4, 9.3, 10.19, and 11.22, emphasizing that YHWH is Israel's only God.

Recognizing the phenomenon to be the glory of YHWH, Ezekiel responds exactly as he did when he first encountered the imposing and weighty presence of YHWH's glory: he falls to the ground face down in worship (1.28; 43.3). The beauty of YHWH's holiness creates a sense of awe that restrains over-familiarity, indifference, and insensibility to YHWH. The awesome presence of YHWH's holy majesty produces reverential respect, fear and wonder, precluding 'any ease or artistic coziness'.[19] Although Ezekiel has seen YHWH's

---

[17] Cf. Stephen C. Barton, *Holiness Past and Present* (London/New York: T&T Clark, 2003), pp. 105-107.

[18] Duguid, *Ezekiel*, p. 489, also notes this observation.

[19] Walter Brueggemann, *Theology of the Old Testament: Testimony, Dispute, Advocacy* (Minneapolis: Fortress, 1997), p. 427.

holy splendor before, this encounter with YHWH's glory, though eas-
ily recognized, is new and astounding, effecting staggering terror and
awed admiration that result only in worship.

Like before in 2.2, the Spirit picks up the prostrate prophet and
takes him to the inner court where he sees the glory of YHWH filling
the temple (40.5) – undoubtedly, an incredible sight for Ezekiel and
his hearers! The significance of YHWH's return to the temple will
not be overlooked by the hearers of Ezekiel: YHWH's return to the
temple reverses the judgment and destruction caused by YHWH's
abandonment[20] and restores all the benefits associated with YHWH's
presence.

Ezekiel's phenomenal spectacle is suspended by the sound of
YHWH's voice coming from the temple (40.6). YHWH's speech asserts YHWH's sovereign governance,[21] affirms YHWH's permanent
residence among YHWH's people, and attests to the holiness of the
temple, a palace befitting the regal magnificence of YHWH's holy
presence. The use of royal language in 43.7 depicts the enthronement
of YHWH and proclaims the temple as YHWH's palace: [22] 'Son of
man, this is the place for my throne and the place for the soles of my
feet'. In 10.3, YHWH's throne-chariot was parked outside the temple,
but here, YHWH declares that the temple is the place for both his
throne and his feet.[23] Now that YHWH has returned to the temple,
Ezekiel and his hearers learn that the temple is the place where
YHWH's glory will reside forever among the people of Israel (43.7,
9).

Furthermore, the return of YHWH's glory to the temple is inti-
mately connected to YHWH's holy name. Previous texts in Ezekiel
noted that Israel's idolatry polluted the holy name of YHWH (cf.
20.39); and, while in 20.22 YHWH does not punish Israel because of

---

[20] Duguid, *Ezekiel*, p. 489.

[21] Cf. Brueggemann, *Theology of the Old Testament*, pp. 283-87.

[22] Paul M. Joyce, 'King and Messiah in Ezekiel', in J. Day (ed.), *King and Messiah in Israel and the Ancient near East: Proceedings of the Oxford Old Testament Seminar* (JSOTSup 270; Sheffield: Sheffield Academic, 1998), pp. 323-37; Block, *The Book of Ezekiel: Chapters 25-48*, pp. 580-81; Bowen, *Ezekiel*, p. 245; and de Vries, *The Kābôd of YHWH*, p. 310.

[23] The temple as YHWH's palace is a reoccurring motif in the Old Testament. Exod. 26.31-35 presents the holy of holies as YHWH's throne room. Isaiah 6.1; Jer. 3.17, 14.21, and 17.12, identify the temple as the place for YHWH's throne, and Isa. 60.13, Ps. 99.5, 9; 132.7; and Lam. 2.1, designate the temple as the place for YHWH's footstool.

concern for his holy name, in 36.20-21, the exile, YHWH's punishment for Israel's repeated and increasing sins, led to the defilement of YHWH's holy name 'among the nations'. Thus, YHWH acts to save Israel from exile because of YHWH's concern for his holy name (cf. 36.22-38). Whereas previous texts in Ezekiel imply a close connection between YHWH's holy name and YHWH's glory, 43.7 concretizes the direct link between the glory of YHWH and the holy name of YHWH. It is the first time in Ezekiel that these two themes, YHWH's glory and YHWH's holy name, appear 'in such close collocation'.[24] Ezekiel's theological message is clear: the holy and only God of Israel 'who resides in this holy temple on this holy mountain demands a holy reputation. [YHWH] will not tolerate an unholy people misrepresenting [YHWH's holy name] before the nations.'[25] Moreover, YHWH's list of Israel's sins mentioned in 43.8-9, further underscores the immediate relationship between YHWH's glory and YHWH's holy name.[26]

Additionally, in the context of glory and holiness, YHWH charges Israel to 'put far away' their spiritual whoredom and their pagan memorials of their kings (43.9), for only then will YHWH dwell forever in their midst (43.9). Interestingly, in Ezekiel 8.6, YHWH uses the word רחק ('to send far away/to put far away') to convey that Israel's idolatrous practices were sending him far away from the temple, while here, in 43.9, he uses the same word רחק to express what Israel must now do with their abominable practices. Previously, Israel's spiritual adultery sent the glory of YHWH far from the temple, here, the people of Israel must now put far away from YHWH their spiritual abominations in order for the glory of YHWH to live among them. Although the implication is the same in both 8.6 and 43.9 (Israel's abominations will drive away YHWH from the temple and from among their midst), in 8.6, Israel's actions profaned the temple and expelled YHWH from the temple; but here in 43.9, Israel must act to keep YHWH's sacred space holy (indicative by the jussive form of רחק). Indeed, YHWH has returned to the temple and has declared the temple as his palace, but YHWH will only live in their midst if the people of Israel terminate their spiritual allegiances to their idols.

24. de Vries, *The Kābôd of YHWH*, p. 311.
25. Block, *The Book of Ezekiel: Chapters 25-48*, p. 582.
26. See also Luc, 'Theology of Ezekiel', pp. 137-43.

To ensure that Ezekiel and his hearers fully grasp the heightened concept of holiness, YHWH declares to Ezekiel: 'this is the law/instruction for the house: "On the top of the mountain [and] all of its territory all around shall be most holy. Behold! This is the law/instruction of the house"'. The phrase קדש קדשים ('most holy') found in 41.4, which is distinctively different from the phrase קדש הקדשים ('the holy of holies'), indicates that not only the temple must be holy, but the entire area all around the temple must be holy and untouched by the profane.[27]

With the return of the glory of YHWH to the temple, Ezekiel gives a description of the laws and ordinances regarding the renewed worship of Israel, the sanctuary, and the land. It is significant that the regulations pertaining to the altar's dimensions, consecration, and sacrifices immediately follow the return of YHWH's glory to the temple (43.13-27). The altar, which was first mentioned in 40.47, represents an essential part of worship in the temple. When the seven days of purification rituals are completed and the priests offer the appropriate sacrifices on behalf of the people, YHWH says, 'Then I will accept you' (43.27), a sublime assurance that the covenantal relationship between YHWH and Israel has been restored.[28]

Next, Ezekiel sees that the East Gate is shut and hears that it will remain closed because the glory of YHWH returned to the temple through the East Gate (44.2). The closing of the East Gate underscores the holiness of the temple.[29] That is, the path of YHWH's glory will not be made common by human traffic.

Then, Ezekiel is led to the front of the temple where he sees the glory of YHWH filling the temple, and once again, the prophet falls to the ground in reverential worship at the sight of YHWH's holy splendor (44.4). While in his prostrated state, YHWH commands Ezekiel to 'pay attention, see with your eyes, and with your ears hear everything I tell you concerning all the statutes of the temple of YHWH and all its laws' (43.5), reminding Ezekiel and his hearers that

---

[27] Cf. Block, *The Book of Ezekiel: Chapters 25-48*, p. 592.
[28] See Wright, *Message of Ezekiel*, pp. 344-46; Block, *The Book of Ezekiel: Chapters 25-48*, pp. 611-12; and Thompson and Carpenter, *Ezekiel, Daniel*, p. 251.
[29] Some scholars such as Zimmerli, *Ezekiel 25-48*, p. 440; Fisch, *Ezekiel*, p. 302; H.G. May, 'The Book of Ezekiel: Introduction and Exegesis', in G.A. Buttrick (ed.), *IB* (Nashville: Abingdon, 1956), p. 307; Block, *The Book of Ezekiel: Chapters 25-48*, p. 614; and Cooper, *Ezekiel*, p. 388, claim that the closing of the East Gate signify that YHWH will never again leave the temple.

YHWH's laws and instructions are visual and aural in nature. YHWH contends that Israel's abominable practices, allowing uncircumcised (both spiritually and physically) foreigners into YHWH's sanctuary, and the failure to guard YHWH's 'holy things' have violated the holiness of YHWH's sanctuary (44.7-8). Thus, in order to defend the sacred space of YHWH's sanctuary, YHWH forbids anyone who does not belong to the covenant community from entering the sanctuary.[30] Additionally, YHWH distinguishes the roles of the Levites from the roles of the Zadokites. Owing to the Levites' apostasy, they are not allowed to serve as priests, restricted from coming near YHWH, and barred from touching YHWH's holy things. Nevertheless, YHWH makes the Levites overseers of the temple's gates and guards of the temple. In addition to guarding the temple, the Levites are permitted to slaughter the people's sacrificial offerings, but they are not allowed to sacrifice the offering upon the altar (44.10-14).

Conversely, the Zadokites will serve as priests before YHWH, and they will be given access to the innermost court (44.17, 27), to the sanctuary (44.16, 27), to YHWH himself (44.28), and to YHWH's table (44.16, 29-30), because they remained faithful to YHWH while the people of Israel wandered away from YHWH (44.15). Significantly, all of the responsibilities of the Zadokite priests are directed to YHWH:[31] they 'will come near me to minister to me. They will stand before me … they will enter my sanctuary and approach my table to minister to me. They will keep my charge' (44.15-16). Along with their ministry to YHWH, the Zadokite priests must (1) teach YHWH's people the difference between 'the holy and the profane' and 'what is unclean and what is clean' (44.23) and (2) act as judges when disputes occur (44.24). Furthermore, in order to safeguard the Zadokite's holiness and maintain their ability to enter into the innermost sacred room of YHWH, the Zadokites are given a list of regulations that govern every aspect of their lives (44.17-22, 25-31). Undoubtedly, both the Levites and the Zadokites serve to guard the holiness of the sanctuary, the residence of YHWH's glory.[32]

---

[30] Block, *The Book of Ezekiel: Chapters 25-48*, p. 622; Thompson and Carpenter, *Ezekiel, Daniel*, p. 252.

[31] Bowen, *Ezekiel*, p. 252.

[32] de Vries, *The Kābôd of YHWH*, p. 320.

The theme of holiness extends from the temple to the land surrounding the temple (45.1-8; 47.13-48.35).[33] In 45.1-8, Ezekiel hears
that a portion of the land should be reserved as 'an offering' to
YHWH (45.1). The whole area belonging to YHWH is characterized
as 'holy' (45.1), and no one is permitted to 'sell ... exchange ... trade
this prime piece of land because it is holy to YHWH' (48.14). Of
YHWH's holy territory, one section of the land (קֹדֶשׁ קָדָשִׁים) is des-
ignated for the sanctuary (45.3) and for the Zadokite priests who
serve YHWH in the sanctuary (45.3-4; 48.11-12).[34] Another section
is assigned to the Levites (45.5; 48.13). Adjoining YHWH's holy territory is the city (45.6; 48.15-20), which is available to the entire house
of Israel. Two areas of land on the east and west of YHWH's holy
region are reserved for the prince (45.7-8). The significance of the
division of the land is threefold. First, YHWH is the ultimate owner
of the land; and thus, YHWH is the sole distributor of the land. Second, Ezekiel emphasizes that the temple and the land that surrounds
the temple are holy. References to the holiness of the temple and its
surrounding districts are exclusive to Ezekiel.[35] Third, the division of
the land serves to protect and maintain the indwelling of the holy
presence of YHWH among the people of Israel, underlining the theocentricity of the community.

The next section (45.8-46.24) calls for the just rule of the princes
(45.8-12), focuses on the liturgical and ministerial duties of the prince
(45.9-17, 22-25), outlines the regulations of festivals and sacrifices,
such as the purification of the sanctuary (45.18-20), the commemo-
ration of both the Passover (45.21-24) and the Feast of Tabernacles
(45.25),[36] records the sacrifices associated with the Sabbath and other
festivals, lists the requirements regarding the entrance and exit of the
prince and the people into the sanctuary (46.1-15), gives instructions
that control the management of the prince's land (46.16-18), and

---

[33] Tuell, *Law of the Temple*, p. 62, notes that 45.1-8 serve as an introduction to
the division of the land in 47.13-48.35.

[34] Block, *The Book of Ezekiel: Chapters 25-48*, p. 652; de Vries, *The Kābôd of
YHWH*, p. 320.

[35] Rimon Kasher, 'Anthropomorphism, Holiness, and Cult', pp. 201-202.

[36] See Kasher, 'Anthropomorphism, Holiness, and Cult'; Jacob Milgrom,
'Israel's Sanctuary: The Priestly "Picture of Dorian Gray"', *Revue Biblique* 83.3
(1976), pp. 390-99; and *idem*, 'Sin-Offering or Purification-Offering', *VT* 21.2
(1971), pp. 237-39; repr. in Jacob Milgrom, *Studies in Cultic Theology and Terminology*
(SJLA 36; Leiden: Brill, 1983), pp. 67-69.

shows the kitchen where the priests prepare the various offerings that are not allowed to be taken out to the outer court (46.19-24). Ezekiel 45.8-46.24 clearly highlights the provisions for the people of Israel to encounter the glory and holiness of YHWH through worship that reflects devotion, fear, and awe of YHWH.

YHWH's River

The man with the bronze appearance returns to the scene and leads Ezekiel back to the entryway of the temple (47.1). The reemergence of Ezekiel's guide leading the way for Ezekiel cues the beginning of a new literary division.[37] At the entrance of the temple, Ezekiel sees 'water flowing under the threshold of the house toward the east … down from the right side of the house, from south of the altar (47.1). Then, Ezekiel is led to 'the outer gate that faces east' (47.2), and there he sees 'the water trickling[38] out from the south side' (47.2). With a measuring line in his hand, the guide leads Ezekiel into the water. Ezekiel notices that each time the man measures the water, the water becomes increasingly deeper until eventually the water becomes 'waters for swimming, a river that no one could cross' (47.3-5), underscoring the increasing depth and powerful strength of the river.

The significance of the river soon becomes clear to Ezekiel and his hearers: the river will produce healing, life, fruitfulness, and food (47.8-13). Unable to cross the river, the guide leads Ezekiel back to the river's shore and directs Ezekiel's attention to the banks of the river, which is fringed by a diverse profusion of lush trees (46.6-7). The trees produce fresh fruit every month and their evergreen leaves possess healing virtues (47.12). The trees' abundance, fruitfulness, and healing properties are accredited to the fact that their source of water flows directly from the sanctuary (47.12).[39] The waters flowing out of the sanctuary also brought healing to the Dead Sea (47.8), giving life and effecting healing wherever its waters flowed (47.9). The threefold repetition of the word כל in v. 9 highlights the comprehensive and far-reaching healing power of the river: 'Every living creature that swarms wherever the river flows will live. There will be

---

[37] Block, *The Book of Ezekiel: Chapters 25-48*, p. 686; Bowen, *Ezekiel*, p. 261.

[38] Zimmerli, *Ezekiel 25-48*, pp. 511-12, accurately notes that the Hebrew word מפכה is a *hapax legomenon*, depicting the flow of water to be no greater than the flow of water that is poured out from the aperture of a small bottle/flask.

[39] The trees that Ezekiel sees are reminiscent of the Garden of Eden and appear to foreshadow John's vision in Rev. 22.12.

vast numbers of fish because these waters flow there. It will be healed because everything will live where the river flows' (47.9).[40]

The life-giving and healing river is a direct and necessary correlative of YHWH's glory and holiness, an essential outcome of the restoration of the people and the land. More specifically, the river may represent YHWH's רוח.[41] While there is not a direct link between the Spirit and the river in Ezekiel, there seems to be a firm indication that the river Ezekiel sees flowing out of the temple is a representation of YHWH's רוח. The strongest connections between the river and רוח are the healing and life-giving characteristics of the river.[42] In other parts of Ezekiel, YHWH's presence that brings about healing and life is expressed through YHWH's רוח. For example, in ch. 37, it is YHWH's רוח that brings life to the dry bones of Israel and restores them to their land. Moreover, Ezek. 39.29 makes a clear connection between water and רוח. The verb שפך ('pour out') is usually associated with water, but here it is used in reference to YHWH's Spirit: 'I will no longer hide my face from them, when I pour out my Spirit upon the house of Israel'. The allusion depicts YHWH pouring out 'my Spirit' as water is poured out from a vessel. Thus, the river flowing out of the temple may be another expression of the life-giving presence of YHWH, particularly YHWH's רוח.

The return of the glory of YHWH to the temple signifies the powerful presence of YHWH in the temple. The glory of YHWH is not confined to the temple but is flowing out of the temple to the entire world, confirming that the glory of YHWH is mobile. The river presents Ezekiel and his hearers with an extraordinary and fresh understanding of the glory and holiness of YHWH: the glory of YHWH is not simply an experience for the Israelites, but for the entire world. That is, YHWH is available to everyone who needs healing, life, and salvation. The river reminds Ezekiel and his hearers that that the return of the glory of YHWH to the temple and to the people of Israel does not mean an insular existence for YHWH. The meticulous preparation of YHWH's holy place is intended to allow YHWH's soteriological gifts of healing, life, and salvation to flow out

---

[40] Cf. Block, *The Book of Ezekiel: Chapters 25-48*, p. 694.

[41] I am indebted to Lee Roy Martin for bringing my attention to this significant connection between the river and YHWH's רוח.

[42] Cf. de Vries, 'The Relationship between the Glory of Yahweh and the Spirit of Yahweh in Ezekiel 33-48', p. 346.

of the temple,[43] emphasizing the world's (Israelites and non-Israel-ites) immediate access to YHWH's soteriological benefits associated with the glory and holiness of YHWH. The river, therefore, repre-sents the universal salvific mission of YHWH accomplished through the giving of the Spirit.

YHWH is There

The last few verses of the book of Ezekiel (48.30-35) redirect hear-ers' attention to the city that Ezekiel first saw in 40.2, forming an inclusio that frames this entire literary unit (chs. 40-48). Like the tem-ple, the measurements of the city form a square (48.16), [44] a shape that is associated with perfection and holiness in the book of Ezekiel. The city's twelve gates named after the twelve tribes of Israel are symmetrically located on the four sides of the city's square, with three gates on each side – north, east, south, and west (48.31-34). Identify-ing each gate that opens in all four directions suggest universal and unlimited access to the city.[45]

The book of Ezekiel closes with the name of the new city re-sounding in the ears of Ezekiel's hearers: יהוה שמה, 'YHWH is there' (48.35). These last two words of the book, יהוה שמה, convey several crucial and meaningful realities to Ezekiel's hearers. First, the name יהוה שמה signifies a full reversal of the exile. YHWH who had de-parted the temple and the city of Jerusalem has now returned to dwell among the people of Israel. As I argued in Chapter 4, the theme of the glory of YHWH provides a literary structure that unifies the en-tire book of Ezekiel. Thus, the name of the city clearly reflects that theme to the very end of the book: YHWH is there! Second, the name of the city indicates that this city is not the old city of Jerusalem rebuilt and brought up to the holiness code, but an utterly new city

---

[43] Cf. Zimmerli, *Ezekiel 25-48*, p. 516. See also, Denis R. McNamara, *Catholic Church Architecture and the Spirit of the Liturgy* (Chicago: Hillenbrand, 2009), pp. 72-77; Tuell, 'Divine Presence and Absence', pp. 111-16; Eichrodt, *Ezekiel*, pp. 584-85; and Anthony Kelly, *Eschatology and Hope* (MaryKnoll, NY: Orbis Books, 2006), p. 31.

[44] Duguid, *Ezekiel*, p. 546; Wright, *Message of Ezekiel*, p. 366.

[45] Block, *The Book of Ezekiel: Chapters 25-48*, pp. 738-39. Cf. John's vision of the new city in Rev. 21.12-21. See Thomas and Macchia, *Revelation*, p. 376; John Sweet, *Revelation* (London: SCM Press, 1990), p. 304; Stephen S. Smalley, *The Revelation to John* (Downers Grove, IL: InterVarsity Press, 2005), p. 548; and J.L. Resseguie, *The Revelation of John: A Narrative Commentary* (Grand Rapids: Baker Academic 2009), p. 254.

that has never been marred by the spiritual, moral, social, and political crimes of the people of Israel.[46] The fact that Ezekiel avoids calling the new city 'Jerusalem' or 'New Jerusalem' in the last nine chapters of the book reinforces the belief that the city that Ezekiel sees is not a reconstructed city. Third, the name of the city reveals that YHWH's return is not merely limited to the sacred precincts of the temple, but that YHWH's glory is immediate, present, and available to the people of Israel beyond the temple, even in the 'profane' or 'common' places where the people work and dwell (cf. 48.15). The book of Ezekiel ends with an incontrovertible assurance of the presence of the glory of YHWH: YHWH is there! While the term 'holy' is not explicit in this text, the very presence of YHWH at the end of the book evinces and demonstrates the holiness of YHWH.

Summary

Chapters 40-48 record the third and final vision of the glory of YHWH in the book of Ezekiel. Specifically, these chapters recount the long and awaited return of the glory of YHWH to the temple, the city, and the people of Israel. In Ezekiel's first vision of YHWH's glory (chs. 1-3), the link between the glory of YHWH and the holiness of YHWH is made clear by the image of the fiery cloud, the four living creatures, the grand throne-chariot, and the dazzling radiance of the image on the throne. If the glory of YHWH is 'holiness uncovered',[47] then Ezekiel's inaugural vision is a gradual unveiling of the holiness of YHWH. In the second vision of YHWH's glory (chs. 8-11), the direct connection between the glory of YHWH and the holiness of YHWH is depicted in terms of YHWH's departure from the temple and the city of Jerusalem. Israel's spiritual apostasy, ethical violations, and political malfeasance cause YHWH to leave Israel. Thus, the absence of the glory of YHWH is the absence of holiness in Israel.[48]

In Ezekiel's third vision of the glory of YHWH (chs. 40-49), the interrelationship between the glory of YHWH and the holiness of YHWH is made explicit by YHWH's return to a holy temple, land,

---

[46] Cf. Wright, *Message of Ezekiel*, p. 368.

[47] Edmond Jacob, *Theology of the Old Testament* (trans. Arthur W. Heathcote and Phillip J. Alcock; London: Hodder & Stoughtoon, 1958), pp. 79-80.

[48] Cf. Wells, *God's Holy People*, p. 163.

and city (cf. 43.12; 45.1; 48.35). To ensure the indwelling of YHWH among the people of Israel, prominence is given to regulations concerning Israel's worship and directives for guarding YHWH's holy things (cf. 44.8). Finally, my seeing and hearing of the three visions of the glory of YHWH clearly reveal that the blessings associated with the holy presence of YHWH are not limited to the temple, land, city, and people of Israel. Indeed, the holy splendor of YHWH is immediate, near, and universal.

8

CONCLUSIONS AND IMPLICATIONS

Summarizing this Study

The goal of this study was to present a literary and theological study of the interrelationship between the glory and holiness of YHWH in the book of Ezekiel from a Pentecostal context. To achieve this goal, this study focused on the vision-narratives that describe the glory of YHWH (chs. 1-3, 8-11, and 40-48) and employed a critically informed Pentecostal hermeneutical strategy of seeing and hearing the book of Ezekiel.

My survey of previous scholarship has demonstrated that published materials have not fully explored the relationship between the glory of YHWH and the holiness of YHWH in Ezekiel. Academic studies have either treated the themes of YHWH's glory and YHWH's holiness almost autonomously or have portrayed the motif of YHWH's glory as an incidental corollary to YHWH's holy name. While there are several publications on either the glory of YHWH or the holiness of YHWH, to this date, there is no monograph that is exclusively dedicated to the correlative relationship between the glory of YHWH and the holiness of YHWH; and there is no published work on Ezekiel that addresses the specific beliefs and practices of the Pentecostal community. Thus, there still remains a demand and opportunity for a fresh approach to the book of Ezekiel.

After justifying the need for this research in the first chapter, Chapter 2 provided a brief survey of the significant critical approaches to the book of Ezekiel. The overview revealed a paradigm shift from the traditional historical-critical methods to the literary/rhetorical studies in the book of Ezekiel. The effect of this shift in methodology not only shows that my narrative approach to the book of Ezekiel stands with the prevailing scholarly approach to the book of Ezekiel, but it also allows Pentecostal scholars, like myself, to forge a hermeneutical strategy that is both critically evaluated and in accordance with the ethos of the Pentecostal community.

Once I established the legitimacy of my synchronic approach to the book of Ezekiel, I set out in Chapter 3 to develop an appropriate Pentecostal hermeneutical strategy for the book of Ezekiel. My interpretive approach of *seeing* and *hearing* the message of Ezekiel builds upon Lee Roy Martin's concept of *hearing* the word of YHWH, a suitable theological term that resonates deeply and powerfully with the Pentecostal community. I argued that since Ezekiel's message places emphasis on seeing and hearing the word of YHWH, then the hearers of this message must be willing to see and hear the prophecy of Ezekiel. Neglecting to see and hear the word of YHWH precludes seeing, hearing, and encountering YHWH. A failure to see and hear YHWH results in rebellion against YHWH (cf. Ezek. 12.2). Thus, the themes of *seeing* and *hearing* serve as a suitable biblical model for a Pentecostal approach to Ezekiel.

After I presented the book's literary structure, a brief overview of the book, and Ezekiel's major theological themes in the fourth chapter, Chapters 5 through 7 aimed to apply *seeing* and *hearing* to the book of Ezekiel. My *seeing* and *hearing* of the book of Ezekiel has revealed an interrelationship between the glory of YHWH and the holiness of YHWH. The effect of this interrelationship is a unique theological description of YHWH.

I have shown that the visions of YHWH's glory (chs. 1-3, 8-11, and 40-48) reveal a direct connection between the glory and holiness of YHWH in the book of Ezekiel. From the very beginning of the book, hearers see a grand unveiling of YHWH's holiness, and these themes continue to weave together to the very end of the book of Ezekiel. Therefore, any work or discussion on Ezekiel that precludes a clear correlation between the glory of YHWH and the holiness of YHWH or treats the glory of YHWH as peripheral to the holiness of YHWH, forms an incomplete characterization of YHWH. YHWH is not only majestic, and holy; YHWH is gloriously holy.

Thus, from the book of Ezekiel we can conclude that (1) the presence and absence of YHWH is the presence and absence of YHWH's holiness; (2) an encounter with the glory of YHWH is an encounter with the holiness of YHWH; (3) the glory and holiness of YHWH depict the sovereignty and power of YHWH; (4) experiencing the glory and holiness of YHWH requires seeing and hearing the word of YHWH; (5) the Spirit of YHWH gives access to YHWH's holy presence; (6) disregarding the holiness of YHWH and the holy things of YHWH is a willful breach of the glorious presence of YHWH; (7) YHWH will depart when we violate YHWH's holy splendor; (8) YHWH manifests his glory and holiness in his judgment of us; (9) YHWH demonstrates his glory and holiness in his salvation and love for us; and (10) YHWH's holy presence is immediate, near, and universal.

Glory, Holiness, and the Pentecostal Community

The themes of glory and holiness are of paramount significance to the Pentecostal community of faith. Pentecostals persistently emphasize a deep longing to encounter God's glory and pursuit of holiness. Like Moses, we individually and corporately yearn for God to 'show me/us your glory' (cf. Exod. 33.18). Pentecostals believe that an encounter with the glory and holiness of YHWH will 'alter and renarrate'[1] present realities. This aspiration to see God's holy presence finds expression in our prayers, songs, and sermons. Indeed, our entire church gathering revolves around encountering the glory of God. Not only do we desire God's presence, but we desperately long for the indwelling of God.[2] Accordingly, Pentecostals understand that in order for a holy God to dwell with us, we must be holy, because a holy God will not coexist with sinful people. Thus, Psalm 51 becomes

---

[1] Daniel Castelo, *Pentecostalism as a Christian Mystical Tradition* (Grand Rapids, MI: Eerdmans Publishing Co., 2017), p. 81.

[2] See R. Jerome Boone, 'Community and Worship: The Key Components of Pentecostal Christian Formation', *JPT* 8 (1996), pp. 129-42; Daniel Castelo, 'Tarrying on the Lord: Affections, Virtues, and Theological Ethics in Pentecostal Perspective', *JPT* 13.1 (2004), pp. 31-56; Cecil M. Robeck, Jr., 'The Nature of Pentecostal Spirituality', *Pneuma* 14.2 (1992), pp. 103-106; and Veli-Matti Kärkkäinen, '"Encountering Christ in the Full Gospel Way": An Incarnational Pentecostal Spirituality', *JEPTA* 27.1 (2007), pp. 9-23, who describes Pentecostal worship as 'the longing for meeting with the Lord', pp. 17-20.

the paradigmatic prayer of repentance for Pentecostals. We frequently cry, 'Create within me a clean heart, O God! Renew a right/resolute spirit within me' (Ps. 51.10).

Moreover, like Ezekiel, Pentecostals affirm that an authentic encounter with God results in genuine worship. It is necessary, however, for the Pentecostal community of faith to guard against a presumptuous, complacent, and tepid attitude towards the presence of God. God's holy presence should effect staggering terror and reverential respect in the minds and hearts of every Pentecostal worshiper. The integrity of our Pentecostal worship must be rooted in an awesome and trembling fear of God.

Since Pentecostalism has its roots in the nineteenth-century holiness movement,[3] holiness is a fundamental trait of Pentecostals.[4] Yet, Pentecostals struggle to define the term holiness. For many Pentecostals, holiness is still associated with the strict observance of precise moral conventions that govern the individual behavior and dress. My study, therefore, benefits the Pentecostal community by redirecting legalistic views of holiness to an understanding of holiness that is in relation to God. If we are to be holy as God is holy, then our pursuit of holiness must begin with the holiness of God. Since God is holy, God is the source of all holiness. Only God can cleanse us, sanctify us, and make us holy. As I explained in Chapter 4, holiness is the fundamental, distinguishing, unique, and unchangeable nature of YHWH. That is to say, holiness is YHWH's 'DNA'. YHWH exists, functions, and acts as holy. Thus, a holy people are people who are transformed into the image and likeness of a holy God. Holiness, therefore, is the unchangeable nature, the divine DNA of the church. Accordingly, we must exist, function, and act as God's holy people.

From the foregoing discussion, it is clear that Ezekiel's themes of the glory of YHWH and the holiness of YHWH intersect with the goals of Pentecostal spirituality, making the message of Ezekiel relevant for the Pentecostal community.

---

[3] Donald W. Dayton, *Theological Roots of Pentecostalism* (Studies in Evangelicalism; Metuchen, NJ: Scarecrow Press, 1987), p. 16.
[4] Lee Roy Martin, *A Future for Holiness: Pentecostal Explorations* (Cleveland, TN: CPT Press, 2013), p. 1.

Contributions of this Study

This study makes several significant contributions to the Old Testament scholarship on the book of Ezekiel. First, my research offers the most comprehensive narrative study of the direct relationship between the glory and holiness of YHWH in the book of Ezekiel to date. While there is ample research on the glory of YHWH and the holiness of YHWH in the book of Ezekiel, previous academic studies have either investigated each theme independently of each other or have treated the subject of YHWH's glory as a postscript to the holiness of YHWH.

Second, this monograph is the first study to present a critically informed Pentecostal hermeneutical strategy of 'seeing' and 'hearing' the book of Ezekiel. This has implications for worship, and suggests the possible benefits of engaging the Eastern Orthodox tradition, which emphasizes the visual aspect of worship and recognizes not only preaching through words, but also the aesthetics of worship.

Third, my research is the first to construct the literary structure of the book of Ezekiel around the three sequential visions of the glory of YHWH.

Fourth, this work is the first detailed monograph-length academic analysis of the book of Ezekiel to be presented from a Pentecostal perspective. As such, it is the first study to construct a Pentecostal theology of the glory and holiness of YHWH from the book of Ezekiel, encouraging contemporary Pentecostals to see and hear afresh the text of Ezekiel.

Suggestions for Future Explorations

The preceding conclusions and contributions highlight several areas of study for future research. First, apart from the themes of YHWH's glory and holiness, it would be interesting to see what new insights could be discerned by applying all five senses to the book of Ezekiel.

Second, in order to demonstrate the usefulness of my Pentecostal hermeneutical strategy, it might be profitable to apply this paradigm of 'seeing' and 'hearing' to other biblical texts.

Third, the book of Ezekiel reveals that true worship comes from a direct encounter with the glory and holiness of YHWH. Thus, I hope to explore further the sensory nature of biblical worship.

Fourth, the cornucopia of Ezekiel's theology has not been fully explored by Pentecostals, an exploration that would inevitably make the book of Ezekiel more relevant to the life and mission of the Pentecostal community of faith.

BIBLIOGRAPHY

Early Pentecostal Periodicals

The Bridegroom's Messenger (Atlanta, GA).
The Church of God Evangel (Cleveland, TN).
The Latter Rain Evangel (Chicago, IL).
The Pentecostal Evangel (St. Louis, MO).
The Pentecostal Herald (Chicago, IL).

OTHER WORKS CITED

Abrams, M.H., *A Glossary of Literary Terms* (Fort Worth: Harcourt Brace College Publishers, 7th edn, 1999).

Alexander, Kimberly E., *Pentecostal Healing Models in Theology and Practice* (JPTSup 29; Blandford Forum, UK: Deo Publishing, 2006).

Allen, Leslie C., 'The Structure and Intention of Ezekiel I', *VT* 43.2 (1993), pp. 145-51.

—*Ezekiel 1-19* (WBC 28; Dallas: Word, 1994).

Alter, Robert, *The Art of Biblical Narrative* (New York: Basic Books, 1981).

Archer, Kenneth, *A Pentecostal Hermeneutic for the Twenty-First Century: Spirit, Scripture and Community* (JPTSup 28; New York: T&T Clark International, 2004).

Archer, Melissa L., *'I Was in the Spirit on the Lord's Day': A Pentecostal Engagement with Worship in the Apocalypse* (Cleveland, TN: CPT Press, 2014).

Arrington, French L., 'Historical Perspectives on Pentecostal and Charismatic Hermeneutics', in S.M. Burgess and G.B. McGee (eds.), *Dictionary of Pentecostal and Charismatic Movements* (Grand Rapids: Regency Reference Library/Zondervan, 1988), pp. 376-89.

—*Encountering the Holy Spirit: Paths of Christian Growth and Service* (Cleveland, TN: Pathway Press, 2003).

Aune, David, *The Westminster Dictionary of New Testament and Early Christian Literature and Rhetoric* (Louisville: Westminster John Knox, 2003), pp. 315-17.

Auvray, Paul, *Ezéchiel. Sainte Bible/Traduite En Français Sous La Direction De L'ecole Biblique De Jérusalem* (Paris: Cerf, 1949).

Baker, Robert O., 'Pentecostal Bible Reading: Toward a Model of Reading for the Formation of the Affections', *JPT* 7 (1995), pp. 30-38.

Bal, Mieke, *Narratology: Introduction to the Theory of Narrative* (Toronto: University of Toronto Press, 1985).

Bar-Efrat, Shimon, *Narrative Art in the Bible* (Bible and Literature Series 17; Sheffield: Almond, 1989).

Barton, Stephen C., *Holiness Past and Present* (London/New York: T&T Clark, 2003).

Baumgärtel, Friedrich, 'Die Formel Ne'um Jahwe', *ZAW* 73 (1961), pp. 277-90.

Bechtel, Christopher R., 'Ezekiel and the Politics of Yahweh: A Study in the Kingship of God' (PhD thesis; University of Edinburgh, 2011).

Becker, Joachim, 'Erwägungen zur Ezechielischen Frage', in Lothar Ruppert *et al.* (eds.), *Künder des Wortes* (Würzburg: Echter, 1982), pp. 137-49.

Behrens, Achim, *Prophetische Visionsschilderungen im Alten Testament: sprachliche Eigenarten, Funktion und Geschichte einer Gattung* (AOAT; Münster, Germany: Ugarit-Verlag, 2002).

Berlin, Adele, 'Characterization in Biblical Narrative: David's Wives', *JSOT* 23 (1982), pp. 69-85.

Bernhardt, K.H., 'אָוֶן', in G.J. Botterweck and H. Ringgren (eds.), *TDOT* (Grand Rapids, MI: Eerdmans, 1974), I, pp. 140-48.

Berry, George Ricker, 'The Authorship of Ezekiel 40-48', *JBL* 34.1/4 (1915), pp. 17-40.

—'Was Ezekiel in the Exile?', *JBL 49* (1930), pp. 83-93.

—'The Title of Ezekiel (1.1-3)', *JBL* 52 (1932), pp. 54-57.

—'The Glory of Yahweh and the Temple', *JBL* 56 (1937), pp. 115-17.

Blenkinsopp, Joseph, 'Structure and Style in Judges 13-16', *JBL* 82 (1963), pp. 65-76.

—*Ezekiel* (IBC; Louisville: John Knox Press, 1990).

Block, Daniel, *The Book of Ezekiel Chapters 1-24* (NICOT; Grand Rapids, MI: Eerdmans, 1997).

—'"Israel" – "Sons of Israel": A Study in Hebrew Eponymic Usage', *SR* 13 (1984), pp. 301-26.

—'Text and Emotion: A Study in the "Corruptions" in Ezekiel's Inaugural Vision (Ezekiel 1:4-28)', *CBQ* 50 (1988), pp. 418-42.

—'The Prophet of the Spirit: The Use of RWḤ in the Book of Ezekiel', *JETS* 32 (1989), pp. 27-49.

—*The Book of Ezekiel: Chapters 1-24* (NICOT; Grand Rapids: Eerdmans, 1998).

—*The Book of Ezekiel: Chapters 25-48* (NICOT; Grand Rapids: Eerdmans, 1998).

—'Divine Abandonment: Ezekiel's Adaptation of an Ancient near Eastern Motif', in Margaret S. Odell and John T. Strong (eds.), *The Book of Ezekiel: Theological and Anthropological Perspectives* (SBLSymS 9; Atlanta: SBL, 2000), pp.15-42.

—*Deuteronomy: From Biblical Text ... To Contemporary Life* (The NIV Application Commentary; Grand Rapids, MI: Zondervan, 2012).

Bloome, Edward C., 'Ezekiel's Abnormal Personality', *JBL* 65 (1946), pp. 277-92.

Boadt, Lawrence, 'Textual Analysis in Ezekiel and Poetic Analysis of Paired Words', *JBL* 97 (1978), pp. 489-99.

—'Rhetorical Strategies in Ezekiel's Oracles of Judgment', in Johan Lust (ed.), *Ezekiel and His Book: Textual and Literary Criticism and Their Interrelation* (BETL, 74; Leuven: Leuven University Press, 1986), pp. 182-200.

—'The Function of the Salvation Oracles in Ezekiel 33-37', *HAR* 12 (1990), pp. 1-21.

—'A New Look at the Book of Ezekiel', *TBT* 37 (1994), pp. 4-9.

—'Mythological Themes and the Unity of Ezekiel', in L.J. Regt *et al.* (eds.), *Literary Sructure and Rhetorical Strategies in the Hebrew Bible* (Winona Lake, IN: Eisenbrauns, 1996).

Bodi, Daniel, *The Book of Ezekiel and the Poem of Erra* (OBO 104; Freiburg: Universitatsverlag, 1991).

Boone, R. Jerome, 'Community and Worship: The Key Components of Pentecostal Christian Formation', *JPT* 8 (1996), pp. 129-42.

Born, Adrianus van den, 'Ezechiel-Pseudo-Epigraaf?', *StC 28* (1953), pp. 94-104.

Bosch, D.J., *Transforming Mission: Paradigm Shifts in the Theology of Mission* (Maryknoll: Orbis, 1991).

Bowen, Nancy R., *Ezekiel* (AOTC; Nashville, TN: Abingdon Press, 2010).

Bron, B., 'Zur Psychopathologie und Verkündigung des Propheten Ezechiel: Zum Phänomen der Prophetischen Ekstase', *Schwiezer Archiv für Neurologie, Neurochirugie und Psychiatrie* 128 (1981), pp. 21-31.

Broome, E.C., 'Ezekiel's Abnormal Personality', *JBL* 65 (1946), pp. 277-92.

Cheryl Bridges Johns, *Pentecostal Formation: A Pedagogy among the Oppressed* (JPTSup 2; Sheffield: Sheffield Academic Press, 1993).

Brown, Francis, *et al.*, *The New Brown, Driver, Briggs, Gesenius Hebrew and English Lexicon: With an Appendix Containing the Biblical Aramaic* (trans. Edward Robinson; Peabody, MA: Hendrickson, 1979).

Browne, Laurence E., *Ezekiel and Alexander* (London: S.P.C.K., 1952).

Brownlee, William H., *Ezekiel 1-19* (WBC; Waco, TX: Word Books, 1986).

—'Ezekiel', in *ISBE* (Reprinted as the introduction to his commentary; Grand Rapids, MI: Eerdmans, 1982).

Brueggemann, Walter, *Interpretation and Obedience: From Faithful Reading to Faithful Living* (Minneapolis, MN: Fortress Press, 1989).

—*Theology of the Old Testament: Testimony, Dispute, Advocacy* (Minneapolis: Fortress, 1997).

—*Texts That Linger, Words That Explode* (Minneapolis: Fortress Press, 2000).

—*An Introduction to the Old Testament: The Canon and Christian Imagination* (Louisville, KY: John Knox Press, 2003).

Bunn, John T., 'Ezekiel', in *The Broadman Bible Commentary* (Nashville, TN: Broadman Press, 1971), p. 6.

Cargal, Timothy B., 'Beyond the Fundamentalist-Modernist Controversy: Pentecostals and Hermeneutics in the Post-Modern Age', *Pneuma* 15.2 (1993), pp. 163-87.

Cartledge, M.J., 'Text-Community-Spirit: The Challenges Posed by Pentecostal Theological Method to Evangelical Theology', in Kevin L. Spawn and Archie T. Wright (eds.), *Spirit and Scripture: Exploring a Pneumatic Hermeneutic* (London: London: Bloomsbury T&T Clark, 2012), pp. 130-42.

Castelo, Daniel, *Pentecostalism as a Christian Mystical Tradition* (Grand Rapids, MI: Eerdmans Publishing Co., 2017).

—'Tarrying on the Lord: Affections, Virtues, and Theological Ethics in Pentecostal Perspective', *JPT* 13.1 (2004), pp. 31-56.

Chan, Simon, *Pentecostal Theology and the Christian Spiritual Tradition* (JPTSup 21; London: Sheffield Academic Press, 2003).

Chatman, Seymour, *Story and Discourse: Narrative Structure in Fiction and Film* (New York: Cornell University Press, 1980).

Hill, Jim, and Rand Cheadle, *The Bible Tells Me So: Uses and Abuses of Holy Scripture* (New York: Anchor Books/Doubleday, 1996).

Childs, Brevard, 'The Canonical Shape of the Prophetic Literature', *Interpretation* 32 (1978), pp. 46-55.

—*Introduction to the Old Testament as Scripture* (Philadelphia: Fortress, 1979).

—*Biblical Theology of the Old and New Testaments* (Minneapolis: Augsburg Fortress, 1993).

Clark, Matthew S., 'An Investigation into the Nature of a Viable Pentecostal Hermeneutic' (DTh thesis, University of South Africa, 1996).

Collins, Terence, *The Mantle of Elijah: The Redactional Criticism of the Prophetical Books* (The Biblical Seminar, 20; Sheffield: JSOT Press, 1993).

Conrad, Edgar W., *Reading the Latter Prophets: Toward a New Canonical Criticism* (JSOTSup 376; New York: T & T Clark International, 2003).

Cooke, G.A., 'Review of G. Hölscher, *Hesekiel: Der Dichter und das Buch*', *JTS* 27 (1925), pp. 201-203.

—*A Critical and Exegetical Commentary on the Book of Ezekiel* (ICC; Edinburgh: T&T Clark, 1936).

Cooper, Lamar Eugene, *Ezekiel: An Exegetical and Theological Exposition of Holy Scripture* (The New American Commentary; Nashville, TN: B&H Publishing Group, 1994).

Coulter, Dale M., 'What Meaneth This? Pentecostals and Theological Inquiry', *JPT* 10.1 (2001), pp. 38-64.

Craigie, Peter C., *Ezekiel* (Philadelphia: The Westminster Press, 1983).

Crenshaw, James L., *Story and Faith: A Guide to the Old Testament* (New York: Macmillan, 1986).

Culver, Robert D., 'ראה', in R.L. Harris, G.L. Archer, and B.K. Waltke (eds.), *TWOT* (2 vols.; Chicago: Moody Press, 1980), II, p. 823.

Darr, Katheryn Pfisterer, 'Ezekiel among the Critics', *CR:BS* 2 (1994), pp. 9-24.

—'The Book of Ezekiel: Introduction, Commentary, and Reflections', in Leander E. Keck, *et al.* (eds.), *The New Interpreter's Bible: A Commentary in Twelve Volumes* (Nashville: Abingdon Press, 2001), VI, pp. 1073-607.

Davies, Andrew, 'What Does It Mean to Read the Bible as a Pentecostal?', in Lee Roy Martin (ed.), *Pentecostal Hermeneutics: A Reader* (London/Boston: Brill, 2013), pp. 248-62.

Davis, Ellen F., *Swallowing the Scroll: Textuality and the Dynamics of Discourse in Ezekiel's Prophecy* (Bible and Literature Series 21; Sheffield: Almond Press, 1989).

—'Swallowing Hard: Reflections on Ezekiel's Dumbness', in J.C. Exum (ed.), *Signs and Wonders: Biblical Texts in Literary Focus* (Atlanta: Scholars Press, 1989), pp. 217-37.

Dayton, Donald W., *Theological Roots of Pentecostalism* (Studies in Evangelicalism; Metuchen, NJ: Scarecrow Press, 1987).

de Vries, Pieter, 'Ezekiel: Prophet of the Name and Glory of YHWH – the Character of His Book and Several of Its Main Themes', *JBPR* 4 (2012), pp. 94-108.

—'The Relationship between the Glory of Yahweh and the Spirit of Yahweh in Ezekiel 33-48', *OTE* 28.2 (2015), pp. 326-50.

—*The Kābôd of YHWH in the Old Testament: With Particular Reference to the Book of Ezekiel* (trans. Alexander Thomson; Leiden: Koninklijke Brill, 2016).

Delcor, M., and E. Jenni, 'שׁלה', in E. Jenni and C. Westermann (eds.), *THAT* (2 vols.; Munich: Kaiser, 1976), II, pp. 909-16.

Dempster, S.G., 'Canon, Canonization', in Mark J. Boda and J. Gordon McConville (eds.), *Dictionary of the Old Testament Prophets: A Compendium of Contemporary Biblical Scholarship* (Downers Grove, IL: InterVarsity Press, 2012), pp. 71-77.

Diringer, David, *The Alphabet: A Key to the History of Mankind* (2 vols.; New York: Funk & Wagnalls, 3rd edn, 1968).

Driver, G.R., *Aramaic Documents of the Fifth Century B.C.* (Oxford: Clarendon, 1954).

—*Canaanite Myths and Legends* (Edinburgh: T&T Clark, 1956).

Driver, S.R., *Introduction to the Literature of the Old Testament* (New York: Scribner, 1913).

Duguid, Iain M., *Ezekiel and the Leaders of Israel* (VTSup 56; Leiden: Brill, 1994).

—*Ezekiel* (Grand Rapids: Zondervan, 1999).

Eichrodt, Walther, *Ezekiel* (trans. Cosslett Quin; OTL; Philadelphia: Westminster, 1970).

Ellington, Scott A., 'Pentecostalism and the Authority of Scripture', in Lee Roy Martin (ed.), *Pentecostal Hermeneutics: A Reader* (Leiden/Boston: Brill, 2013), pp. 149-70.

Ervin, Howard M., 'Hermeneutics: A Pentecostal Option', *Pneuma* 3.1 (1981), pp. 11-25.

Even-Shoshan, Abraham, *A New Concordance of the Old Testament: Using the Hebrew and Aramaic Text* (Jerusalem: Kiryat-Sefer, 2nd edn, 1989).

Ewald, H., *Commentary on the Prophets of the Old Testament* (London: William & Norgate, 1880).

Feinberg, C.L., *The Prophecy of Ezekiel: The Glory of the Lord* (Chicago: Moody, 1969).

Feist, Udo, *Ezechiel. Das literarische Problem des Buches forschungsgeschichtlich betrachtet* (BWANT, 138; Stuttgart: Kohlhammer, 1995).

Fisch, S., *Ezekiel* (London: Soncino, 1950).

Fishbane, Michael, *Text and Texture: Close Readings of Selected Biblical Texts* (New York: Schocken Books 1979).

Floyd, M.H., 'Prophecy and Writing in Habakkuk 2,1-5', *ZAW* 105 (1993), pp. 462-81.

Fohrer, Georg, *Die Hauptprobleme des Buches Ezechiel* (BZAW 72; Berlin: Töplemann, 1952).

Fokkelman, J.P., *Reading Biblical Narrative: An Introductory Guide* (Louisville, KY: Westminster John Knox Press, 1999).

Fox, Michael V., 'The Rhetoric of Ezekiel's Vision of the Valley of the Bones', in R.P. Gordon (ed.), *'The Place Is Too Small for Us': The Israelite Prophets in Recent Scholarship* (Winona Lake: Eisenbrauns, 1995), pp. 176-90.

Freedman, David Noel, 'The Book of Ezekiel', *Int* 8 (1954), pp. 446-71.

Freehof, Solomon B., *Book of Ezekiel: A Commentary* (Jewish Commentary for Bible Readers; New York: Union of American Hebrew Congregations, 1978).

Frendenburg, Brandon, *Ezekiel* (The College Press NIV Commentary; Joplin, MO: College Press Publishing Company, 1966).

Fuhs, Hans F., *Ezechiel 1-24* (NEchtB; Würzburg: Echter, 1986).

—'ראה', in J.G. Botterweck, H. Ringgren, and H.-J. Fabry (eds.), *TDOT* (15 vols.; Grand Rapids, MI: Eerdmans, 2004), XIII, pp. 208-42.

Gaebelein, A.C., *The Prophet Ezekiel: An Analytical Exposition* (New York: Our Hope, 1918).

—'Ezekiel', in John Barton and John Muddiman (eds.), *The Oxford Bible Commentary* (New York: Oxford University Press, 2001), pp. 533-62.

Galambush, Julie, *Jerusalem in the Book of Ezekiel: The City as Yahweh's Wife* (Atlanta: Scholars Press, 1992).

Gammie, John G., *Holiness in Israel: Overtures to Biblical Theology* (Minneapolis: Augsburg Fortress Press, 1989).

Ganzel, Tova, 'Transformation of Pentateuchal Descriptions of Idolatry', in William A. Tooman and Michael A. Lyons (eds.), *Transforming Visions: Transformations of Text, Tradition, and Theology in Ezekiel* (Eugene, OR: Pickwick Publications, 2010), pp. 33-49.

Garber, David G., 'Traumatizing Ezekiel, the Exilic Prophet', in J. Harold Ellens and Wayne G. Rollins (eds.), *Psychology and the Bible: From Genesis to Apocalyptic Vision* (Westport, CT: Praeger, 2004), pp. 215-36.

Garscha, Jörg, *Studien zum Ezechielbuch: Eine redaktionskritische Untersuchung von Ez 1-39* (EHS, 23; Frankfurt: Peter Lang, 1974).

Gesenius, H.F.W., *Gesenius' Hebrew Grammar* (trans. A.E. Cowley; New York: Oxford University Press, 1910).

Goldingay, John, 'The Breath of Yahweh Scorching, Confounding, Anointing: The Message of Isaiah 40-42', *JPT* 11 (1997), pp. 3-34.

—*Old Testament Theology: Israel's Faith* (Downers Grove, IL: InterVarsity Press, 2006).

Gray, G.B., *A Critical Introduction to the Old Testament* (London: Duckworth, 1913).

Green, C.E.W., *Toward a Pentecostal Theology of the Lord's Supper: Foretasting the Kingdom* (Cleveland, TN: CPT Press, 2012).

Greenberg, Moshe, 'The Vision of Jerusalem in Ezekiel 8-11: A Holistic Interpretation', in J.L. Crenshaw and S. Sandmel (eds.), *The Divine Helmsman: Studies on God's Control of Human Events* (New York: KTAV, 1980), pp. 143-64.

—'Ezekiel's Vision: Literary and Iconographic Aspects', in Hayim Tadmor and Moshe Weinfeld (eds.), *History, Historiography and Interpretation: Studies in Biblical and Cuneiform Literatures* (Leiden: Brill, 1983), pp. 159-68.

—*Ezekiel 1-20: A New Translation with Introduction and Commentary* (AB; New York: Doubleday, 1983).

—'The Design and Themes of Ezekiel's Program and Restoration', *Int* 38 (1984), pp. 181-208.

—'What Are Valid Criteria for Determining Inauthentic Matter in Ezekiel?', in Johan Lust (ed.), *Ezekiel and His Book: Textual and Literary Criticism and Their Interrelation* (BETL, 74; Leuven: Leuven University Press, 1986), pp. 123-35.

—*Ezekiel 21-37: A New Translation and Commentary* (AB; New York: Doubleday, 1997).

Gros Louis, Kenneth R.R., James Stokes Ackerman, and Thayer S. Warshaw, *Literary Interpretations of Biblical Narratives* (2 vols.; Nashville: Abingdon, 1974-1982).

Gunkel, Hermann, 'Die Israelitische Literatur', in P. Hinneberg (ed.), *Die Kultur der Gegenwart* (Berlin & Leipzig: B.G. Teubner, 1906).

—*Die Propheten* (Göttingen: Vandenhoeck & Ruprecht, 1917).

Gunn, David and Danna Nolan Fewell, *Narrative in the Hebrew Bible* (Oxford: Oxford University Press, 1993).

Gurney, O.R., 'Tammuz Reconsidered: Some Recent Developments', *JSS* 7 (1962), pp. 156-77.

Halperin, David J., *Seeking Ezekiel: Text and Psychology* (University Park, PA: Pennsylvania State University Press, 1993).

Hals, Ronald M., *Ezekiel* (FOTL, 19; Grand Rapids: Eerdmans, 1989).

Hamilton, James M., *God's Glory in Salvation through Judgment: A Biblical Theology* (Wheaton, IL: Crossway, 2010).

Hänel, Johannes, *Die Religion der Heiligkeit* (Gütersloh: Der Rufer, 1931).

Harmon, William, and C. Hugh Holman, *A Handbook to Literature* (Upper Saddle River: Prentice Hall, 8th edn, 1999).

Heller, Roy L., *Narrative Structure and Discourse Constellations: An Analysis of Clause Function in Hebrew Prose* (Winona Lake, IN: Eisenbrauns, 2004).

—'Hebrew Language', in Bill T. Arnold and H.G.M. Williamson (eds.), *Dictionary of the Old Testament Historical Books: A Compendium of Contemporary Biblical Scholarship* (Downers Grove, IL: Intervarsity Press, 2005), pp. 380-86.

Herntrich, Volkmar, *Ezechielprobleme* (BZAW 61; Giessen: Töpelmann, 1932).

Herrmann, J, *Ezechielstudien* (BWANT, 2; Leipzig: J.C. Hinrich, 1908).

Heschel, Abraham J., *The Prophets* (New York: Harper & Row, 1962).

Hiebel, Janina Maria, *Ezekiel's Vision Accounts as Interrelated Narratives: A Redaction-Critical and Theological Study* (Berlin/Boston: Walter de Gruyter, 2015).

Hildebrandt, Wilf, *An Old Testament Theology of the Spirit of God* (Peabody, MA: Hendrickson Publishers, 1995).

Holladay, William L., *A Concise Hebrew and Aramaic Lexicon of the Old Testament* (Grand Rapids, MI: Eerdmans, corrected 10th edn, 1988).

Hollenweger, W.J., *The Pentecostals* (Peabody, MA: Hendrickson, 1988).

—*Pentecostalism: Origins and Developments Worldwide* (Peabody, MA: Hendrickson Publishers, 1997).

Hölscher, G., *Hesekiel, Der Dichter und das Buch* (BZAW 39; Giessen: Töpelmann, 1924).

Horton, Stanley M., *What the Bible Says About the Holy Spirit* (Springfield, MO: Gospel Publishing House, 1986).

Hossfeld, Frank-Lothar, 'Die Tempelvision Ez 8-11 im Licht unterschiedlicher methodischer Zugänge', in Johan Lust (ed.), *Ezekiel and His Book: Textual and Literary Criticism and Their Interrelation* (BETL 74; Leuven: Leuven University Press, 1986), pp. 151-65.

—*Untersuchungen zur Kompositon und Theologie des Ezechielbuches* (Würzburg: Echter, 1977).

Hossfeld, Frank-Lothar, and Erich Zenger, *Die Psalmen I, Psalm 1-50* (NEchtB; Würzburg: Echter Verlag, 1993).

Houk, C.B., 'The Final Redaction of Ezekiel 10', *JBL* 90 (1971), pp. 42-54.

Howie, C.G., *The Date and Composition of Ezekiel* (JBL Monograph Series 4; Philadelphia: SBL Press, 1950).

Hunter, H.D., *Spirit Baptism: A Pentecostal Alternative* (Lanham, MD: University Press of America, 1983).

Israel, Richard D., Daniel E. Albrecht, and Randall G. McNally, 'Pentecostals and Hermeneutics: Texts, Rituals and Community', *Pneuma* 15.1 (1993), pp. 137-61.

Jacob, Edmond, *Theology of the Old Testament* (trans. Arthur W. Heathcote and Phillip J. Alcock; London: Hodder & Stoughton, 1958).

Jacobsen, Thorkild, 'Toward the Image of Tammuz', in W.L. Moran (ed.), *Toward the Image of Tammuz and Other Essays* (Cambridge, MA: Harvard University Press, 1970), pp. 73-103.

Jenson, P., *Graded Holiness: A Key to the Priestly Conception of the World* (Sheffield: JSOT Press, 1992).

Johns, Cheryl Bridges, *Pentecostal Formation: A Pedagogy among the Oppressed* (JPTSup 2; Sheffield: Sheffield Academic Press, 1993).

Johns, Jackie David, 'Pentecostalism and the Postmodern Worldview', *JPT* 7 (1995), pp. 73-96.

Johns, Jackie David and Cheryl Bridges Johns, 'Yielding to the Spirit: A Pentecostal Approach to Group Bible Study', in Lee Roy Martin (ed.), *Pentecostal Hermeneutics: A Reader* (Leiden/Boston: Brill, 2013), pp. 33-56.

Johnson, Elliott E., *Expository Hermeneutics: An Introduction* (Grand Rapids, MI: Academie Books Zondervan Publishing House, 1990).

Joyce, Paul M., *Divine Initiative and Human Response in Ezekiel* (JSOTSup; Sheffield: JSOT Press, 1989).

—'Synchronic and Diachronic Perspectives in Ezekiel', in Johannes C. De Moor (ed.), *Synchronic or Diachronic?: A Debate on Method in Old Testament Exegesis* (New York: Brill, 1995), pp. 115-28.

—'King and Messiah in Ezekiel', in J. Day (ed.), *King and Messiah in Israel and the Ancient near East: Proceedings of the Oxford Old Testament Seminar* (JSOTSup 270; Sheffield: Sheffield Academic, 1998), pp. 323-37.

—*Ezekiel: A Commentary* (New York: T&T Clark, 2009).

—'Ezekiel and Moral Transformation', in William A. Tooman and Michael A. Lyons (eds.), *Transforming Visions: Transformations of Text, Tradition, and Theology in Ezekiel* (Eugene, OR: Pickwick Publications, 2010), pp. 139-58.

Kaiser, Otto, *Isaiah 1-12* (Philadelphia: Westminster, 1972).

Kärkkäinen, Veli-Matti, 'Pentecostal Hermeneutics in the Making: On the Way from Fundamentalism to Postmodernism', *JEPTA 18* (1998), pp. 76-115.

—'"Encountering Christ in the Full Gospel Way": An Incarnational Pentecostal Spirituality', *JEPTA* 27.1 (2007), pp. 9-23.

Kasher, Rimon, 'Anthropomorphism, Holiness and Cult: A New Look at Ezekiel 40-48', *ZAW* 110 (1998), pp. 192-208.

Kaufmann, Yehezkel, *The Religion of Israel: From Its Beginnings to the Babylonian Exile* (trans. Moshe Greenberg; Chicago: University of Chicago Press, 1960).

Keck, Elizabeth, 'Beside the Chebar River: The Glory of Yahweh, Name Theology, and Ezekiel's Understanding of Divine Presence' (PhD, Boston College, 2011).

Kelly, Anthony, *Eschatology and Hope* (MaryKnoll, NY: Orbis Books, 2006).

Klein, William W., Craig L. Blomberg, Robert L. Hubbard Jr., *Introduction to Biblical Interpretation* (Nashville: Thomas Nelson, 2004).

Knierim, Rolf P., *The Task of Old Testament Theology: Substance, Method, and Cases* (Grand Rapids, MI: Eerdmans, 1995).

Koehler, Ludwig, and W. Baumgartner, *Supplementum Ad Lexicon in Veteris Testamenti Libros* (Leiden: Brill, 1958).

Konkel, Michael, 'The System of Holiness in Ezekiel's Vision of the New Temple (Ezek 40-48)', in Christian Frevel and Christophe Nihan (eds.), *Purity and the Forming of Religious Traditions in the Ancient Mediterranean World and Ancient Judaism* (Leiden/Boston: Brill, 2013), pp. 429-56.

Kort, Wesley A., *Story, Text and Scripture: Literary Interests in Biblical Narrative* (University Park: Pennsylvania State University Press, 1988).

Kraeling, Emil G., *The Brooklyn Museum Aramaic Papyri* (New Haven: Yale University Press, 1953).

Kraetzschmar, R., *Das Buch Ezechiel* (*HKAT* 3: Göttingen: Vandenhoeck & Ruprecht, 1900).

Kutsko, John F., *Between Heaven and Earth: Divine Presence and Absence in the Book of Ezekiel* (Biblical and Judaic Studies; Winona Lake, IN: Eisenbrauns, 2000).

Kydd, R.A.N., *Charismatic Gifts in the Early Church* (Peabody, MA: Hendrickson, 1984).

Land, Steven Jack, *Pentecostal Spirituality: A Passion for the Kingdom* (Cleveland, TN: CPT Press, 2010).

Launderville, Dale F., *Spirit and Reason: The Embodied Character of Ezekiel's Symbolic Thinking* (Waco: Baylor University Press, 2007).

Levitt Kohn, Risa, *A New Heart and a New Soul: Ezekiel, the Exile, and the Torah* (London: Sheffield Academic, 2002).

—'Ezekiel at the Turn of the Century', *CBR* 2 (2003), pp. 9-31.

Lilley, J.P.U., 'A Literary Appreciation of the Book of Judges', *Tyndale Bulletin* 18 (1967), pp. 94-102.

Lind, Millard C., *Ezekiel* (Believers Church Bible Commentary; Scottdale, PA: Hearald Press, 1996).

Lindsey, H, *The Late Great Planet Earth* (Grand Rapids, MI: Zondervan, 1970).

Livingston, G. Herbert, 'אוּר', in R.L. Harris, G.L. Archer, and B.K. Waltke (eds.), *TWOT* (2 vols.; Chicago: The Moody Bible Institute, 1980), 1, pp. 48-49.

Longacre, R.E., 'Discourse Perspective on the Hebrew Verb: Affirmation and Restatement', in W. Bodine (ed.), *Linguistics and Biblical Hebrew* (Winona Lake, IN: Eisenbrauns, 1992), pp. 177-89.

Luc, Alex, 'A Theology of Ezekiel: God's Name and Israel's History', *JETS* 26.2 (1983), pp. 137-43.

Lust, Johan, *Ezekiel and His Book: Textual and Literary Criticism and Their Interrelation* (BETL, 74; Leuven: Leuven University Press, 1986).

Lyons, Michael A., 'Transformation of Law: Ezekiel's Use of the Holiness Code (Leviticus 17–26)', in William A. Tooman and Michael A. Lyons (eds.), *Transforming Visions: Transformations of Text, Tradition, and Theology in Ezekiel* (Eugene, OR: Pickwick Publications, 2010), pp. 1-32.

Maarsingh, B., 'Das Schwertlied in Ez 21, 13-22 und das Erra-Gedicht', in Johan Lust (ed.), *Ezekiel and His Book: Textual and Literary Criticism and Their Interrelation* (BETL 74; Leuven: Leuven University Press 1986).

Malbon, Elizabeth Struthers, 'Narrative Criticism: How Does the Story Mean?', in Janice Capel Anderson and Stephen D. Moore (eds.), *Mark & Method: New Approaches in Biblical Studies* (Minneapolis: Fortress, 1992), pp. 23-49.

Marguerat, Daniel, and Yvan Bourquin, *How to Read Bible Stories: An Introduction to Narrative Criticism* (London: SCM, 1999).

Marshall, Christopher D., *Beyond Retribution* (Grand Rapids, MI/Cambridge: Eerdmans, 2001).

Martin, Lee Roy, *The Unheard Voice of God: A Pentecostal Hearing of the Book of Judges* (JPTSup 32; Blandford Forum: Deo Publishing, 2008).

—*Introduction to Biblical Hebrew* (Cleveland, TN: CPT Press, 3rd edn, 2009).

—'Hearing the Voice of God: Pentecostal Hermeneutics and the Book of Judges', in Lee Roy Martin (ed.), *Pentecostal Hermeneutics: A Reader* (Leiden/Boston: Brill, 2013), pp. 205-32.

—(ed.), *Pentecostal Hermeneutics: A Reader* (Leiden/Boston: Brill, 2013).

—(ed.), *A Future for Holiness: Pentecostal Explorations* (Cleveland, TN: CPT Press, 2013).

—'"Oh give thanks to the Lord for he is good": Affective Hermeneutics, Psalm 107, and Pentecostal Spirituality', *Pneuma* 36.3 (Fall 2014), pp. 1-24.

—*Fasting: A Centre for Pentecostal Theology Short Introduction* (Cleveland, TN: CPT Press, 2014).

—'Towards a Biblical Model of Pentecostal Prophetic Preaching', *Verbum et Ecclesia* 37.1 (2016), pp. 1-9.

Masenya, Madipoane, 'An African Methodology for South African Biblical Sciences: Revisiting the Bosadi (Womanhood) Approach', *OTE* 18.3 (2005), pp. 741-51.

Matties, Gordon H., *Ezekiel 18 and the Rhetoric of Moral Discourse* (Atlanta: Scholars Press, 1990).

May, H.G., 'The Book of Ezekiel: Introduction and Exegesis', in G.A. Buttrick (ed.), *IB* (Nashville: Abingdon, 1956), VI, pp. 39-338.

Mayfield, Tyler D., *Literary Structure and Setting in Ezekiel* (Tübingen: Mohr Siebeck, 2010).

Mays, James Luther, *Ezekiel, Second Isaiah* (Proclamation Commentaries; Philadelphia: Fortress Press, 1978).

McClendon, James W., *Systematic Theology: Doctrine* (Nasville: Abingdon, 1994).

McConville, Gordon J., 'ברית', in Willem Van Gemeren (ed.), *NIDOTTE* (5 vols.; Grand Rapids, MI: Zondervan, 1997), I, pp. 747-55.

McKay, John, 'When the Veil Is Taken Away: The Impact of Prophetic Experience on Biblical Interpretation', *JPT* 5 (1994), pp. 17-40.

McKeating, Henry, *Ezekiel* (Sheffield: Sheffield Academic Press, 1993).

McLean, Mark, 'Toward a Pentecostal Hermeneutic', *Pneuma* 6.2 (1984), pp. 35-56.

McNamara, Denis R., *Catholic Church Architecture and the Spirit of the Liturgy* (Chicago: Hillenbrand, 2009).

McQueen, Larry, *Joel and the Spirit: The Cry of a Prophetic Hermeneutic* (JPTSup 8; Sheffield: Sheffield Academic Press, 1995).

—*Toward a Pentecostal Eschatology: Discerning the Way Forward* (JPTSup 39; Blandford Forum, UK: Deo Publishing, 2012).

Mein, Andrew, *Ezekiel and the Ethics of Exile* (Oxford Theological Monographs; Oxford: Oxford University Press, 2001).

Merenlahti, Petri, *Poetics for the Gospels? Rethinking Narrative Criticism* (London: T&T Clark, 2002).

Messel, Nils, *Ezechielfragen* (Oslo: Dybward, 1945).
Milgrom, Jacob, 'Sin-Offering or Purification-Offering', *VT* 21.2 (1971), pp. 237-39, repr. in Jacob Milgrom, *Studies in Cultic Theology and Terminology* (SJLA, 36; Leiden: Brill, 1983), pp. 67-69.
—'Israel's Sanctuary: The Priestly "Picture of Dorian Gray"', *Revue Biblique* 83.3 (1976), pp. 390-99.
Miller, Patrick D., 'Popularizing the Bible', *ThT* 53 (1997), pp. 435-38.
Mobley, Gregory, 'Know, Knowledge', in David Noel Freedman, Allen C. Meyers, and Astrid B. Beck (eds.), *Eerdmans Dictionary of the Bible* (Grand Rapids, MI/Cambridge, UK: Eerdmans, 2000), p. 777.
Mol, Jurrien, *Collective and Individual Responsibility: A Description of Corporate Personality in Ezekiel 18 and 20* (Boston: Brill, 2009).
Montague, George T., *The Holy Spirit: Growth of a Biblical Tradition* (New York: Paulist Press, 1976).
Moore, Rickie D., *The Spirit of the Old Testament* (JPTSup 35; Blandford Forum: Deo Publishing, 2011).
—'A Pentecostal Approach to Scripture', in Lee Roy Martin (ed.), *Pentecostal Hermeneutics: A Reader* (Leiden/Boston: Brill, 2013), pp. 11-14.
—'Canon and Charisma in the Book of Deuteronomy', *JPT* 1 (1992), pp. 75-92.
—'Deuteronomy and the Fire of God: A Critical Charismatic Interpretation', *JPT* 7 (1995), pp. 11-33.
Moore, R.D., J.C. Thomas, S.J. Land, 'Editorial', *JPT* 1 (1992), pp. 3-5.
Morgan, Robert and John Barton, *Biblical Interpretation* (Oxford Bible Series; New York: Oxford University Press, 1988).
Muilenburg, J., 'Form Criticism and Beyond', *JBL* 88 (1969), pp. 1-18.
—'Ezekiel', in M. Black and H.H. Rowley (eds.), *Peake's Commentary on the Bible* (London: Routledge, 1999), pp. 568-90.
Mullo Weir, Cecil J., 'Aspects of the Book of Ezekiel', *VT* 2 (1952), pp. 97-112.
Nel, Marius, '"Pentecostals" Reading of the Old Testament', *Verbum et Ecclesia* 28.2 (2007), pp. 524-41.
—'Attempting to Define a Pentecostal Hermeneutics', *Scriptura* 114.1 (2015), pp. pp. 1-21.
Niditch, Susan, 'Ezekiel 40-48 in a Visionary Context', *CBQ* 48 (1986), pp. 208-24.
Nielsen, Kirsten, 'Ezekiel's Visionary Call as Prologue: From Complexity and Changeability to Order and Stability', *JSOT* 33.1 (2008), pp. 99-114.
Odell, Margaret S., 'Ezekiel Saw What He Said He Saw: Genres, Forms, and the Vision of Ezekiel 1', in Marvin A. Sweeney and Ehud Ben Zvi (eds.), *The Changing Face of Form Criticism for the Twenty-First Century* (Grand Rapids: Eerdmans, 2003), pp. 168-76.
—*Ezekiel* (The Smith & Helwys Bible Commentary; Macon: Smith & Helwys, 2005).
Odell, Margaret S., and John T. Strong, *The Book of Ezekiel: Theological and Anthropological Perspectives* (SBLSymS 9; Atlanta: SBL, 2000).
Oeder, Georg Ludwig, *Freye Untersuchung über einige Bücher des Alten Testaments* (ed. G.J.L. Vogel; Halle: Johann Christian Hendel, 1771).
Ohnesorge, Stefan, *Jahwe gestaltet sein Volk neu: Zur Sicht der Zukunft Israels nach Ez 11, 14-21; 20,1-44; 36,16-38; 37,1-14.15-28* (FZB, 64; Würzburg: Echter, 1991).

Orelli, Conrad von, *Das Buch Ezechiel* (Munich: Ch. Beck, 1896).

Ostow, Mortimer, *Ultimate Intimacy: The Psychodynamics of Jewish Mysticism* (London: Karnac Books, 1995).

Oswalt, John N., *The Book of Isaiah: Chapters 1-39* (NICOT; Grand Rapids, MI: Eerdmans, 1986).

Otto, Rudolph, *The Idea of the Holy* (trans. John W. Harvey; Oxford: Oxford University Press, 1928).

Parunak, H. Van Dyke, 'The Literary Architecture of Ezekiel's *Mar'ot 'Ělōhîm'*, *JBL* 99 (1980), pp. 61-74.

Parunak, Henry Van Dyke, 'Structural Studies in Ezekiel' (PhD, Harvard University, 1978).

Pasala, Solomon, *The 'Drama' of the Messiah in Matthew 8 and 9: A Study from a Communicative Perspective* (Bern: Peter Lang, 2008).

Patte, Daniel, *Ethics of Biblical Interpretation: A Reevaluation* (Louisville, KY: Westminster John Knox, 1995).

—'The Guarded Personal Voice of a Male European-American Biblical Scholar', in Ingrid Rosa Kitzberger (ed.), *Personal Voice in Biblical Interpretation* (London: Routledge, 1999), pp. 12-24.

Pedersen, Johannes, *Israel: Its Life and Culture* (4 vols; London: Oxford Univeristy Press, 1926).

Peterson, Brian Neil, *Ezekiel in Context: Ezekiel's Message Understood in Its Historical Setting of Covenant Curses and Ancient Near Eastern Mythological Motifs* (Princeton Theological Monograph Series; Eugene, OR: Pickwick Publications, 2012).

Petter, Donna Lee, *The Book of Ezekiel and Mesopotamian City Laments* (OBO 246; Fribourg: Academic Press, 2011).

Pinnock, Clark H., 'The Work of the Holy Spirit in Hermeneutics', *JPT* 2 (1993), pp. 3-23.

—*The Scripture Principle* (Eugene, OR: Wipf and Stock Publishers, 1998).

—'The Work of the Spirit in the Interpretation of Holy Scripture from the Perspective of a Charismatic Biblical Theologian', in Lee Roy Martin (ed.), *Pentecostal Hermeneutics: A Reader* (Leiden: Brill, 2013), pp. 233-48.

Plüss, Jean-Daniel, *Therapeutic and Prophetic Narratives in Worship: A Hermeneutic Study of Testimonies and Visions* (Bern: Peter Lang, 1988).

Pohlmann, Karl-Friedrich, *Das Buch des Propheten Hezekiel (Ezechiel) Kapitel 1-19* (Göttingen: Vandenhoeck & Ruprecht, 1996).

—*Ezechiel: Der Stand der Theologischen Diskussion* (Darmstadt: Wissenschaftliche Buchgesellschaft, 2008).

Porter, Stanley E., 'Literary Approaches to the New Testament: From Formalism to Deconstruction and Back', in Stanley E. Porter and David Tombs (eds.), *Approaches to New Testament Study* (JSNTSup 120; Sheffield: Sheffield Academic Press, 1995), pp. 77-128.

Powell, Mark Allan, *What Is Narrative Criticism?* (Minneapolis: Fortress, 1990).

Rabinowitz, Chaim Dov, *Da'ath Sofrim: The Book of Yehezkel* (Jerusalem: Vagshal, 2001).

Rea, John, *The Holy Spirit in the Bible* (Lake Mary, Florida: Creation House, 1990).

Reid, Stephen Breck, 'Endangered Reading: The African-American Scholar between Text and People', *CCur* 44.4 (1994), pp. 476-88.

Rendtorff, Rolf, 'Zum Gebrauch der Formel *ne'um jahwe im* Jeremiabuch', *ZAW* 66 (1954), pp. 27-37.

—'Canonical Reading of the Old Testament in the Context of Critical Scholarship', *The Asbury Theological Journal* 54.1 (1999), pp. 6-13.

Renz, Thomas, *The Rhetorical Function of the Book of Ezekiel* (Leiden: Brill, 1999).

Resseguie, J.L., *Narrative Criticism of the New Testament: An Introduction* (Grand Rapids, MI: Baker Academic, 2005).

—*The Revelation of John: A Narrative Commentary* (Grand Rapids: Baker Academic 2009).

Rhoads, David, 'Narrative Criticism and the Gospel of Mark', *JAAR* 50 (1982), pp. 411-34.

—*Reading Mark, Engaging the Gospel* (Minneapolis: Fortress, 2004).

Rhoads, David, Joanna Dewey, and Donald Michie, *Mark as a Story: An Introduction to the Narrative of a Story* (Minneapolis, MN: Fortress Press 2012).

Rimmon-Kenan, Slomith, *Narrative Fiction: Comtemporary Poetics* (London: Methuen, 1983).

Ringgren, Helmer, and Horst Seebass, 'פשׁע', in G.J. Botterweck and H. Ringgren (eds.), *TDOT* (Grand Rapids, MI: Eerdmans, 1974), XII, pp. 133-51.

Robeck, Cecil M., Jr., 'The Nature of Pentecostal Spirituality', *Pneuma* 14.2 (1992), pp. 103-106.

Roberts, J.J.M., *The Hand of the Lord* (Baltimore: John Hopkins University Press, 1977).

Robinson, Henry Wheeler, *Two Hebrew Prophets: Studies in Hosea and Ezekiel* (London: Lutterworth, 1948).

Robson, James, *Word and Spirit in Ezekiel* (LHB/OTS 447; New York: T. & T. Clark, 2006).

Rodas, M. Daniel Carrol, 'Seek Yahweh, Establish Justice: Probing Prophetic Ethics. An Orientation from Amos 5.1-17', in Cynthia Long Westfall and Bryan R. Dyer (eds.), *The Bible and Social Justice: Old Testament and New Testament Foundations for the Church's Urgent Call* (Eugene, OR: Wipf and Stock Publishers, 2015), pp. 64-83.

Rowley, H.H., *Men of God: Studies in Old Testament History and Prophecy* (London: Nelson, 1963).

Sanders, James, *Torah and Canon* (Philadelphia: Fortress, 1972).

Schmidt, H., 'Die Grossen Propheten übersetzt und erklärt', in H. Gressmann (ed.), *SAT* (Göttingen: Vandehoeck und Ruprecht, 1915), II, pp. xi-lxxii.

Schulz, H., *Das Todesrecht im Alten Testament* (BZAW 114; Berlin: de Gruyter, 1969).

Schweinhorst, Ludger, 'מרד', in G.J. Botterweck and H. Ringgren (eds.), *TDOT* (Grand Rapids, MI: Eerdmans, 1974), IX, pp. 1-5.

Schweinhorst, Ludger, 'מרי', in G.J. Botterweck, H. Ringgren, and H.-J. Fabry (eds.), *TDOT* (Grand Rapids, MI: Eerdmans, 1998), IX, pp. 5-8.

Scofield, C.I., *The Scofield Reference Bible* (New York: Oxford University Press, 1917).

Scott, Jack B., 'אבל', in R.L. Harris, G.L. Archer, and B.K. Waltke (eds.), *TWOT* (2 vols.; Chicago: Moody Press, 1980), I, pp. 39-40.

Seamands, Stephen A., 'An Inclusive Vision of the Holy Life', *The Asbury Theological Journal* 42.2 (1987), pp. 79-88.

Sedlmeier, Franz, *Das Buch Ezechiel* (NSKAT 21; Stuttgart: Katholisches Biblewerk, 2002).

Segovia, F.F., and M.A. Tolbert, *Reading from This Place: Social Location and Biblical Interpretation in the United States* (Minneapolis: Fortress, 1994).

Sheppard, G.T., 'Word and Spirit: Scripture in the Pentecostal Tradition – Part One', *Agora* 1.4 (1978), pp. 4-5, 17-22.

—'Word and Spirit: Scripture in the Pentecostal Tradition – Part Two', *Agora* 2.1 (1978), pp. 14-19.

Simian-Yofre, Horacio, *Die theologische Nachgeschichte der Prophetie Ezechiels: Form-und traditionskritische Untersuchung zu Ez 6; 35; 36* (Würzburg: Echter, 1974).

Simon, Bennett, 'Ezekiel's Geometric Vision of the Restored Temple: From the Rod of His Wrath to the Reed of His Measuring', *HTR* 102.4 (2009), pp. 411-38.

Skinner, John, *The Book of Ezekiel* (The Expositor's Bible; New York: Armstrong & Son, 1895).

Smalley, Stephen S., *The Revelation to John* (Downers Grove, IL: InterVarsity Press, 2005).

Smend, R., *Der Prophet Ezechiel* (Leipzig: S. Hirzel, 1880).

Spiegel, S., 'Toward Certainty in Ezekiel', *JBL 54* (1935), pp. 145-71.

Sprinkle, Joe M., 'Literary Approaches to the Old Testament: A Survey of Recent Scholarship', *JETS* 32.3 (1969), pp. 299-310.

Stalker, D.M.G., *Ezekiel* (Torch Bible Commentaries; London: SCM, 1974).

Steinmann, Jean, *Ézéchiel* (Connaître La Bible; Paris: Brouwer, 1953).

Sternberg, Meir, *The Poetics of Biblical Narrative; Ideological Literature and the Drama of Reading* (Bloomington, IN: Indiana University Press, 1985).

Stevenson, Kalinda Rose, *The Vision of Transformation: The Territorial Rhetoric of Ezekiel 40-48* (Atlanta: Scholars Press, 1996).

Strong, John T., 'God's Kabod: The Presence of Yahweh in the Book of Ezekiel', in Margaret S. Odell and John T. Strong (eds.), *The Book of Ezekiel: Theological and Anthropological Perspectives* (SBLSymS 9; Atlanta: SBL Press, 2000), pp. 69-96.

Stronstad, Roger, *The Charismatic Theology of St. Luke* (Peabody, MA: Hendrickson, 1984).

—*The Prophethood of All Believers: A Study in Luke's Charismatic Theology* (JPTSup 16; New York: Sheffield Academic Press, 2003).

Stubert, Johanna, *The Exile and the Prophet's Wife: Historic Events and Marginal Perspectives* (Collegeville, MN: Liturgical Press, 1998).

Sweeney, Marvin, *Reading Ezekiel: A Literary and Theological Commentary* (Reading the Old Testament; Macon, GA: Smith & Helwys 2013).

Sweeney, Marvin, and Ehud Ben Zvi, *The Changing Face of Form Criticism for the Twenty-First Century* (Grand Rapids, MI: Eerdmans, 2003).

Sweet, John, *Revelation* (London: SCM Press, 1990).

Synan, V., *The Holiness-Pentecostal Movement in the United States* (Grand Rapids: Eerdmans, 1971).

Tate, W. Randolph, *Biblical Interpretation: An Integrated Approach* (Peabody, MA: Hendrickson Publishers, 1991).

Taylor, John B., *Ezekiel: An Introduction and Commentary* (TOTC; Downers Grove, IL: Inter-Varsity Press, 1969).

Taylor, Preston A., *Ezekiel: God's Prophet and His Puzzling Book* (Maitland, FL: Xulon Press, 2006).

Tellenbach, H., 'Ezechiel: Wetterleuchten einer "Schizophrenie" (Jaspers) oder prophetische Erfahrung des Ganz-Anderen', *Daseinsanalyse* 4 (1987), pp. 227-36.

Thomas, J.C., 'Pentecostal Theology in the Twenty-First Century', *Pneuma* 20.1 (1998), pp. 3-19.

—'Pentecostal Interpretation', in Steven L. McKenzie (ed.), *OEBI* (New York, NY: Oxford University Press, 2013), II, p. 94.

—*1 John, 2 John, 3 John* (Pentecostal Commentary Series; London: T&T Clark International, 2004).

—*The Spirit of the New Testament* (Blandford Forum, UK: Deo, 2005).

—'"What the Spirit Is Saying to the Church": The Testimony of a Pentecostal in New Testament Studies', in K.L. Spawn and A.T. Wright (eds.), *Spirit and Scripture: Exploring a Pneumatic Hermeneutic* (London: Bloomsbury T&T Clark, 2012), pp. 115-29.

—'Women, Pentecostalism, and the Bible: An Experiment in Pentecostal Hermeneutics', in Lee Roy Martin (ed.), *Pentecostal Hermeneutics: A Reader* (Leiden/Boston: Brill, 2013), pp. 81-94.

Thomas, J.C., and Frank D. Macchia, *Revelation* (The Two Horizons New Testament Commentary; Grand Rapids, MI: Eerdmans, 2016).

Thompson, David L., and Eugene Carpenter, *Ezekiel, Daniel* (Cornerstone Biblical Commentary; Downers Grove, IL: Tyndale House, 2010).

Torrey, Charles Cutler, *Pseudo-Ezekiel and the Original Prophecy* (New York: KTAV, 1970).

Tuell, Steven, *The Law of the Temple in Ezekiel 40-48* (HSM 49; Atlanta: Scholars Press, 1992).

—*Ezekiel* (Old Testament Series: New International Biblical Commentary; Peabody, MA: Hendrickson Publishers, 2009).

—'Divine Presence and Absence in the Book of Ezekiel', in Margaret S. Odell and John T. Strong (eds.), *The Book of Ezekiel: Theological and Anthropological Perspectives* (SBLSymS 9; Atlanta: SBL Press, 2000), pp. 96-117.

Vanhoozer, Kevin J., 'Word of God', in Kevin J. Vanhoozer *et al.* (eds.), *DTIB* (Grand Rapids: Baker Publishing Group, 2005), pp. 850-54.

Vawter, Bruce and Leslie J. Hopp, *Ezekiel: A New Heart* (International Theological Commentary; Grand Rapids: Eerdsman Publishing Company, 1991).

Voltaire, F.M.A. de, *The Complete Works of Voltaire*, xxxv. *Dictionnaire Philosophique, ii* (Oxford: Oxford University Press, 1994).

Waddell, Robby, *The Spirit of the Book of Revelation* (JPTSup 30; Blandford Forum: Deo Publishing, 2006).

Bruce K. Waltke, 'גלול', in R.L. Harris, G.L. Archer, and B.K. Waltke (eds.), *TWOT* (2 vols.; Chicago: Moody Press, 1980), I, pp. 163-64.

Warrington, Keith, *Pentecostal Theology: A Theology of Encounter* (London: T&T Clark, 2008).

Weinfeld, M., 'The Covenant of Grant in the Old Testament and in the Ancient near East', *JAOS* 90.2 (1970), pp. 184-203.

—'ברית', in G.J. Botterweck and H. Ringgren (eds.), *TDOT* (Grand Rapids, MI: Eerdmans, 1974), II, pp. 253-79.

—'כבוד', in G.J. Botterweck and H. Ringgren (eds.), *TDOT* (Grand Rapids, MI: Eerdmans, 1974), VII, pp. 22-38.

—'Covenant, Davidic', in Keith R. Crim (ed.), *IDBSup* (Nashville: Abingdon, 1976), pp. 188-92.

—*The Promise of the Land: The Inheritance of the Land of Canaan by the Israelites* (Berkeley: University of California Press, 1993).

Wells, Jo Bailey, *God's Holy People: A Theme in Biblical Theology* (Sheffield: Sheffield Academic Press, 2000).

Wessels, Willie J., 'Biblical Hermeneutics', in Adrio and S.S. Maimela König (eds.), *Initiation into Theology: The Rich Variety of Theology and Hermeneutics* (Pretoria: Van Schaik, 1998).

Westermann, Claus, *Basic Forms of Prophetic Speech* (trans. H.C. White; Philadelphia: Westminster Press, 1967).

Wevers, John W., *Ezekiel* (London: Butler & Tanner, 1969).

Whitley, C.F., 'The "Thirtieth" Year in Ezekiel', *VT* 9 (1959), pp. 326-30.

Wilson, Robert R., 'Prophecy in Crisis: The Call of Ezekiel', *Int* 38.2 (1984), pp. 117-30.

—'Ezekiel', in James L. May (ed.), *Harper Collins Bible Commentary* (San Francisco: Harper San Francisco 2000), pp. 583-622.

Wolde, Ellen Van, 'The God Ezekiel 1 Envisions', in Paul M. Joyce and Dalit Rom-Shiloni (eds.), *The God Ezekiel Creates* (London: Bloomsbury T&T Clark, 2015).

Wong, Ka Leung, *The Idea of Retribution in the Book of Ezekiel* (Leiden: Brill, 2001).

Wright, Christopher J.H., *The Message of Ezekiel: A New Heart and a New Spirit* (The Bible Speaks Today; Leicester: Inter-Varsity, 2001).

Wright, K.L. Spawn and Archie T., *Spirit and Scripture: Exploring a Pneumatic Hermeneutic* (London: Bloomsbury T&T Clark, 2012).

Yamauchi, E.M., 'Tammuz and the Bible', *JBL* 84 (1965), pp. 283-90.

Zimmerli, Walther, *Ezekiel 1: A Commentary on the Book of the Prophet Ezekiel, Chapters 1-24* (trans. Ronald E. Clements; Hermeneia; Philadelphia: Fortress, 1979).

—*I Am Yahweh* (trans. D.W. Scott; Atlanta: John Knox, 1982).

—*Ezekiel 2: A Commentary on the Book of the Prophet Ezekiel, Chapters 25-48* (trans. James D. Martin; Hermeneia; Philadelphia: Fortress Press, 1983).

—'Life before God', in Ben C. Ollenburger (ed.), *Old Testament Theology: Flowering and Future* (Winona Lake, IN: Eisenbrauns, 2003), I, pp. 120-39.

Index of Biblical References

INDEX OF AUTHORS

About the Author

Rebecca Basdeo Hill is a Lecturer in Old Testament and Hebrew at the Pentecostal Theological Seminary in Cleveland, Tennessee, USA. She is a native of Trinidad, where she grew up in a pastor's home. Her education includes the BA from Lee University, the MDiv from the Pentecostal Theological Seminary, and the DTh from the University of South Africa. She is married to Jason Hill, and they have served together as youth pastors.

QR Code linking to the Pentecostal Theological Seminary. https://www.ptseminary.edu

QR Code linking to Rebecca's sermon on Psalm 91. https://vimeo.com/163286615

QR Code linking to Rebecca's sermon on Psalm 30. https://vimeo.com/235960440